The Tie That Binds

Conversations with Jewish Writers

Harold U. Ribalow

SAN DIEGO • NEW YORK
A. S. BARNES & COMPANY, INC.
IN LONDON:
THE TANTIVY PRESS

For Shoshana,
>whose love and understanding
have enriched and lengthened
the days of my life.

The Tie That Binds copyright © 1980 by A. S. Barnes & Co.

First Edition
Manufactured in the United States of America

For information write to:
A. S. Barnes & Company, Inc.
P. O. Box 3051
La Jolla, California 92038

The Tantivy Press
Magdalen House
136–148 Tooley Street
London, SE1 2TT, England

Library of Congress Cataloging in Publication Data

Ribalow, Harold Uriel, 1919–
>The tie that binds.

1. Authors, American—20th century—Interviews.
2. Jewish authors—United States—Interviews.
3. Authors, Yiddish—United States—Interviews.
4. Jews in the United States—Identity. I. Title.
PS153.J4R5   810'.9'8924   80-19433
ISBN 0-498-01963-2

1 2 3 4 5 6 7 8 9   84 83 82 81 80

Contents

Also by Harold U. Ribalow:

Acknowledgments

Some of the interviews have been published, in other versions, as follows:

Charles Angoff and Chaim Grade in *Congress Monthly*. The interview with Angoff also appeared, almost intact, in *The Old and the New* (Essays in honor of Charles Angoff), edited by Alfred Rosa, published by Fairleigh Dickinson University Press, 1978. The Introduction, in a shortened version, also appeared in *Congress Monthly*.

Isaac Bashevis Singer and Meyer Levin in *Midstream*.

Susan Fromberg Schaeffer in *Pioneer Woman*.

The photographs of the authors are by Harold U. Ribalow, with the exception of that of Jack Ansell, which appears with the permission of John Robaton.

Introduction

Some of my best friends are Jewish writers. This fact, plus my own involvement with American Jewish writing over a period of forty years, has led to this book of conversations which, I know now, seems almost to have been ordained. The marvelous portable cassette tape recorder has played an important role in the precision and accuracy of the dialogues presented here.

It was only when I had completed copy editing this volume and thought of the interviews in a detached way that it came to me that I had actually spent my life among writers who, we are told by nonwriters, are an odd, unique, and quite mysterious group of individuals.

My father was the founder (in 1921) and editor of *Hadoar,* for many years the only Hebrew weekly in the world outside the borders of the State of Israel. During his tenure of more than thirty years, I was raised among Hebrew and Yiddish poets, novelists, scholars, essayists, and journalists.

When I was very young—and I recall it only dimly—Chaim Nachman Bialik, the most notable Hebrew poet of the generation, had dinner in our home on his single visit to the United States. I remember somewhat more clearly the stunned sorrow that assaulted my father when news of Bialik's death reached us in 1934.

The second member of the great triumvirate of modern Hebrew writers, the poet Saul Tchernichovsky, also was our house guest. For some hardly explicable reason, I remember him quite clearly. He was a robust, finely moustached man with a poet's head, or at least what I assumed to be a poet's head—wild hair, untamed, striking. He had been a dentist, I think, because he examined my teeth closely and, in a happy, booming voice, complimented my mother on the excellent condition of my molars and gums.

Zalman Schneour, the third member of the group, was a poet in Hebrew and in Yiddish as well as a gifted novelist. He had first come to the home of my parents in 1938 and I remembered him as a hilarious mimic and a man of gusto and ego. I met him next on an unhappy occasion in 1940. He had fled

Paris after it had been occupied by the Germans. He and his family had managed to board a Spanish ship and traveled from Cadiz to Seville to Lisbon to Bermuda to Cuba. The trip had been hellish. He was bitter about the French, although he had been living fairly comfortably in Marseilles. Once a tall, Apollo-like figure, handsome, bearded, and virile, he now was tired, a worn-out fugitive. I had been assigned to interview him by the editor of the Jewish news syndicate for which I was then working. Disoriented, his life shattered, he was willing to meet me and talk with me again only because he remembered our social ties and was close to my father. We met a few times more before he died, a broken man. As I recall it, his wife and children also had great difficulty in assimilating to life in America.

Although my father was a Hebrew editor and literary critic, he, unlike most other Hebraists, also wrote for Yiddish literary journals and maintained close friendships with many Yiddish writers. Aaron Zeitlin, a pale, emaciated, aesthetic Hebrew and Yiddish poet, was a frequent visitor. I found it difficult to understand how so timid and tentative a man could have been so highly regarded by my father, who treated Zeitlin with enormous respect. Years later, I learned that Isaac Bashevis Singer also looked up to Zeitlin as a great writer, and he said as much in his address when he received the Nobel Prize for Literature, naming Zeitlin as one of the notable figures in Yiddish literature. To me, Zeitlin was a thin, quiet man who ate sparingly and seemed always prepared to be sent home by his host. He was a tormented man because of the Holocaust. He could not account for it and was unwilling to accept the philosophy that it was all God's will. Gentle though he appeared to be, I remember him as a bitter man and was later surprised to discover how highly he was regarded as a writer.

I have more affectionate memories of Joseph Opatoshu, the Yiddish novelist, whose son David later became a fairly well-known actor who had translated some of his father's work into English and had arranged for one of his father's stories to be made into a movie. Joseph Opatoshu resembled the old-time actor Louis Wollheim; that is to say, he resembled a prize fighter who had caught too many punches. His face looked battered, but he was a kindly, generous man. He used to call my father every Saturday morning to catch up on literary news and to discuss the world of Hebrew and Yiddish journalism and Jewish literature. The telephonic conversations seemed endless, although my father normally was curt on the phone. He and Opatoshu enjoyed their relationship. I vaguely remembered that years earlier, when my father had taken me to a cafeteria to meet with Opatoshu, I had accidentally turned over a glass of tea on the writer's lap. It was a family joke for years.

Yiddish writers always seemed to me to be more relaxed and friendly than their Hebrew counterparts. I guess there was a good reason for this.

Nearly all Hebrew writers earned their livelihood as Hebrew teachers. They had few literary outlets, the *Hadoar* being the primary one. The Yiddish writers were working journalists; they could publish their poems, sketches, and stories regularly in their own newspapers or in the Yiddish journals in New York, Europe, or South America. The Hebraists were pedantic, tense. The Yiddishists sat in cafes, carried on flamboyant love affairs, went to the flourishing Yiddish theater, and enjoyed themselves, which may be why I preferred them.

When I was a child, I was impressed with Aleph Liessin, the Yiddish poet who lived in my neighborhood and walked its streets with an air of importance. During the High Holidays, when the streets outside our synagogue teemed with people, Liessin would walk by, never in. To this day, I recall with a touch of surprise that Liessin once told my father that he wished he had the *ability* to walk into a shul on a holiday, but that he had cut himself off from religious practices as a rebellious Jewish youth and now was psychically unable to enter a synagogue. The desire, he said, was strong, but somehow he could not manage to do so.

Liessin had a daughter who was badly crippled. She had a very large head and a twisted body. Many shied away from her. Somehow, I did not and when we conversed, I found that she was quite brilliant and that the enlarged head and the unfortunate body in no way implied a lack of intelligence or intellect, as some suspected. Liessin's wife had died long years before and the housekeeper was Liessin's sister-in-law, who took care of him and his handicapped daughter, her own niece. It was an odd and tragic family. When I later read Hutchins Hapgood's *The Spirit of the Ghetto* and looked at Jacob Epstein's charcoal drawings, Liessin's face jumped off the page at me and I immediately remembered the poet and editor (of the Yiddish-language *Zukunft*) as an older, unhappier man than the one depicted by Epstein.

While working with the American Jewish Congress, I became acquainted with two excellent Yiddish poets, two men who were quite dissimilar, except that they had great talent. Jacob Glatstein was an impressionist poet and a novelist. He was Americanized and was proud of his son, who had become a stockbroker and had issued one single volume of a Jewish magazine, which then promptly died. Glatstein was talkative, vibrant, well acquainted with American poetry and prose, which was rather uncommon for a Yiddish writer. We talked often of Faulkner, Hemingway, Graham Greene, and other contemporary writers. In later years, prior to his death, he grew bitter because his prose works made no impression on either critics or readers when they were translated into English. He grew obsessive over the success of Isaac Bashevis Singer.

Menahem Boraisha, who wrote epic poetry in Yiddish, was a handsome, brooding man, and was chief editorial writer for *Congress Weekly*. He seldom smiled, always worked laboriously over his editorials for he had reverence for words and felt sharply his lack of enough English words to convey his thoughts. Together, we polished his prose and he would sigh that his efforts to write in English drained him of the stamina he required to write his Yiddish poetry. When Sholem Asch began to write his Christological novels, Boraisha developed a deep hostility toward him and was distressed that Asch was enhancing his reputation in the general literary and commercial world. Boraisha was a passionate man, often intolerant of the opinions of others, but he had enormous integrity and although more than thirty years have passed since I worked with him and since he died, I think of him frequently and hold his memory in high regard.

More naturally, I met and got to know scores of Hebrew writers, almost all of whom contributed to the *Hadoar.* The most picturesque of these men was Daniel Persky, a columnist of note in his day and a Hebrew grammarian who was engaged in a lifelong love affair with the Hebrew language. He also had been one of my Hebrew teachers at Herzliah Hebrew Academy, then housed in a dilapidated, crumbling building on the Lower East Side, close to the newspaper offices of the Yiddish daily newspapers, the *Morning Journal, The Day,* and *The Forward.*

Persky never married and lived on Fourteenth Street in Lower Manhattan. He was an eccentric for whom many people felt sorry. On Friday nights, he would visit and celebrate the Sabbath with Abraham Spicehandler, a businessman who was a dedicated Hebraist. All the Spicehandlers (one son later became a prominent rabbi-scholar, and a second a novelist) spoke Hebrew and Persky never allowed another language to cross his lips, it was said. Sometimes, however, I wondered about that. After all, Dwight Macdonald wrote a profile on Persky for the *New Yorker* magazine and Hebraists rejoiced that one of their own people had "made" a general American magazine. Persky must have communicated with Macdonald, who had no knowledge of the Hebrew language. Persky, who loved Hebrew and everything connected with it, was unable, or unwilling, to settle in Israel after statehood was declared. Unashamedly, he admitted that he was a coward and was afraid of living in Israel while the nation was under siege. His candor softened the barbs of scoffers who wondered why so many Hebrew scholars and writers remained on what they themselves called the "barren" soil of Jewish America.

Ephraim Lisitzky, the Hebrew poet who lived in New Orleans, was a close personal friend of my father's. He stayed with us every summer for a few days when he was en route to Boston to visit with members of his family. He and I became friends and we conversed, in Hebrew, for hours on end. When he translated Shakespeare's *The Tempest* into Hebrew, he insisted, to my astonishment, that I write an introduction to the play, in English, of course, and he would have my essay translated into Hebrew for the edition he would publish.

One of the most interesting Hebrew writers I have known is Moshe Meisels, who later settled in Israel, where he still lives. Meisels had come from Poland as a disillusioned yeshiva student. He was the assistant editor of the *Hadoar* and early in his American career tutored me in Hebrew at my home. Soon thereafter, he had a second student, and the three of us composed a class of two with a teacher who smoked Old Gold cigarettes and seemed indifferent to our progress. The other student was a young boy, also newly arrived from Poland, Avreml Karp, now the noted Jewish historian Abraham J. Karp. Meisels must have taught us something that lasted because we both remember him with affection and visit him in Israel whenever we are there.

A quiet man, with a sardonic streak, Meisels is a philosopher who is the author of a massive two-volume history on Jewish thought. He wrote it under a pseudonym, sent the manuscript pages for setting in what was then Jewish Palestine, and, once the book was made available, did not lift a finger to promote it or even discuss it with his friends and acquaintances. A handful of years after publication in Hebrew, he quite uncharacteristically actively worked to have it translated and published in English. I helped find a publisher for the book, which, following its publication, passed into obscurity. Nonetheless, the work earned him a reputation as a genuinely thoughtful writer and, from time to time, his book is referred to by various scholars. In Israel he works as a book editor and remains known only to an appreciative few.

With the passing years, as I edited English-language Jewish periodicals, I dealt constantly with writers. It was part of my daily existence and I seldom gave it any special thought. Years later, on reflection, I was grateful for having had the experiences.

Harry Golden came to my office at *Congress Weekly*. He was then an obscure New Yorker who had settled in the South. He had liked some of my pieces, he said, and wanted to meet me. He was selling advertising space for a newspaper and was considering establishing a paper, which later became *The Carolina Israelite*. I was intrigued that an East-Side, New York Jew had found a spiritual home in the South and I suggested he write a piece for *Congress Weekly* on his Southern experiences. The article he produced was the first writing he had ever done for a national journal. Of course, he continued in that vein and became a nationally known author. He never changed character and remained a pleasant, easygoing successful writer. We exchanged views and letters throughout the years and, though we are separated in distance, we remain aware of one another.

I met Anzia Yezierska when she was quite old, yet she lived at least fifteen years beyond that time. We both were members of a literary panel on Jewish books, a regular Jewish Book Month feature years ago. I was astonished at her vigor and her youthfulness. She had recently published her autobiography, *Red Ribbon On a White Horse*, with an introduction—quite improbably—by W. H. Auden, so she was temporarily back in the limelight. She had been one of the most popular Jewish immigrant writers of the 1920s, and her book *Hungry Hearts* was extremely popular in its day. *Salome of the Tenements* and *Bread Givers* advanced her reputation as the novelist of the East Side Jewish ghetto, of life on Hester Street. Later, she was called to Hollywood for the filming of *Hungry Hearts* and I own a copy of *Salome of the Tenements,* which is illustrated with glossy pictures from the Paramount Picture "photoplay." Yezierska met many famous Hollywood personalities during her tenure as a script writer. But it did not take her long to realize that the never-never world of filmmaking was not for her, and she fled California. Her account is vividly reported in *Red Ribbon On a White Horse*.

We became friends and she began to turn to me to help her solve the problems of daily living. She lived in a dingy flat on the West Side and her eyesight was going. She was willing to enter an old age home, but not when she discovered that she could not have a telephone. She would feel cut off from the world, she explained. She would also have to give up every penny she had—and she had very little. She needed a skirt shortened. She required that someone put together her unpublished stories for a book. There were many things she needed. Another friend of mine, pleased to learn that Anzia was alive, volunteered—together with his wife—to help her out. But she was too demanding for them; she snapped at them; old age had made her intolerant. And then, one day, I read in the *Times,* years after I had met her, that she had died. But I continued to remember her candor, and how her open, blue eyes shone when she talked of her future, this old woman who had only a past, and a difficult one at that.

Another intriguing personality was Harry Sackler, a playwright and novelist, whose *Festival at Meron,* now a forgotten novel, made a profound impression on me and led to the reading of dozens of books on Jewish mysticism. It was in *Festival at Meron* that Sackler humanized Rabbi Simon Bar Yohai, considered by many as the author of the *Zohar.* Sackler was married to a woman who thought him a genius. He appeared to agree with her judgment. He read widely and took malicious pleasure in tearing down world-renowned writers, talking with a towering self-confidence that shook the belief of a young man who had thought that Thomas Mann was an important writer; that James Joyce was an uncommon literary experimenter; that D. H. Lawrence was an interesting novelist. Sackler was, however, an engaging conversationalist and it flattered me that he was willing to hear my opinions, even though he was obdurant in his own literary views and enjoyed puncturing the reputations of others. In later years, he was ill and suffered doubly because of his inability to write. He was unhappy that, as a Hebrew writer, he had few outlets for his work. He was pleased that there were those who admired his novel and regretful that so few of his dramas reached the stage.

When I served as managing editor of the *American Zionist,* I worked closely with Marvin Lowenthal, a cultured man who had been a careful stylist as an essayist, editor, and biographer. We became colleagues long after he had lost his stamina and desire to write. But he enjoyed life. He and his wife Sylvia understood each other. He, however, lacked the tension of most of the Jewish writers I knew. He was no longer driven. He was something of a gourmet and often persuaded me to join him at a local hotel bar after work. He was the first Jewish writer I knew who was a relaxed individual.

Lowenthal was friendly with Ludwig Lewisohn and we used to speak, sometimes amusedly, of Lewisohn's Messianic fervor. Lewisohn himself remains vivid in my mind. He had been a celebrated author before he turned to Zionism. In a sense, this step destroyed him. He had been an important literary critic and, as the drama critic for *The Nation,* was a force to reckon with. His early novels, fiercely Freudian, were international best sellers. When Lewisohn converted to Zionism—Judaism, really—he started to lecture on the Jewish circuit. The moment he began, his reputation diminished. He became "too Jewish" for the general public. To the Jews, now that he was "one of us," he could not really be important, could he? I remember attending a Zionist meeting only because I knew Lewisohn was the scheduled speaker. I had wanted to meet him and thought it would be difficult. To my surprise, he sat alone, unattended, scarcely recognized. When he mounted the podium and commenced, in his impassioned manner, to stress the values and meaning of the Zionist dream, I looked about me and felt that his audience was not taking him seriously. As a fellow Zionist, he was no longer looked up to. On the other hand, Pierre van Paassen, the Dutch journalist who had become a convinced Zionist, always was admired and cheered.

As Lewisohn committed himself more and more deeply to Zionism, the more his luster faded. I read his work regularly and admired him. We corresponded and finally met again, not long before his death, when he was a teacher and librarian at Brandeis University. He was old, given now to boastfulness, as though prodding himself to justify his life to a younger man. He talked of his translations from the German, which should have been familiar to anyone who knew him. But he kept talking. We remained in touch with one another until he died, suddenly. From time to time, he is mentioned in passing in a critical essay; Jewish academics occasionally publish something about him. A few of his books were reissued. In the main, however, his name and his reputation have faded and Lewisohn has become a footnote in literary history.

A contemporary of Lewisohn's was Maurice Samuel, who learned to write English as a boy in Manchester, England. Samuel gained early recognition as a translator of the poet Bialik, but he confessed to my father, who was a Bialik specialist, that his own command of Hebrew was not quite rich enough to reproduce Bialik adequately in English. For years he was noted as a fine translator. Perhaps he earned that reputation as the translator of Sholem Asch's major novels. I had heard Asch's Yiddish was inexact and sloppy and that Samuel's excellent English style salvaged Asch's work. Perhaps this is true. I do know that Samuel was a superlative lecturer, a good essayist, and polemicist. He wrote many books about Zionism, Palestine, Israel, and about Jewish cultural subjects. He was truly a "maggid," or a sermonic lecturer to his fellow Jews. He also wrote novels, which, although ambitious, seemed less successful than his general works.

We met from time to time and I was deeply impressed with his professionalism. In his hotel room on the Upper West Side (before he married his wife Edith), he had organized his lectures and filed them in heavy folders. The lectures, each and every one, were written out, and he had only to read from any one to have an evening's lecture in hand. Later, many of these were transformed to the printed page and they glowed with knowledge, warmth, and charm. Samuel's *The World of Sholom Aleichem*, more than *Fiddler on the Roof*, sparked a revival in Sholom Aleichem. His book on Y. L. Peretz and his later books on the Yiddish language are brilliantly written essays that bring a language to life for people who have been unacquainted with it. Although he may have been somewhat uncertain in his knowledge of Hebrew, Samuel's popularization of Yiddish literature and Yiddish writers—as well as his own evocative segments of his autobiography—made him a valued man of Jewish letters.

He did not take himself all that seriously and once told me—and I heard him out with semidisbelief—that he never accepted an advance from Alfred A. Knopf because he did not want to feel the pressure of commitment. "Knopf," he said, "will publish what I offer him because he has faith in me and knows how careful I am with my work. I'd rather have it that way." When I wondered how he could earn a living without the cushion of advance royalties, he assured me that his lectures helped sell his books and his books kept him popular on the lecture circuit. He was a man who had found his métier, understood his talents, and worked within them.

Through a casual comment made to me in 1958 by Charles Angoff, I learned that Henry Roth, author of the neglected novel, *Call It Sleep,* was alive and working on a duck farm near Augusta, Maine. I initiated a correspondence with Roth, traveled to Maine to meet with him in 1959, and arranged for the republication of *Call It Sleep* in 1960. A few years later, Avon published it in paperback; Irving Howe reviewed it on the front page of the *New York Times Book Review,* and *Call It Sleep* had a remarkable revival. (The paperback went into almost thirty printings at this writing, with more than a million copies sold and the novel is required reading in more than 450 high schools and colleges throughout the United States.) Its continuing success is one of the most gratifying experiences of my own literary life.

Roth and I—as well as his own wife Muriel and my own wife—have remained friends through the years. Our friendship has transcended our literary relationship, and, since he moved from Maine to New Mexico, we have kept in constant touch with one another. He is a complex, moody man, withdrawn from ordinary social life. Once hostile to organized Jewish life, Zionism, and Israel, he has experienced a metamorphosis and today is obsessed with Israel, its fate and its future. He and Muriel have visited the country and are thinking of settling there. In New Mexico, he has involved himself in Jewish community life and sometimes his letters, brilliantly phrased, aphoristic, highly stylized, list as many activities as that of an active member of B'nai B'rith. His voice went silent after *Call It Sleep,* except for an occasional short story.

I regret very much that Roth was unwilling to "sit" for another interview with me for this volume. We had talked together frequently, but without the benefit of a tape recorder. (A report on our conversations appears in the hardback edition of *Call It Sleep* published by Pageant Books in 1960.) When I suggested that I come out to New Mexico for a lengthy, updated conversation, Roth replied that "the very thought of tapes, interviews, questionnaires just deflates my breath. Am weary." Roth is a very private person, withdrawn, complex—and I was not surprised, although I was sorry.

While on the subject of regrets, I must also note that Bernard Malamud felt that his "definitive" interview had already taken place and had been published in the *Paris Review.*

Cynthia Ozick, whose work I so much admire, wrote to me again and again, explaining her reluctance to "submit" to an interview. Originally, when we talked about the possibility, she was uncertain. She would think about it. Later, she wrote, "An essay sets its own premise; an interview is governed by the interviewer's premises. ... An essay is written in writer's language; the interview is conducted in 'conversation' language.... I am beginning to realize more and more that I must stick with the written word only." She amplified in a later letter: "You are perfectly right when you argue that an interview has its own separate life. *It's another thing.* I believe each of us ought to do the thing we *can* do best."

Wilfred Sheed, reviewing a volume of *Paris Review* interviews (*New York Times Book Review,* August 1, 1976), on the other hand, observed, "Can the interview as a form pass beyond the realm of necessary small talk into art itself? Perhaps. Whenever a good writer uses words literature is a possibility. . . ."

This book had its genesis in 1974 when, after having known him for twenty-seven years, it occurred to me to interview—with the support of a cassette recorder—my good friend Charles Angoff. I knew him, his literary career and his work well. All the project called for, at the time (the summer of 1974), was for the two of us to get together and discuss his career, his many Jewish novels and stories, and his life as an editor and educator. I transcribed the two hours of tapes in longhand on yellow, lined, legal-sized pads. It was slow, laborious work. Only then did I edit, cut, shift material to where it fit best, and produced a 6,000-word interview, which was published in *Congress Bi-Weekly.*

As a result of the publication of this interview, I was asked by the editors of the magazine to talk with the Yiddish poet and novelist Chaim Grade. Again, it was an interesting and exciting experience.

It was then that I began to think of other writers I admired and did not necessarily know personally. Other interviews followed, although there was a considerable lapse of time because I had suffered a serious ailment, which did not allow me to do any work at all for about a year. I had known Isaac Bashevis Singer, Meyer Levin, and Chaim Potok. But through this project I met, for the first time, Susan Fromberg Schaeffer, Robert Kotlowitz, Hugh Nissenson, and Jack Ansell.

The process of interviewing writers on their total work is time consuming, requires planning and organization of materials and constant wrestling with mechanical devices. Most writers, including this one, are not especially handy with electronic equipment, batteries, microphones, cassettes, and the constant pushing of buttons on the cassette recorder (fast forward, reverse, record, and stop) to make sure all the words are clearly understood and properly recorded on paper. An added complication was photographing the writers. I was required to carry (in addition to recording equipment) a camera with alternate lenses, a strobe unit, and film of varying speeds and sensitivity.

I found it necessary to read or, as the case may be, reread *all* of a writer's work, not merely to familiarize myself with his body of writing, but to extract intelligent questions, which would elicit meaningful replies.

In the case of Isaac Bashevis Singer, for example, I reread all his novels, one hundred twenty stories, sixty-seven sketches, four books of literary criticism devoted to his writings and perhaps a dozen earlier interviews. Each time I thought of a question I might ask, I wrote it on an index card. When I visited Singer, I was "armed" with two hundred thirty cards, representing at least one question on a card.

Lining up the questions took weeks of work for each author. The actual interviews took the least amount of time, usually from two to three hours. Transcribing the tapes, editing them (usually eliminating repetitions of phraseology or redundancies) took weeks of careful work for each interview. In all, each interview represents the labor of a month, and longer.

All of the writers included here—with the lamentable exceptions of Charles Angoff and Jack Ansell—are vigorous, prolific and productive. I shall be cursory about some, a bit lengthier about others.

Robert Kotlowitz turned to fiction comparatively late in life. When I met him, he was—and is—an executive with Channel 13 in New York City. Prior to that he had been the successful editor of *Harper's* magazine. The son of a cantor in Baltimore, Kotlowitz is a pleasant man who, with a rising sense of astonishment, has realized that he is actually a good novelist. Closely tied to his family, he has drawn from that solid and secure background to produce a book about Jews in Warsaw and London before World War I, and a second novel, *The Boardwalk*—published after our interview—about Jewish family life in a summer resort in Atlantic City just before World War II breaks out in Europe. I found it illuminating that American Jewish literature continues to turn out writers who have the background, and the will, to write knowingly and affectionately about Jewish family life on two continents

Some of the other writers included in this volume are well known to the general American reader and, although I have interviewed them at length, I cannot say that I know them at all well. Their work speaks to me; I know the people almost fleetingly. I have in mind here Hugh Nissenson, Chaim Potok, and Susan Fromberg Schaeffer. Chaim Grade, Isaac Bashevis Singer, Meyer Levin and the late Charles Angoff and Jack Ansell, were closer to me, and I to them, for reasons which may become more obvious in the telling.

I met Hugh Nissenson only that one single time we sat down to talk, with a tape recorder between us. A handsome man in his mid-forties, he has enormous confidence in his gifts. What struck me about him is his passion for Israel and its people, especially those living on the kibbutz, his constant awareness of the Holocaust, and his uniformly generous observations and comments about almost any and all Israelis. This is why I have retained so many of his observations of a nonliterary nature.

As a child, he felt a sense of shame that Jews were victims and, it seems to me, that Israel's ability to defend itself permitted Nissenson to shed a personal badge of shame and inadequacy as a Jew. He contended, again and again, that he does not believe in God and that life is essentially meaningless. When I remarked that some critics consider him the most religiously oriented of modern American Jewish writers, he conceded that this was so, not because he is a believer but because he is obsessed with questions about God. He is a gifted, thoughtful man, and it is obvious why those who read him look forward to everything he writes.

Chaim Potok and I attended some of the same schools, at different times. In reading his phenomenally popular best sellers, I recognized the *milieu*, the people and the problems he poses. We first met in Jerusalem in the home of Dr. Moshe Davis of the Hebrew University, himself a noted Jewish scholar and historian. Even then, Potok appeared to be totally involved in the novelistic problems that were confronting him in the writing of *My Name is Asher Lev*. A few years later, when we met for the interview reproduced in this book, we both recalled the period when he was questioning anyone he met about the issues he could not quite handle while wrestling with *Asher Lev*. Prolific and commercially successful, he nevertheless emanates a sense of modesty and a knowledge that he still was struggling to attain artistic heights he had not yet reached. He was sharply aware of the "freakishness" of a religious man spending his time, or wasting it, on imaginative writing. I had the impression that Potok would soon move away from Jewish themes to more general subjects. He confirmed this when he said that his very first novel had been written on a non-Jewish theme (it was never published because, Potok said, it was a bad novel) and that his next work of fiction would also be on a general, not a Jewish, subject. Nonetheless, his next ambitious book was *Wanderings,* a personal view of generations of Jewish history.

Susan Fromberg Schaeffer and I met the one time late in 1974 when we talked in her large rambling, interestingly furnished house close to Brooklyn College, where both she and her husband are professors of English. She is a poet and novelist and I was initially attracted to her work when she published *Anya,* a sensitive narrative about a woman who has survived the Holocaust. The house in which she lives with her husband (she had one child when we met; she now is the mother of two) is pleasantly cluttered, sort of Edwardian and reminds one of what a Bloomsbury flat might be like, although King Edward was gone when the Bloomsbury Group came into notoriety. Schaeffer is a compulsive writer. Many are, but few match her intensity and stamina. A few years after we conversed, she published *Time in Its Flight,* a very long novel set in New England. She sent me Xeroxed manuscript pages and the novel ran to over one thousand pages. It was somewhat shorter in its published version, and it became a major book club selection.

Susan Schaeffer rises at three in the morning to scratch out a poem on a snippet of paper and then hides it in a jewelry box. By morning she may have forgotten that she had written anything. Weeks later she would accidentally find the poem and read it, not remembering she had produced it. In this fashion, she creates poem after poem and her published poetry (the books keep coming) is original, vivid, and excellent. Her face is young, as though always anticipating surprises, but she talks often of psychoanalysis and there is, somewhere deeply imbedded in her psyche, a grain of gloom. Although we got together only a few times, we talk on the phone and send each other letters and cards. Her postal cards are outsize, colorful: pictures of the Marx Brothers, or reproductions of *Saturday Evening Post* covers, or floral arrangements. What astonished me most about her was the knowledge that her first experience with the Holocaust came through seeing the stage version of *The Diary of Anne Frank*. It seemed to me, having lived through the era, that *everyone* knew about these historical events and tragedies through the newspapers and newsreels of the day. It was a new thought to me that a writer could produce so good a book as *Anya* and not know of the Holocaust until it was itself part of history. She also was delighted with her new-found popularity as a writer. She was accustomed to writing in comparative obscurity. Her poems and book reviews were published in out-of-the-way literary journals of limited circulation. Now she was "almost" famous. Her transparent pleasure was pleasant to see. When she talked of her childhood and Jewish upbringing, I was again surprised to learn that she had enjoyed studying in a dank, small Brooklyn classroom with an old-fashioned religious Hebrew teacher, and that she very much disliked the hollowness of the classes she attended in a suburban temple. There is passion within her and one senses it in her presence as well as in her work.

I first met Meyer Levin when he was already famous and had written many of his notable books. It amazed me that this well-known author was so quiet and withdrawn a man. He mumbled rather than spoke out. He did not look a person in the eye. He sat in the front row of a press area at a Zionist convention as though he were a stranger; he, a man who had spent his life in promoting and defending Israel and its people, who had written (in *Yehuda*) the first novel in any language about life on a kibbutz.

We met in the 1940s. Since then, as he has grown older, he has become more outgoing, aggressive, if that is the proper word. He learned how to sell his own books. He has been, people say, too argumentative, but if you listen to him closely, his arguments make sense. Especially on the subject of Anne Frank, about which he has perhaps been obsessive (he wrote an entire book about this), but on the other hand, he also may very well have been right.

When *In Search*, his probing, fascinating autobiography lost its American publisher (due to a political conflict between Levin and an editor), Levin issued the book privately in Paris. He then brought all the copies to the United States, hoping to find a new publisher. He enlisted my aid in the task and eventually Ben Raeburn of Horizon Press, who was one of my own publishers at the time, read the book and reissued it (by photo offset; it did not require new composition). Since then, Levin and I have remained friends. His commitment to writing and to Jews is extraordinarily deep; and he has enormous integrity. Yet, he wrestles with doubts about his influence and his impact. In the interview we had, he displays a touching diffidence about himself and his body of work. Many writers—some might argue that all writers—have a self-sustaining ego. I am sure Levin does, too. But he looks back at a long career, much indifference, some hostility—and wonders. For example, after he completed both *The Settlers* and *The Harvest,* a critic writing for *Commentary* used the occasion not only to denigrate both books, but also to belittle Levin's entire literary career. It was not only inaccurate; it was poisonous, and it makes one sympathize with Levin and understand his vulnerability.

Charles Angoff, whose talk with me was the conversation that prompted the idea of this book, died in May of 1979, five years after our interview. Of all the writers included here, I felt closest to him, although he was considerably older than I, and far more experienced. He had been an editor with H. L. Mencken in the glorious days of the *American Mercury,* but I first got to know him when he published *When I Was a Boy in Boston.* At the time, I was collecting Jewish short stories for the first of a group of anthologies I was editing. I was astonished that this noted editor, the friend of Mencken, George Jean Nathan, and other famous American writers, knew so much about Jewish life and was able to describe immigrant Jews with such tenderness, affection, and understanding. I reviewed his book, included one of his stories in my initial collection and have admired his work ever since.

Now that he is dead and his saga of David Polonsky and his family has not been completed, it is worth stressing, and appreciating, what it was that he attempted. He tried to paint the entire American Jewish experience on a fictional canvas, and his work did not receive the attention it deserved while he lived, and I fear that, now that he is gone, there will not be any rising interest in it. It is a pity.

Angoff taught me a lesson about writing that should be committed to memory by all who would write. The message is: write! For forty years and more, no matter what else he did in the course of any given day (and he had been a university professor, editor, lecturer, college executive, television professional), he wrote *every single day of his life.* If he returned from a lecture at eleven o'clock at night, he wrote for an hour or two. If he had an afternoon class, he wrote in the morning. No day was complete until he had written. As a result, he produced some dozen novels, three collections of short stories, books of poetry and short stories, a literary history, a collection of memoiristic essays, a biography of Mencken, a group of books on music—in all, some forty-five volumes.

He was, in addition, an extremely generous man, who loved to discover new literary talent and as the editor of *The Literary Review,* he opened the pages of this fine journal to unknown poets and short story writers. He once called me, with excitement, to say that he had found a beautiful new writer. It was Edward Lewis Wallant, at the time scarcely known and touted by no one. It was Angoff who informed me that Henry Roth was alive in Maine, but somewhat depressed. He said to me, "Please let him know that you, too, admire him. His letters to me are so gloomy, maybe you can cheer him up." He also had the candor to confess that Roth had stopped writing to him. "I suppose I can't communicate with him, somehow. Maybe you will be able to. It is important to him."

I remain puzzled and angry that none of Angoff's novels are in paperback, that his name is mentioned only in passing when contemporary critics write comprehensive essays on American Jewish writing. His work is substantive, suffused with love for his people, and written out of a deep knowledge of the American Jew. It is easy to understand why he was sometimes bitter when lesser writers won attention that he deserved but, in his lifetime, did not get.

Isaac Bashevis Singer is, of course, very well known all over the world now, since he won the Nobel Prize for Literature in 1978. I had first heard of him in the early 1940s when I attended a performance of Habimah, the Hebrew-language theater of what was then Palestine. Sitting behind me and my father was I. J. Singer, then famous as the author of the popular Yiddish drama, *Yoshe Kalb,* which had been staged by Maurice Schwartz. My father pointed out I. J. Singer to me and declared, "He has a younger brother who has more talent that he has, although he is very good." That brother was Isaac Bashevis Singer who, incidentally, always pays tribute to his older brother when he is asked about the major influences on his life, literary, or otherwise.

I had occasion to review Singer's work early in his American writing career and found his writing intriguing even then. He and his wife Alma visited us once in Queens, just about when the *Saturday Evening Post* had accepted a group of three of his stories. Ultimately, the *Post* published them in a single issue, shortly before the periodical ceased publication (years later it was revived, in a different format by a different company). Singer was astonished at the huge size of the check he had been sent. He was accustomed to writing almost for nothing. I later learned that any fugitive magazine, started up by collegians, or academics or hopeful culture promoters, could ask for—and obtain—a story by Singer. He was actually thrilled when he was invited to offer one of his stories to an English-language publication.

Since then, of course, Singer has learned to accept his success. He gives the impression, occasionally, of being "on stage" with both questioners and admirers. I have seen him benign, accommodating, and gentle; I have felt that he sometimes represses an inherent sharpness. He can be brusque and, a moment later, considerate. He is reluctant to confront the reality that many Yiddish critics and readers are shocked by his sensuality and eroticism. They mistakenly assume that these elements are introduced into his work for "commercial" reasons. I am convinced that the Yiddish-language reader, unfamiliar with the Western or American writing tradition, cannot understand that sexuality and man-woman relationships are the common material of the writer of fiction. "There is no story without a love story," Singer has told me, and others. He is convinced of it. The reader raised on Peretz and Sholom Aleichem cannot understand this. Singer is modern; too many of his potential Yiddish readers are not. "This could not have happened," they often complain, when they read one of his wildly imaginative tales, a fable or parable. "Anything the human mind can imagine, can happen," Singer replies. In the interview in this volume, Singer explains this at length, and eloquently. Singer and these Yiddish readers inhabit different worlds, although they speak the same language. It is therefore intelligent of Singer to deny that his critics exist. In effect, for him they do not exist. He is wise to behave as he does.

Although he is a believer in "fate," and imps and demons, Singer is in possession of an extremely sophisticated sense of humor. It is obvious not only in his work, but in his conversation, his interviews, and his lectures. He uses his humor to help him adjust to a world that must be strange to him: the literary and publishing world and the academic world. He adapts; he copes. He is a survivor and his work will survive. His imagination is so glistening; his world peopled with so many extraordinary human beings placed in extraordinary situations, that his stories and novels hypnotize readers who are strangers to Yiddish, Jews, and his imagined world. The Nobel Prize was placed in good hands when it was given to Isaac Bashevis Singer.

Chaim Grade is a passionate, emotional Yiddish poet and novelist who carries lightly and modestly an enormous amount of Jewish knowledge and learning. A product of a yeshiva, he, more than any other Yiddish creative writer, is respected for his deep acquaintance with the sacred and legal volumes incorporated in the Gemara and Mishna and the Chumash. He also is a student of philosophy and Jewish history; not a superficial scholar but a serious one. His home spills over with books, in many languages. He is a book-buying addict. No matter where he finds himself, whether in New York City, his upstate summer home, or on the lecture circuit, somehow he manages to find books that interest him—not single copies, but large collections. His literary appetite is insatiable; his curiosity always at a peak.

Interestingly, he keeps his own books, his poems, stories, and novels in Yiddish and the translations into other languages tucked away in a far corner of a distant bookcase, where one can hardly notice his own work. He feels, quite clearly, that fiction and poetry—imaginative writing—do not belong on the same shelves with books of scholarship, religion, and history. Although he is a former yeshiva student and was not raised to appreciate the visual arts, he owns many outsize volumes of modern art and he constantly bewails his own inability to read and speak English fluently. It is as though he senses a world floating past him; he is reaching for it but it eludes his grasp.

Grade is shrewd and naive, generous and caustic, undisciplined and yet controlled. Unfortunately, I am not qualified to judge the caliber of his poetry, but I have been profoundly impressed with his few novels translated into English, as well as with some of his philosophical essays and, in particular, one elegaic prose poem on his return to the Vilna ghetto ("Sanctuaries in Ruin"). His fictional sketches in *The Well* and his novel *The Agunah* recreate East European shtetl life with vividness, clarity of vision, and artistic detachment. When I interviewed him, we talked of his massive Yiddish work of fiction, *Tsemach Atlas,* which had not yet been translated into English. Since then the book has appeared in two volumes as *The Yeshiva,* brilliantly translated by Curt Leviant. On the basis of *The Yeshiva*, Grade is a major world literary figure. He makes references to it in our conversation, but I had no idea at the time of its scope, its depth, and its remarkable evocation of a life now destroyed and vanished. It is a profound book, one which probes deeply into the Jewish psyche and which clarifies for Jews everywhere the strengths—and weaknesses—of the traditions from which they stem.

Grade is a skilled narrator with a sharp comprehension of the religious Jews of Poland and Lithuania. He does not concern himself with devils, but with tortured men and women—tortured in the spiritual sense—who constantly wrestle with God, question Him and debate with Him. Grade does not sentimentalize, although he depicts great scholars, and, occasionally, saints.

His books are inhabited by drunks and lechers as well as by heads of yeshivas and saintly men and women. He re-creates a world that has been shattered, but one that lives in his imagination and in the mind of the reader. It is, I think, remarkable that Grade is so fine and effective a novelist, after having spent most of his life as a practicing poet. Few poets, in any language, are good novelists. He is an exceptional one.

As a human being, he is even more uncommon. There is an innocence about him that is winning. In the same moment, he seems both vain and humble. He is sure that his work, in Yiddish, will be respected and win attention. When a book of his appears in translation, he is kept awake at night by the frightening possibility (to him) that English-language critics, not being familiar with his work and his world, will cut him up. He cannot persuade himself to believe that a literary critic unacquainted with yeshivas and yeshiva students and the Lithuanian shtetl can understand his work. He is, of course, entirely wrong for he writes so well of the particular that his work is transformed into the universal. His Tsemach Atlas in *The Yeshiva* is a gigantic character, just as is Prince Myshkin in Dostoevsky's *The Idiot*. One need not be a Russian to understand the Prince, just as one need not be a Jew or yeshiva student to empathize with Tsemach Atlas.

Although my command of Yiddish is less than fluent, Grade and I talk in Yiddish with some frequency. His health is sometimes uncertain. His spirit and his drive and his desire to excel force him beyond his physical abilities at times. To know him is to worry over him, to think of him. His wife, Inna, cultured, charming, and utterly devoted to his well being, makes life much easier for him, although he gruffly denies it from time to time. I have been "charged" with liking Yiddish writers beyond others. If this is true, it is because I know men like Chaim Grade.

As mentioned earlier, I regret that Cynthia Ozick was unwilling to be interviewed for reasons already given by her. When I first read her unique and highly intellectual short story, "The Pagan Rabbi," I thought of her as an intellectual writer. Her long, dense and overlooked novel, *Trust*, to which I turned after reading her stories, strengthened this view. While I recognized her inner passion, I missed her warmth in the writing. When she spoke in public, she sometimes sounded like an angry Biblical prophet. I heard her admonish, castigate, and read beautifully phrased sermons to an audience of rabbis and Jewish communal workers. I also heard her, rather less confident sounding, as a member of various panels on Jewish culture and literature. In personal discussion, in brief notes, in letters, on the telephone, she is emotional, outgoing, affectionate, and wonderfully understanding. Her pleasure is genuine, bubbling, instinctive when she hears of an achievement of genuine merit by others. There is no malice in her, although in one of her celebrated stories she is sharp and knowing about the Yiddish literary jungle.

In many of the interviews in this book, I have quoted from her work in order to elicit the views of other writers on her statement that when she writes in the English language she is writing in a Christian language. Some have agreed with her and some have not. Also—when I mentioned her name—many prefaced their own remarks with observations about Ozick's gifts, her wonderful stories, her "genius." Although she has refused to be included in this volume, I cannot think of a more interesting writer and yet I have found that the writer and the individual person are not always the same individual and I await the written work which shall represent them both at their best.

Jack Ansell's name is not well known to the reader of Jewish fiction, although his books have been quite successful commercially. His novels and stories about the South are uncommonly good and socially important. He also has written books about the entertainment industry and about the business world, which include Jewish characters who were obviously drawn—and sometimes quartered—by a novelist who is a Jew. It is not my intent here to write about his novelistic abilities, a subject dealt with in the interview in this book. It is as a person that I shall remember him best. We met under circumstances that were very difficult for him, and became so for me. Originally, I wrote to him about my project of interviewing Jewish writers and asked whether he would be willing to sit for an interview. He was extremely pleased and I sensed in his acceptance a degree of satisfaction over the invitation. But not quite yet, he said. He had to enter a hospital for a checkup. Politely, I hoped it was a small matter. Calmly, he said, "Well, I'm used to it. I was hospitalized six times last year and I'm lucky to be alive." He spoke in a soft Southern drawl, without self-pity. He kept calling me to let me know what progress he was, or was not, making. One morning a woman called me. It was Ansell's sister. She had come to New York from Hawaii because, within the hour, her brother was to undergo radical surgery for cancer. He had asked her to call me so that I should not bother to contact him for the time being. He would, she said with a quaver, call me when he was able.

A few weeks later, he did call. Speaking with great effort, he informed me that he had just been moved out of intensive care, at the Lenox Hill Hospital in New York City, to a private room. He was not well enough to meet with me yet, he reported. He would call me again when he came home. I wanted to know how he was feeling, what the doctors had said. Ansell informed me he had been on the operating table for nine hours and that he was told that he would recover. I was relieved and we agreed to wait until he was strong enough to talk at length.

He continued to call me, and I was puzzled. We had not yet met, he knew little about me and I knew a little of him. But, it seemed to me, that he was latching onto me as though I were to be a kind of literary executor for him. He got home and we set a date to meet. Before that date arrived, he called one more time. He was back in the hospital: a complication. Sorry. He would call again. I began to suspect we would never meet. Then, one day in June 1976, he phoned to say that while he had to remain in the hospital, his doctors agreed to allow me to come; it would be good therapy for him, he suggested. "I look terrible," he said. "Usually I weigh about 160. I'm down to 90 pounds." Usually I carry a camera to interviews and take portrait shots of the writers. I knew that in this instance, I would be unwilling to enter Ansell's hospital room with a camera, for he talked again and again about his loss of weight.

Finally, early in July 1976, a few days before the Tall Ships extravaganza that enraptured New York City, I walked over to Lenox Hill with my paraphernalia, minus a camera, and under nervous tension.

He looked like an Auschwitz inmate who could not be saved. I had never seen so skeletal a figure. Again, his first words to me were about his mean thinness. He excused himself for his appearance and reminded me that his natural weight was 160 pounds. He was beyond medical aid. He had neither energy nor stamina. I saw immediately that, if we talked at all, it would have to be done in brief stages, over a longish period of time. For half an hour we gossiped, becoming acquainted. I then set the cassette recorder and we began our formal interview. Within twenty minutes, Ansell was unable to concentrate. He had no strength at all. I assured him that I would be back the next day and as many days as was necessary.

Over the next few days, we became good friends. He had been raised in Monroe, Louisiana, had gone to temple and had become a radio and then a television executive. He was a prolific writer and had written many of his novels, as well as a full-length play, from hospital beds. Some days he was quite strong for an hour or an hour and a half, never longer. He was unable to swallow. He was obliged to take more than twenty different drugs each day and he methodically listed what he had to take, and when. If a nurse brought him the wrong pill at the wrong time, he knew it immediately. He was at home in the small hospital room, which was filled with books, his own and others, and beautiful fresh flowers sent to him daily by old friends. He had a gift for friendship. His first editor, at Doubleday, was still one of his best friends, although every other one of his books was published by someone else. This editor called him daily.

I had never met a writer—or anyone—who was able to work in such tranquility in such adverse circumstances. His mind was flooded with plans. He had worked out what he called a "saga" about American Jewish family life, set in the South. He was writing a second play. He was completing two books, one a collection of short stories. He never talked about the possibility of being terminally ill. He continued to explain that he was having "plumbing problems," not health complications.

I kept visiting him long after we completed our professional work. At the outset, he was sensitive about his appearance. I had told him that generally I took pictures of writers I talked with. He smiled and said, "Not me; not now." I did not reply. When we taped his comments, he at first asked me to delete references to our being in a hospital room; he did not want to admit that so much of his writing was done on a legal-size pad in a bed. Later he waved a thin hand and whispered, "What the hell, this is where I am, why hide it?"

When I talked of my son's interest in and involvement in the theater, he asked if my son could come to his bedside. It was his indirect way of letting me know that he would permit another member of my family to see him in this emaciated state. My son and he also became friends. They discussed plays and producers and agents. Ansell and I lent each other books, copies of our articles, and exchanged views on politics, the TV industry, and paperback book publishing. In a week, we were close friends. I missed him when I did not see him. I no longer saw a dying man. I saw a vital, determined, very brave human being. One day, I said that even for a man in good health, his writing program was enormously ambitious and few men could live to see these plans fulfilled. For the only time, he allowed a note of pessimism to break through. "I must act and think as though I shall live tomorrow," he said, with some passion in his gentle drawl. "If I don't make it," he said, "God bless me."

God bless him, indeed, for he died in the hospital in September 1976.

I should like to think that the reader of this book will be attracted to the works of the writers represented here. At the same time, I believe that the creative artists who talked with me also give the reader some idea of their personalities, their thought processes, their views of writing, Judaism, Jews, and their own wrestling with the Muse that makes them artists who have enriched American and Jewish literature.

A Conversation with

Charles Angoff

(Charles Angoff died at the age of seventy-seven on May 3, 1979, some five years after this interview took place. In the introduction to this volume, I have written about him at length, and thus the notes that follow remain intact, as first noted, prior to his passing).

Charles Angoff is a sandy-haired, gangling man with a loping stride and a soft voice which still carries the sounds and echoes of Europe, although he is a Harvard graduate and an eminent literary figure. His career has been varied as a writer, editor, teacher, lecturer. For years he worked with H. L. Mencken and George Jean Nathan on the old, justifiably famous *American Mercury.* He has written a basic book on Mencken and has spent years editing the collected works of Nathan. He has edited many periodicals, is a prolific critic, recognized poet, a memoirist, and, of course, the author of an ongoing series of novels about American-Jewish life, with David Polonsky as the central character in all the books. No Jewish writer in the English language, or for that matter in any other language, has undertaken so ambitious a literary project.

We have known each other since the 1940s and met often. This "formal" talk took place at my home on June 9, 1974.

RIBALOW: You worked with H. L. Mencken, George Jean Nathan and others and you have known some world-famous writers like William Faulkner, Thomas Wolfe, F. Scott Fitzgerald, and Sinclair Lewis. As I remember it, you were involved in the first publications of both Faulkner and Wolfe. Then, suddenly, at some point in the 1940s, you began to write fiction. Now why did you turn to fiction?

ANGOFF: It happened suddenly. I can't really explain it. Incidentally, I felt a certain kinship with, of all people, Dr. Theodor Herzl. I had just read a new biography of him by Desmond Stewart. Maybe you've read it. Stewart speaks of Herzl's sudden conversion to Zionism. Herzl himself didn't understand it. He said it came out of his complete unconscious, and apparently the same thing happened to me. I was walking down Fifth Avenue with Mencken. Just about then G. B. Stern's *The Matriarch* had been published. I think it was a Book-of-the-Month Club selection. People began to compare Stern to Tolstoy and Dostoevsky. The novel, of course, is completely forgotten now. We were walking down the street and suddenly, I don't know why, I said to Mencken, "You know, G. B. Stern's *The Matriarch* is a very bad book." So Mencken turns to me and says, "That's no way to talk. After all, great men like Henry Seidel Canby, and so forth, have said it is a very great book." "Well," I said, "I still think it's a very bad book."

Mencken then told me that I had bad manners because I was disagreeing with my superiors. Well, I didn't take that kind of talk too seriously because he had been talking to me that way frequently. But then he asked me why I didn't like it. I said, "She writes about her Jewish grandmother from on high looking down, as if she were an editor for *Vanity Fair*." That was one of the fancy magazines. Frank Crownenshield was the editor. Mencken said, "Well, how do you know about it?" I said, "What do you mean, how do you know about it? I have a grandmother, I have a great grandmother, I know her very well. I know my *family* very well." Well, Mencken said, "If you feel that way, why don't you write a story about her?" Suddenly, I felt a revelation.

RIBALOW: What year was this?

ANGOFF: This must have been in the late twenties, maybe in the middle thirties. I forget exactly when. Then we started talking about some other people. We talked about Mike Gold, by the way. I wasn't so sure about him. We talked about Gold and I said I didn't like his stuff either. Mencken asked why and I told him that Gold gives me a picture of the East Side that I don't know about. I don't know the East Side as well as I know the Boston slums but I know it quite well; I've been down there a great deal. And Gold speaks of rabbis who have been in cahoots with capitalists and that they were part owners of houses of prostitution and if you go into any home you'll see cockroaches crawling around the table and in the soup. Well, I said, that's a very partial picture. I've been to many East Side homes. There's a considerable beauty there—especially Friday nights. I said another thing that interests me: you go to these terrible tenements and you will see shoe boxes in the windows with flowers sprouting out of them. The kids bought seeds in school. Then if you look in the corner, you'll find an old Victrola with records. What kind of records? Not only records of cantors like Rosenblatt and Qwartin and Sirota, but also records of Alma Gluck and Mischa Elman. Well, Mencken said, "If you feel that way why don't you write about it?" So I went home and I wrote my first story—"Alte Bobbe," published in the *Prairie Schooner,* I think.

RIBALOW: Not in a Jewish magazine.

ANGOFF: Oh. I want to tell you about that. I sent the story to virtually every Anglo-Jewish magazine in America. It came back. . . . One editor, Henry Hurwitz, who was then editing the *Menorah Journal,* wrote me a letter—I have the letter someplace—I think it's in the Boston University Collection of my papers. You know, they're collecting my papers. They're collecting yours too. And Hurwitz said, "Dear Charlie, I like you. But from you I didn't expect any *bobbe maaysess.* From you I thought I would get a serious, three-dimensional essay on the socio, politico, economic flux, you know, and all that." So I wrote him back and I said, "Dear Henry, I know nothing about socio, politico, and economic flux. But I do know my alte bobbe. Well, as I say, it went around everyplace. Everyplace. So I sent it to some general or *goyish* magazines. And Lowry C. Wimberley, who was the editor of the *Prairie Schooner,* wrote me a beautiful letter. He said, "This I like. It comes out of your innards." I was so pleased because, you know, Dr. Sam Johnson said the praise of one man you respect is like the accolade of the angels. So then I wrote another story about her husband, Zayde Tzalel.

RIBALOW: Then ultimately the stories were published in *When I Was a Boy in Boston.*

ANGOFF: Ultimately I brought them all together, I had about fifteen stories published. I added another three or four and went around from publisher to publisher. I'll never forget: I had a talk with Max Perkins of Scribners. He was very friendly to me. He said, "I like these stories very much. But you know, stories don't sell." He added, "You know, Anton Chekhov didn't sell very well. Even Hemingway doesn't sell." "Well," I said, "Mr. Perkins, I'll tell you something. I think I'm a lot better than Hemingway." By the way, I still think so. "Chekhov—he's pretty stiff competition."

Then a new publisher had started business, Thomas Yoseloff. So I called up Thomas Yoseloff—Thomas Yoseloff, Inc. himself answers me. He says, come on up. So I went up. He knew about me from the *American Mercury* and elsewhere and he said, "Look, I like your stories. I'll probably lose money on them, but if I do, I like to lose money on *this.*" And that's how my long relationship with Tom Yoseloff began. Then I said to him that I was so hot about the whole project, it was as if I had at long last found myself. I told him I'd like to do a novel about the whole situation, the whole *mishpacha.* From about 1899 down to now. Up to date. The forties. I finished six hundred pages. I was up to 1908. So I gave it to Yoseloff, who read it in two nights. Again he said to me, "I like it." I said, "Tom, honest to God, I think I'll do the rest of it in another volume." Well, the rest you know. I did another volume. I was up to 1912.

RIBALOW: You have written ten novels, a couple of books of short stories. I didn't count them, but you've got thousands of pages of fiction. From what I know of the books and the people in them, I wouldn't call the works autobiographical, but a lot of it is based on actual people. Why did you decide to do all this fictionally instead of as a memoir, or auto-biographically, even though I know you've written some biographical essays on many of the same people?

ANGOFF: In fiction you go at inner essences far better than you can in nonfic-tion. Take alte bobbe. You know, I knew my alte bobbe actually for only about fourteen months, but I didn't realize it at the moment. She sank into my inner being so much that she's part of me now. I can discuss her fictionally, portray her, reveal her, far better than I can nonfictionally.

RIBALOW: Take another instance. You wrote a memoir of H. L. Mencken called *H. L. Mencken, A Portrait from Memory.* In your novels you write about a fellow named Brandt who is based on Mencken. What have you done in the fiction that you didn't do in the memoir, which, inci-dentally, aroused a great deal of controversy? You know, out of curiosity, every time I see a book on Mencken, I look at the index and the authors always refer to you and your book on him.

ANGOFF: They have to—for a simple reason. I'm the only man who knew him all that time. That's number one. Number two, nobody in all the years of controversy has been able to knock down a single fact. My trouble was that I was too kind. For example, in my chapter on Mencken and the Jews, I was far too easy on him. He was a violent anti-Semite. He himself proved it. If you should read, for example, his introduction to *The Anti-Christ,* you will see what he says there about the Jews. He said they deserved ten times as many pogroms as they have received.

Now to come back to Mencken: in a biography, even in a portrait from memory, which the book *is,* it's impossible to go into motives. But in fiction I have a great opportunity to go into motives. It's also possible to go into meanings of what in a biography would seem like *minutiae.* Fiction gives you more elbow room and I think Brandt, based largely on

Mencken, is a far fuller portrait of Mencken than is my nonfiction book on him.

RIBALOW: Now again, nearly all your creative work deals with Jewish characters, Jewish themes, Jewish problems. Why have you chosen to focus almost exclusively on Jews? I wouldn't say that about other writers, but you've been involved in the so-called outside world to such a great degree and to such a wide extent.

ANGOFF: I'm a schizophrenic. I have one foot in the non-Jewish world; the other foot in the Jewish world.

RIBALOW: There must be people who know you only from the non-Jewish world and other people who know you the other way.

ANGOFF: There are. There are a great many people who know me from the other angle. For example, recently I received a letter from the editor of *The South Carolina Quarterly,* which is a very high-toned literary review and he wanted an essay from me on the twenties. From the way he wrote I'm almost positive he has never read a single line of my Jewish fiction. Not a single line. He's read my poetry—in fact he's going to print some of my poems—and he wants an essay.

RIBALOW: *The Tone of the Twenties* is a very good book.

ANGOFF: Thank you.

RIBALOW: A seminal book on that period.

ANGOFF: But the essence of your question contains a great truth. That is I do write, not only extensively but with *geshmak* (relish), on Jewish themes. I never realized, until I became much older, how deep Jewishness was in me. I feel a glow when I am with Jewish people. When I go to Israel I feel very much at home.

Then there's another thing. I have an advantage over other people. My knowledge of Jewish things is quite extensive. I am very glad it is. I not only went to one of the finest Hebrew schools in America, in Boston, called Ivriah. I'm the man, the boy, who was selected by the teachers to give the *kabbolos ponim* (welcoming) speech to Shmaryahu Levin, to Eliezer Ben Yehuda, and to Nahum Sokolow when they came—in Hebrew. I also wrote poetry in Hebrew; unfortunately I can't do it any more. I wrote stories in Hebrew. I was the editor of the Hebrew magazine which was put out by my school and it was called *Bikkurim.* I also went to a yeshiva. I studied *gemora.* I studied the Talmud. One of the great heartaches of my father was that I didn't study to be a rabbi.

RIBALOW: This obviously is not the common background of most contemporary American Jewish novelists.

ANGOFF: No it isn't. Sometimes when I read their books, I say to myself, "These are not the Jews I know." These people don't know the whole field. For example, when I visit any town, one of the first things I do is go to a little shul. I love the *nigunim* (melodies). I like to come on Saturday afternoon and see a group of Jews around a table studying the Talmud. I do this because I feel a compulsion to do it.

RIBALOW: Now we just went over the number of novels you've written. Ten of them. At the moment it's not quite the longest ongoing series. I think C. P. Snow's series is somewhat longer. But how much further do you see these books going? The most recent one, *Mid-Century,* is still not actually contemporary. It's set in the fifties. And here we are in the midseventies. You did say earlier on that when you did one book, you thought you could do it all in one and then you thought that it would take two. Now ten have been published. If I know you, I know that you have some in the vault of your publisher. How many does Yoseloff have?

ANGOFF: He now has in the vault one completed—the eleventh—and one almost finished.

RIBALOW: What do you do? You give it to him as you write it?

ANGOFF: No, no.

RIBALOW: Or do you give it to him as a complete manuscript?

ANGOFF: No. In volume twelve for example, there are a couple of things I want to change. Actually he has two volumes.

RIBALOW: But you're going to alter one of the two.

ANGOFF: The twelfth one—a little bit. In fact, I'm not sure I'll do it yet.

RIBALOW: But he has two manuscripts.

ANGOFF: Two manuscripts.

RIBALOW: That's volume eleven and volume twelve.

ANGOFF: Eleven and twelve. I'm working on thirteen, which is near its end, and I hope to begin volume fourteen early in 1975.

RIBALOW: Now you indicated yourself that when you say you have this Jewish background and you attended yeshiva and you knew Hebrew and you visit Israel—and I should add that your depictions of synagogue life, even the garment industry, Jewish educational and general institutions, because of your characters is a *melamed*—all of these are closely knit with

Jewish life—do you think that the use of such material limits your readership to Jews?

ANGOFF: I don't think so. I think that my relatively small public is not due to
the nature of my material. It is simply due to the fact that at the moment I
seem to be outside the stream of critical acceptance by the "way showers."

RIBALOW: Let me interrupt a moment. Years ago I wrote a book on Arnold
Wesker, the English playwright who is a Jew. He's from London's East
End and when I knew him first and when he became popular and well
known, this was in 1960, three of his plays were on the boards at the same
time. The British at that time claimed it hadn't happened since Shakespeare. Nothing he had written was basically Jewish. When I wrote my
book about him, I had to do some probing and digging and seeking to
find the Jewish elements in his plays. The last time I was back in London,
I met Wesker and discovered that he is now writing a great deal of Jewish
material, and curiously Wesker claims that he too has been placed outside
the stream of English writing for the same reason. So why is it that you
think you're not in the main stream and you make mention of the limited
readership you have?

ANGOFF: I don't know the English-Jewish literary world too well. I think I've
read most of their writers, but I don't know the background that well.
Actually I think on the whole they are about twenty years behind us. But
anyway, to keep it to America, my own feeling—and here I'm doing some
public psychoanalysis—is that now there is a market for *negative* Jewish
fiction. *Positive* Jewish fiction for a long time hasn't had very much of a
public except when it's become mystical. For example, take *The Rise of
David Levinsky* by Abraham Cahan. It didn't do well at all, you know
that. Edward Lewis Wallant didn't do well either. When I say well I mean
as compared to, you know, *Portnoy's Complaint* and so forth. Or take
Hugh Nissenson, whose stories I happen to like. He didn't do so very well.
Leon Uris is successful but in this case you have something special. With
Leon Uris I think I am one of the few people who didn't like his stuff from
the very beginning. I got into deep trouble on account of that with a
certain important Jewish magazine. Anyway, I think his stuff is high
grade soap opera and I'm not sure of the high grade aspect of it. To return
to my work. I wear many caps. I'm a poet; I'm an editor; I'm a professor;
I'm a critic. Frankly I think my stuff is at least as good as that of the
others. But there comes out of it a certain positive emotionalism. Some
people say I whitewash my characters. I wish they would read my novels a
little more carefully; they would see how little I whitewash them. But
there is a difference between being negative and *negative*. Mendele
Mocher Sfarim is certainly very critical of his Jews.

RIBALOW: So are a lot of Hebrew and Yiddish writers.

ANGOFF: Yes, very critical. But it's with affection, with love. In the case of some of the American writers there's a bitterness there. In addition to bitterness, there's simple ignorance. They don't like Jews and try to portray them in such a way that their dislike of them is justified.

RIBALOW: You are saying that the general public prefers portraits of Jews pictured that way?

ANGOFF: The answer is yes, but there is a reason for it. The readers get directions from critics who know as little about Jewish life—many of them—as do some of the very popular writers. And you know who some of the people are, who review for the *New York Times,* for the *New York Review of Books* and so on. However, in justification of myself, I think, people have told me that I have a small public of Hasidim, and it's growing very slowly. And then there's another thing. You take *Journey to the Dawn,* the first novel in my series. The book's still selling.

RIBALOW: I think that was published in 1950.

ANGOFF: Around there. The book is selling. It's in the fifth edition now, I think. It goes on and on and on. Nearly all of the books are in print. And when they go out of print they get reprinted and they remain constantly available. They're all in demand. I know. After all, I get my statements. Every one of them is bought every single year. Sometimes there's an upsurge. By the way, the one book that seems to enjoy the biggest sale of all is the very first one *Journey to the Dawn* and then there's *Memory of Autumn* and *In the Morning Light* and then you jump to *Winter Twilight.*

RIBALOW: I know a number of people who told me they had read your early books but they haven't been able to find the later ones. They know your name and they say, "Oh yes I'm acquainted with the earlier books. I don't seem to know, have there been many others?" And they didn't know that. Now it may be, in part, the critical reception you get. Unhappily if a book isn't fairly widely reviewed in the major media, your potential readers simply don't know the book exists.

ANGOFF: That's true, unfortunately. I should say, out of my ten novels, I think six or seven were reviewed in the *New York Times Book Review.*

RIBALOW: What about the Jewish periodicals? What has been the critical reception there? I am not talking about whether the critics like it or not but do they get reviewed in the Jewish magazines around the country?

ANGOFF: Yes, I'm always reviewed, for example, in the Detroit *Jewish Times,* in the Boston *Jewish Advocate,* in the *Jewish Frontier.* Usually it's much later than when the book is published. On the other hand, it doesn't make too much difference. Many of the other periodicals will review a novel now and then. I've been reviewed in the *Jerusalem Post*. You don't get totally overlooked.

RIBALOW: None of your novels are in paperback as I can remember.

ANGOFF: Unfortunately no. And not one of them, alas, is translated into Hebrew and I don't understand why.

RIBALOW: Now to get to another subject for a moment. You've been a professor for many years now; you lecture all around the United States. I know you have visited Europe on a professional basis and you visit Israel with some frequency. You have lectured in England, in Spain, in Rome, in Jerusalem, in Tel Aviv, and other major cities overseas. What about the Jewish reader around the world today? I ask this, because at one time when I was abroad, some intelligent, well-read people had never at that time heard of Bernard Malamud and they didn't know Isaac Bashevis Singer or other major American Jewish literary figures. Ultimately of course, they got around to them. But as you yourself have indicated to me, this happened eight or nine years after we did. What do you find of Jewish interest in the world in which you moved when you were outside of America? Or for that matter, around the country?

ANGOFF: Let's take Israel first. In Israel, unfortunately, they know only two or three Jewish writers. And whom do they know? They know Philip Roth, of course. By the way, one of the things that depressed me no end a few years ago happened when I was at the bottom of Har Zion. I always go up to see King David who is buried there. And there at the bottom was a little newsstand and I saw a great announcement—bold letters in Hebrew saying that we are very happy to tell our people that *Portnoy's Complaint* can now be had in a Hebrew edition. And I thought to myself, King David, the man up there should hear about that! You see it's unfortunate but the people who teach literature at the Hebrew University in Jerusalem, in Haifa, and in Tel Aviv—at least some of them—follow the lead of the people who they think are the great critics in the United States, like Leslie Fiedler. They also don't seem to be much interested in Jewish Americans. They'd rather write about William Faulkner than write about Meyer Levin or myself. That's part of the general condescension towards things American, I think. And a book that denounces American Jews, as Roth does very often, that they like. But anything that's more positive, they don't generally like.

RIBALOW: What about England or some of the other countries you visited?

ANGOFF: Yes, I've been to England. And it's pretty much the same. They know Roth, a little bit of Malamud. I was amazed. For example, I was given a lunch by the people who run the *Jewish Chronicle* in London. Now they are a knowledgeable group. The first time I was there, about ten years ago, not one of them had read *The Rise of David Levinsky*. Not a single one of them! The name of Anzia Yezierska meant nothing to them. And when I was speaking of Ludwig Lewisohn, they said, "Oh, that's the fellow who had trouble with wives." I said "Now wait a minute, wait a minute, I'm talking about his writing." I even mentioned poets like Charles Reznikoff. I'm afraid they don't follow Jewish-American writing particularly closely.

RIBALOW: Now that we have been ranging around, let me ask you a few questions about Jewish writers. Which contemporary Jewish writers in the creative fields do you think well of? I recall that you reminded me at one point, years ago, that *The Human Season* by Edward Lewis Wallant was a fine book; this was when it first came out. But there are a lot of people so many readers don't know. A year or so ago the Jewish Book Council gave its award to a young writer named Francine Prose. Hardly anybody read her book *Judah the Pious*. After winning the award, I doubt that there was any increase of interest in her. Yet there are, you will agree, a tremendously large number of Jewish writers.

ANGOFF: A great many. And I think this runs counter to the picture I may have presented earlier. I believe that in spite of everything, there is a greater awareness among the general Jewish-American public of fictional work by Jewish American writers. At least they hear about them and so they read a little more. I do quite a bit of lecturing, as you know, and more people come to these lectures than used to come. How many of them read? Not too many. But I think it's more than before.

I probably am responsible for at least half of the sales of Wallant's books. Everywhere I go I talk about him. Why? I know I was one of the first to hail him. I recall writing one of the early reviews of *The Human Season* in the Philadelphia *Jewish Exponent* and I loved it. Later on I met him at the Jewish Book Council meeting where he won the award and I happened to like him personally. He and I then corresponded and later I liked his books. I enjoyed *The Pawnbroker* and I liked *The Tenants of Moonbloom*. Yes, I like him very much. Still, he's hardly known. I read many a book of criticism by the so-called cognoscenti and they will discuss him, if they do at all, on the basis of the movie made of *The Pawnbroker*. Yet I don't think they understand the man or the writer. I see a book up there on your shelf called *In the Days of Simon Stern* by Arthur Cohen. I read that book twice. He is a cultivated taste but I think there's a great deal in that book, a tremendous amount. There's Hasidism there, there's history, there's understanding of Jewish life, of the Holocaust. And wherever I go I talk about the book.

RIBALOW: I'm interested in what you say about Arthur Cohen's novel but let me tell you: I live close by to a bookstore that sells remainder copies of books and the first and only edition of *The Days of Simon Stern* has been remaindered and it has been piled high for a single dollar.

ANGOFF: I'm shocked to hear this. Listen, you know this field as well as I do and we haven't had a book like Cohen's for years, have we? It's just terrible, terrible.

RIBALOW: It isn't only Cohen. Isaac Bashevis Singer whom I like more than you do, is a popular writer. His books seem to remain in print and almost all of his titles are issued in paperback. Yet *Satan in Goray* has also been dumped. I don't really know why, except perhaps that the title is in paperback.

ANGOFF: Yes, I like his short stories better than I do his novels. I don't believe many of his novels "go." Yet there is one book, *In My Father's Court,* a collection of little sketches, and I kind of like that one. I like these things more than the big novels.

RIBALOW: What about some of the other Jewish writers?

ANGOFF: I'm on record about most. As I say, I'm a critic as well as a fiction writer, which gets me into all kinds of difficulties. There's a Mr. Roth, for example. And I don't mean Henry Roth. I mean Philip Roth. These two must never be confused.

RIBALOW: In recent years he has been having a great deal of trouble with his books, both with the critical and the public reception.

ANGOFF: He's naving a lot of trouble. I remember reading *Commentary*'s review of *Portnoy's Complaint. Commentary,* which had published Roth and generally speaking had admired his work, didn't like *Portnoy's Complaint* at all. I never liked him. The only story of his that had any meaning to me was the very last one in *Goodbye, Columbus,* "Eli, the Fanatic." You remember that story about the Hasidim who move into a little town in the suburbs like Spring Valley. That story had something. But I do have to be as objective as I can, and I do not remember anything else that he wrote that had any meaning to me. I believe that he writes not as an artist but as a deeply troubled man. I think he ought to take a little time off and collect himself and do more reading about Jewish life. I wouldn't write about the love life of the Manchu Dynasty in the eleventh century in China, because I don't know it. You take Saul Bellow. Bellow interests me. I think his first two books were really good. That is, *Dangling Man* and *The Victim.* Do you remember them? I couldn't get past page sixty in *Herzog.* It is the same thing over and over again.

RIBALOW: His view of life has become quite sour in *Mr. Sammler's Planet.*

ANGOFF: That's it. That book offended me. I don't mean merely about the sexual things. I'll take anything if it adds up to insight and revelation. You are right; it is a bitter book. Bellow doesn't just dislike his Jews, he seems to dislike the human race. God knows, there is a lot to dislike in the world now. All you have to do is to pick up the *New York Times.* There's a great deal in the world not to like. But you cannot write out of hatred. Out of hatred you don't get art, you only get hatred. And it is possible to be truthful and compassionate, which is exactly what the great prophets were and what all the great writers were.

Who else is there? Bernard Malamud. I liked about three quarters of *The Assistant.* I don't like the ending. I do not believe that the Italian was circumcised, I just don't believe it. But up to this point it's a very compassionate story about a schnook grocery man. It's a wonderful story. Malamud's book on the Jewish blood libel case, *The Fixer,* rings false to me. He's so cold. I believe I wrote a review of that book somewhere and said that. Malamud writes about that case, the Mendel Beiliss case, only intellectually. And I always compare his book with the one on the same subject by the late Maurice Samuel, *Blood Accusation.* Samuel's book throbs. He's emotionally involved. It's far better than the fictional study by Malamud. Yet I do like some of Malamud's short stories. Especially "The Last of the Mohicans."

RIBALOW: We did mention briefly Isaac Bashevis Singer. You seem not to care for him as much as I do and as much as many other writers do. I know that he has been wildly criticized by the Yiddish critics writing in the Yiddish language.

ANGOFF: He's not liked in the Yiddish press. As you know, some of the critics have made an industry out of writing against him.

RIBALOW: He also has become an academic industry. There are books about him and collections of essays on him, individual studies on him.

ANGOFF: Unfortunately, a good many of the critical studies, as you know better than I do, could be a great deal better. As I indicated, I do like his stories far better than his novels. I think he has an ailment that so many writers have—he suffers from what might be called literary asthma.

RIBALOW: It's certainly not writer's block.

ANGOFF: Oh, no, not writer's block. Literary asthma. You see, what happens very often in the general realm of American literature, I've discovered, is that some people will write a story and it's superb. Then they will take that story and blow it up and make a novel out of it. The result is an unsuccessful novel. This is partly due to the fact that in America, far different from Europe, people look down upon the short story. In Europe, people have made world reputations on the short story. De Maupassant, for example, Katherine Mansfield, Anton Chekhov himself. But in this country writers think that you've got to write a novel. Take Katherine Ann Porter, who was superb as a short story writer. Her friends pushed her into writing a novel. She finally did—*The Ship of Fools,* and it was terrible. I think Singer is at his best when he writes short stories. He writes beautiful short stories. Really magnificent ones. The short story, or the small canvas, fits him best. I mentioned earlier *In My Father's Court.* I think the sketches there are wonderful. Maybe I think so because I like the people he writes about in that book.

RIBALOW: Well, I don't entirely agree with you. I think extremely highly of Singer and I believe that the first half of *The Slave* is an absolutely remarkable section in which Singer recreates ancient Polish life and in a way in which the Orthodox Jew manages to retain the essence of his Judaism while enslaved. Later, the book becomes a little more ordinary. But that segment is an outstanding feat of imagination. . . . What about Wiesel?

ANGOFF: You know, of course, that I was one of the first to praise Elie Wiesel and at the time he was very grateful; he called me up; he saw me; he came to my home and I thought he was a remarkable man.

RIBALOW: That book was called *Night.*

ANGOFF: Yes, *Night* and the second was *Dawn.* In *Dawn* I regret to say Wiesel began repeating himself. As he wrote more and more something else happened. He became an authority on a lot of things concerning which he had very little information. I was very sorry to see that happen. I think he's a little angry with me because I've said these things. However, I think anybody who has written *Night* and *Dawn* should be gauged on his best.

RIBALOW: What about our mutual friend Meyer Levin?

ANGOFF: Meyer Levin and I, as you know, have been friends for a great many years. In inscribing one of his books to me, he wrote, "To the other member of the two-member admiration society." I boosted him and he's boosted me. I believe that when the dust settles down he will be regarded without question as one of the very great figures in the history of Jewish-American literature. Even historically, he was the granddaddy of us all. He pretty much started the whole thing. I'm not talking of Abraham Cahan. I mean of the contemporary writers, the contemporary people. I believe *The Old Bunch* is going to live. I think *In Search* is a magnificent book, it's a beautiful book. People forget. I've studied his case in depth and I've written about him at length. I'll mention *The Obsession*, a fairly recent book written by him. People forget that in the issues he raises in *The Obsession* that he is most likely *right*. Yes it's about the Anne Frank book and play. I don't want to go into the details of it again. I've read his version of the play and the version that was staged and there's no question that his is more faithful to the original book than *The Diary of Anne Frank* version that appeared on stage and won the Pulitzer Prize.

RIBALOW: What do you see about the future of the Jewish novel and Jewish novelists in terms of the reception they get, in terms of being able to live as a writer? In my first anthology of Jewish short stories there are a great many of the contributors who wrote one story, and no more. Daniel Fuchs wrote three or four books, went to Hollywood and—as the old line has it—we never heard from him again. Simply to survive, writers have to do some many noncreative chores. You worked on "Meet the Press," you also were involved in television, and you've lectured in summer schools sponsored by various universities. What do these writers do to get by as writers if their work can't keep them financially afloat?

ANGOFF: This ailment is not peculiar to Jewish-American writers. I'm afraid it's the ailment of the whole literary world from time immemorial. Take American literature. Herman Melville had to work in the Custom House. So did Nathaniel Hawthorne. Edwin Arlington Robinson in the post office. He also was a streetcar conductor in Brooklyn. Longfellow was a Harvard professor. Take the poet, Wallace Stevens; he was a vice president of an insurance company. People born to wealth who are writers can afford only to write. Marcel Proust was very well-to-do. For a while Somerset Maugham had to be a doctor. Then he had luck; one or two of his plays caught on. Arthur Schnitzler was a doctor for many years. You know, it may be a good thing. That is to say, to write under adversity and duress and pressure. It may also be useful from another angle. If you write only, you become solipsistic. You don't meet people but if you are in the outside world you're always getting new material and that has great value. William Carlos Williams, the poet and short story writer, was a pediatrician. I knew Williams extremely well. He used to write poetry between patients. I said, "What were the poems about?" He said, "The preceding patient." And there's a great deal in that.

I remember talking years ago with a man far inferior to Williams, Robert P. Tristram Coffin. He and I taught in summer school at the University of New Hampshire. He said the best time to write is in that time which you steal from your other activities. If you have a lot of time available, you waste it. There's a lot of sense in that. I remember years ago asking T. S. Eliot—you know he was one of the editors of Faber and Faber—and I went up to him and said, "You used to work as a teller in the Midland Bank in Westminster." I said, "How did you do it?" He answered, "At first I cursed my fate, and then I blessed my fate. I had duties to do. But after a while I did them in a mechanical way. People ask for change, you know, so you just make the change." But he told me he was always writing poetry when he was doing this work. He also told me that you overhear certain things that are valuable to you. Sometimes one phrase will give you the material for a whole group of poems. Then Eliot became an editor of Faber and Faber. I asked him whether there wasn't a conflict there and he said, "No, I steal ideas, that's all." He added, "I don't steal them, I adapt them." So it may be a good thing.

RIBALOW: On your work habits. You write every day, don't you?

ANGOFF: Every single day. I mean that literally. I couldn't live without writing every single day. To me that's the only way in the world to be.

RIBALOW: Do you structure your novels?

ANGOFF: No. But I do structure the entire work. I have a complete structure for all novels, including those I haven't written. I know fairly well what is going to happen and what I am going to write about, for example, in volumes fifteen and sixteen.

RIBALOW: When did you do this? You structured it before you began?

ANGOFF: Yes. No, the first one was an accident, you know. I thought I could cover the whole business, but as I wrote I became more and more interested in my people. After the first novel, I decided to structure the whole thing.

RIBALOW: I asked the question because I'm thinking of the series of novels published by C. P. Snow. They weren't issued in the same sequence as the interior life of the books. The book for example that came out in 1955 was written at a considerably earlier period, and the books were issued in accidental or casual order. Then when Scribner's published them here, they reissued them in a kind of order. All of the Snow novels in the series were published in a three-volume set and he took the opportunity at this time of rewriting and deleting and compressing so that in the introduction to the first of the three volumes, which contains all of the books, he tells his reader that if the reader read them previously what the differences now were. In many ways, therefore, you can read the entire project as a totally new work. But Snow at some point did structure very carefully.

ANGOFF: I didn't know this but I do the same thing and I do structure every novel. Usually, before I start, I will outline the chapters in two-page summaries. However, as I write these chapters, other things come up.

RIBALOW: That's why I asked you. For example, you have a habit, which I see in nobody else, which intrigues me. In your most recent volume, *Mid-Century,* for example, the hero's girlfriend says if so-and-so will invite you to her home I suggest you attend; it will interest you. Then you as the novelist write twenty, thirty, or forty pages about the hostess. In this way the reader gets to know that hostess pretty well, before he is led into that party. How does that come about? Does it flow?

ANGOFF: It comes as a flow.

RIBALOW: As a flow. You hadn't planned that. In an earlier book, you are very critical of a faker who pretends he's a specialist on the Soviet Union but really isn't. Before we get to meet him, you give us the whole history of this man so that when the reader accosts him, he already knows he's a faker because you've already told it to us. In this fashion, we get a total portrait of all these people—the Hebrew teacher, the garment worker, the rabbi, or the faker on the Russian revolution, or the character you modeled on Dorothy Thompson. Now I can't conceive whether that is planned in advance. Again, you are the only novelist who does this: your character visits a synagogue or a shul, and listens to the rabbi preach his sermon. You, as the novelist, produce a full-length sermon that runs on for seven or eight pages. That can't be planned, can it?

ANGOFF: No, it's not planned. What happens is that as I get into a scene there is a fever which gets me, a fever of creativity. I want to say so much that my problem is in how to say it. In the case of this particular sermon, by the way, I did hear a sermon. But my sermon was not the rabbi's sermon. Completely different. Still the spirit of the sermon was the spirit that I got as I was listening. You see, all men of the cloth fascinate me because they are dealing with eternal things in a very temporary way. And that always gets me. A real *rov* (rabbi) is to me a very noble person, but a man who is a *rov* who really should be a floor walker, well, this I can't take. But I seldom discuss such people.

RIBALOW: But then you write in the evening and you do restructure your work and edit it, right?

ANGOFF: Yes. What happens is that my first draft of a certain chapter might be fifty pages long. I will then cut it down to thirty. But I will do it as I am writing the following chapter. I do a lot of things simultaneously. I write poetry, novels, stories, mark papers, deliver lectures.

RIBALOW: Do you write short stories with the knowledge that they stand alone, or do you plan to include them ultimately as part of one of your novels?

ANGOFF: They are completely isolated. Sometimes I use them, as I did in *When I Was a Boy in Boston.* But ordinarily I write stories as independent works. If I can use them, fine; if not, that's it.

RIBALOW: There are many studies relating to well-known writers and their attitudes toward Jews. I once did a long study on Thomas Wolfe and the Jews and concluded that he both hated and loved them at the same time. I don't know—as you might—about Faulkner and Hemingway, and Fitzgerald, but one of Harry Golden's sons wrote a book on Fitzgerald and his contemporaries and discussed the anti-Semitism or philo-Semitism of these writers. What has been your own experience with some of these people on a personal basis?

ANGOFF: I knew most of these people and, in the case of some, I actually discussed the whole business of their attitude toward Jews. It's very complicated. Some of them were out-and-out anti-Semites. I think Mencken was, for example, without question an out-and-out anti-Semite. In Mencken's series of essays called *Prejudices,* there is no anti-Semitism. But if you study his introduction to the translation of Nietzsche's *Anti-Christ,* you'll see violent anti-Semitism. Also in some of his essays in the old *Baltimore Sun.* He used to run a column there on Monday—violent anti-Semitism. Mencken presents a very complicated business with anti-Semitism. His best friend in New York was a Jew, Philip Goodman; he felt closer to Goodman than, I believe, to any other human being in the world.

RIBALOW: I've read something of Goodman. Who was he? What did he do?

ANGOFF: I have a long chapter on him in my book on Mencken. He was an amazing, mysterious man. Nobody knew how he made a living, but he had a lot of money. He told me once that he was descended from Spinoza, and I said Spinoza was a bachelor. And he said, "That's what they teach you at Harvard." He was one of those vague people. He knew nothing about plays and yet he put on *The Old Soak* that I believe, introduced W. C. Fields. He put on *Poppy* with Madge Kennedy, I think.

Goodman and Mencken were very close but finally Goodman left him on the Nazi issue. Mencken was a Hitlerite, there's no doubt about it. But there again, I say it's very complicated. His publisher was a Jew—not much of a Jew—Alfred Knopf. His other friend, George Jean Nathan, a Jew, but not much of one either. And then of course there's me. I was the person closest to him professionally on the *Mercury*. He said, "I like the Jews because I've never met a Jewish prohibitionist." And then he said, "I've never been to a Jewish home, however lowly, where the food wasn't good." He also said, "I like them because they're against nuns and priests. I like that too." And so forth and so on. Yes, he was anti-Semitic.

RIBALOW: What about Thomas Wolfe?

ANGOFF: Wolfe was anti-Semitic, true. Yet he was liberal. Esther Jack, the woman in his novels, you know who she was—Aline Bernstein. She was his mistress. At the end he had a fight with her. That brings up something else—a general human failing, maybe not anti-Semitism. If you want to lose a friend, do him a favor. And who did Wolfe more favors than Bernstein? She kept him, she fed him, she slept with him—and then he threw her out. If anybody had said to him, "Tom you're an anti-Semite," he would have killed them. But there was a streak of anti-Semitism, I think, in a way. I'm trying to be as fair as I can be. Maybe you should blame the New Testament. You see, what's instilled in you when you're going to Sunday School stays with you. I remember what Freud said: reason is the figleaf of the emotions. Then you get accustomed to certain phrases, you know, that you use without quite meaning them.

RIBALOW: What of some of the other writers?

ANGOFF: I heard Fitzgerald use some four-letter words about Jews, but with him I wasn't too sure. When Theodore Dreiser said the same things, I was positive he was anti-Semitic. He referred to Horace Liveright as a "damn Kike." Dreiser was far more biased than Fitzgerald, but it is a funny thing having to compare this sort of feeling one against another. Remember, this is an old story in American literature. Herman Melville took a trip to Palestine and came back to say that he was amazed there are so many Jews there. Henry James. . . .

RIBALOW: Maxwell Geismar wrote an entire book on James in which he expressed his disgust with James, in large measure, because of his hatred for Jews and "immigrants."

ANGOFF: That's right. And he used to say he was afraid that pure Anglo-Saxon blood was going to be adulterated by Leventine blood. And by Leventine blood he meant you and me. Hawthorne was a little bit anti-Semitic. Look, I can't explain it. If Freud didn't understand it, how should I understand it?

RIBALOW: George Orwell, in his earlier books like, *Down and Out in London and Paris,* had some negative things to say about Jews. Then he started to write a newsletter for the *Contemporary Jewish Record,* the precursor of *Commentary,* and he changed altogether. So that can happen, too.

ANGOFF: What are you going to do? Many were anti-Semitic, many were not. Sinclair Lewis was absolutely free of anti-Semitism. This I'm positive of. He was once in Kansas City, Missouri, at a social gathering, and one of the people present was Logan Clendening, the medical man, who wrote a best seller, *The Human Body.* He and I were quite friendly. The story is told by people I trust. I'll tell you who told me the story—a former colleague of mine, Clarence Decker, then president of the University of Missouri. A group of people started talking and Clendening got up and began to talk about "Kikes." Lewis stood up, banged on the table and said, "I will not be in the same room with a son of a bitch who denounces Jews," and he walked out.

Faulkner—I don't know. He was a little anti-Negro, a bit anti-Semitic, but was he as anti-Semitic as Mencken? Definitely not. I don't know what it is . . . it reminds me of what my zayde said long ago. He said, "Scratch a goy, and you will find an anti-Semite." Well, the older I get, the more I wonder whether there isn't a little bit of truth in it.

RIBALOW: Arthur Koestler said it in one of his books: at the bottom of the wine glass that the peasant drinks is the pogrom . . . but to another subject for a moment. What is the status of the professional writer in America? I remember years ago, when I was free-lancing, naturally I didn't go into the city to an office. People used to ask my wife, "What is he doing at home?" They never did adjust to it; Thomas Mann and others used to say regularly that writing was a profession. As a result, Mann wrote a new book every year, good or bad.

ANGOFF: Yes, in Europe it's different. Mann had an advantage. He came from a pretty well-to-do family.

RIBALOW: I'm not talking about that part of it, but the part that recognizes writing as a profession.

ANGOFF: A writer is a writer. This kind of faithfulness to an author has not yet happened in the United States. You should read an author, no matter what he writes. That's the way it should be. Some of his books are better; some not so good. You keep up with them because he tells you about the world. But we haven't achieved this yet here. And that's a shock. In the Jewish world, of course, it's even worse, for all kinds of special reasons.

RIBALOW: Perhaps we should try to conclude on an upbeat note, if we can. Do you think that the books you write and the books that Meyer Levin writes, and other writers who are producing what you call *positive* fiction, will have a growing audience? Or will it remain, almost by definition, a restricted and small audience?

ANGOFF: This may be whistling in the dark, what I am going to say now. I've discussed this with Meyer Levin at considerable length and I said, "Meyer, what are you complaining about?" And I asked myself the same question, although I say I complain very little. I write something; if it's published, I'm perfectly happy. I said to Meyer, "I have a feeling that when you and I are angels, your books and my books are going to have a wide readership. There will be many doctoral theses on us. But what's even more important, the books will serve as mirrors for the life we discuss." I said, speaking of myself, I don't see how they can possibly discuss Jewish-American life from 1900 down to now without reading me. They have to. "And the same with you," Meyer, I told him.

RIBALOW: He has had best-selling books.

ANGOFF: Yes, he's a national best seller from time to time. And I'll say this about myself, here again I may be whistling in the dark. Naturally, I'd like more readers. Of course I'd like a front page essay on me in *The New York Times, Christian Science Monitor,* or the *Washington Post.* But what pleases me is that wherever I go people come up to me and say they've read me.

Then there is something else. Years ago, when I did more lecturing than I do now, I went to a little town on the border of Texas and Mexico, a little place called Hunt, Texas, and there one night, there was a big dinner in which I was involved and a man came over to me and he says, "Are you Charles Angoff?" I said yes. He then said, "You saved my life." I didn't know what he meant. He told me that he comes from Refugio, which is near Hunt, Texas. It's on the border of Texas and Mexico and it's so much on the border that one part of this man's house is in Texas and the other is in Mexico. Well, he said to me that his was the only Jewish family in Refugio and that he has been there for a long time. "I can't move," he says, "because I've got a general store, a drug store, you know one of those things." And then he said, "I was terribly worried about what's going to happen to my two daughters. You see that girl over there?" I acknowledged that I did. He said to me then, "She's married to a Jewish boy who just got his medical degree from the University of Chicago. You see the other one over there?" He pointed her out. "She's going around with a nice Jewish boy, an architect."

He said, "You know what we used to discuss at night? Your books. I've got every one of your novels and we discussed them and read them and reread them."

"Well," I questioned "what did you do when they were younger when they were six or seven?" He told me that he read the books to them at a certain stage in their lives, when they were younger. "I'll tell you what I did," he said. "Sunday, I had a station wagon. I put two pillows in the back and placed the little girls in there and I traveled one hundred miles to Corpus Christi, Texas, where there's a community center, a B'nai B'rith group." He said that he put them in the Sunday School and he himself went from synagogue Sisterhood to Brotherhood, picked up all kinds of information. Then he said, "And then we'd go back. And between those trips and your books, we remained Jews."

You see, when you hear this, it justifies it all. . . .

A Conversation with
Chaim Grade

Chaim Grade, probably the most celebrated and admired living Yiddish poet, is a verbal, gregarious, volatile, and immensely likable human being. A prolific poet, he has earned his living for some three decades as a professional lecturer. Only late in life did he become a novelist. In recent years, some of his work has been translated into English, but the bulk of it remains untranslated. He is also a short story writer and a man of great Jewish scholarship.

Grade is the product of the Jewish cultural center of Vilna, known before World War II and the Holocaust, as the "Jerusalem of Europe." He studied for years at a Lithuanian yeshiva just outside Vilna and was a favorite student of "Hazon Ish," a great and revered Jewish scholar, who spent his last years in Israel, where he was consulted and loved by many of the leaders of the Jewish State. Grade's two-volume novel, *The Yeshiva*, describes his early life and contains brilliant portraits of Talmudic scholars and yeshiva organizers, including "Hazon Ish."

Grade is an intriguing conversationalist, neither pompous nor self-important. He makes himself the butt of many of his well-told anecdotes and laughs heartily at his own foibles as well as those of others. There is in him an engaging blend of the shrewd peasant and the naive artist.

He lives in the Bronx, in New York City, with his charming, cultured, and very devoted wife, Inna, who herself has taught Russian and French on the university level. Their home is a lovely place, full of bookcases jammed with books in five languages, Talmud sets (the *shas*) cheek by jowl with lavish modern art volumes. The bookcases were built by Inna Grade. Breakfronts, usually full of porcelain and silver, are stacked with books, as are closets

47

normally reserved for clothes. Grade's own books, ten volumes of poetry, six in prose, plus various editions in translation, are tucked away, almost hidden, in a bottom shelf of a bookcase obscurely squeezed into a narrow hallway at some distance from Grade's warmly furnished, comfortable study and workroom.

While Grade understands the English language more than he lets on, he speaks almost entirely in Yiddish, a rich, flowery, graphic Yiddish. This interview, conducted largely in Yiddish, took place at the Grade home on Sunday, November 30, 1974, before *The Yeshiva* appeared in English-language translation, and shortly after *The Agunah* made a considerable stir in the American literary world.

RIBALOW: What has it been like to win recognition as a Yiddish writer in America? Now that *The Agunah* has appeared in English, people know your name because of *The Agunah*. They didn't know it so well from *The Well*. So what's happened to you since the publication of *The Agunah*?

GRADE: Since *The Agunah* has appeared in English, there has been a kind of earthquake in a particular circle. But let me first tell you that anyone who reads Yiddish literature in America knows me. There aren't too many readers of Yiddish literature, but almost all of them are familiar with my work. Certainly with my name. But when S. Niger, the Yiddish critic, wrote about me—and he wrote tens of articles on my work—it never happened that a reader in Los Angeles should call me long distance and say, "Today I read Niger's article about you." It was perfectly natural for him to assume that I should write and that Niger should comment on my work. But when Elie Wiesel's review was published in *The New York Times* about *The Agunah*, I received phone calls from Los Angeles, from Detroit, and from Chicago. I then realized the impact of an article in the *Times*. This was a very good article, not because it was printed in the *Times,* but because of the way he understood the novel. It would have been very good had it been written in Yiddish for a Yiddish-reading public. But had it been published in Yiddish, surely I wouldn't have got calls from Los Angeles telling me they had read it. This is not said in praise, but in criticism because the calls came *because* the article appeared in English and in *The New York Times*, and so they consider it so important. The article itself touched the core of the book. Wiesel asks, "On which side is Grade?" Grade, he says, is on the side of the two rabbis. He understands the viewpoint of each of them. He is, however, against the masses, which shift from one side to the other. I believe he is right in his analysis. There were other articles, of course. Naturally, as a result of all this—including interviews in the *Times* and the *New York Post*—there was attention paid to me by people who previously didn't know my name. But I must reemphasize that among Yiddish readers, this all made no difference at all.

RIBALOW: Let me follow this up. There are thousands of Jewish readers who *don't* read Yiddish. They didn't know you.

GRADE: True. You might say that I've become a "celebrity," in quotation marks.

RIBALOW: I don't know the size of the first printing of *The Agunah* but I understand it is now in a second printing.

GRADE: Yes.

RIBALOW: With the possibility of a third printing soon.

GRADE: That's what the publisher told me.

RIBALOW: That means there are people buying it because they didn't know that *this* writer was writing such books and now they are aware of you and want to read you. But I really wanted to talk of something else. You are a poet and first wrote poetry in Vilna in 1932.

GRADE: Yes, first in newspapers.

RIBALOW: Your first volume of poetry was issued in 1936. Charles Madison, in his book *Yiddish Literature,* reports that you were a member of a "Young Vilna Group" of poets. Who were the other poets?

GRADE: Oh, it was a very fine group. Only three survive.

RIBALOW: Who?

GRADE: I, the poet and editor of *Der Goldener Kait*, Abraham Sutzkever. He's a master poet, a great virtuoso, a language master. And a third *chaver* who lives in Toronto. His name is Mirainsky. This was the last such group in Yiddish literature. You know, in America you had an older group of poets and then *Die Yunge*. Their leaders, the most important members, included Mani Leib and Moshe Lieb Halpern. Then came a second group. They were called the *Insichisten*. They included Leyeless, Glatstein, and Minkoff. They were the three most important. In Poland there also were such groups. In 1920 there was a group—the *Chalastrei.*

RIBALOW: *Chalastrei?*

GRADE: Yes. It means, a company, but this is a kind of slang, vulgar. It means a *tsutumelte chevra.*

RIBALOW: A gang?

GRADE: A gang! That is exact. The *Chalastrei* had many great poets. One of them was Uri Zvi Greenberg, the Hebrew poet, a great poet. Peretz Markish, Melech Ravitch. And one of this group, I think, was Singer, the older brother of Bashevis. And each one of them followed his own separate way in literature. Markish became a Communist poet. Greenberg became a rightist poet, some say "fascist." Ravitch became a cosmopolitan poet.

RIBALOW: What about your group?

GRADE: Our Vilna Group was the most important and last group in Yiddish literature. It was established in 1929, and I entered in 1933.

RIBALOW: You yourself went to Russia in 1941?

GRADE: During the War I went to Russia, I fled there. My wife remained in. . . .

RIBALOW: The Vilna ghetto.

GRADE: Yes, my first wife was a rabbi's daughter, a famous rabbi. She remained and I went to Russia. I was there until 1945 and met Inna, my second wife, in Russia. And I returned to Poland, by this time with Inna. I should tell you that Inna, who has taught Russian and French, has constantly helped me in my work. In one case, she persuaded me against the deletion of a major character in one of my novels. She's always the first reader and has many good suggestions.

RIBALOW: What did you do in Russia?

GRADE: I was a refugee.

RIBALOW: Did you work there? Did you write?

GRADE: No. I want to tell you this. In Russia I was a man of privilege. Why? Before the outbreak of the war, there was organized in Vilna a chapter of the Soviet Writers Union, and I was accepted as a member. So that when the War broke out, I had a card saying that I was a member of the Soviet Writers Union. When I fled to Russia, I had another lucky break. Even before the War started, I took out a Soviet passport. So when I went to Russia, from Vilna to the farthest point near the Iranian border, the first question you are asked is, Passport, meh? Yest?" Do you have a passport? "Passport yest?" I had one. That meant I wouldn't be arrested. Secondly, food. In order for me to be able to eat, and not work, I showed that I was a member of the Soviet Writers Union. In this way, I lived in Asia, on the border of Iran, in a city called Ashchabad for eight months.

And I was a member of the Turkomen Writers Union. And I got a *paryok,* a ration card. With this *paryok,* I was able to live. And as a member of the writers union, I also had the right to live in Ashchabad. Other refugees didn't have this right. From there, I went to a city called Stalinobad, on the Persian border and on the border of mountains adjacent to Afghanistan. On the other side of that was India. I lived there a year and a half, also on the strength of the fact that I was a writer.

RIBALOW: Were there other Jews there?

GRADE: Yes, refugees. And then I came to Moscow. Naturally, all the Jewish writers there knew me and testified for me, saying I was a Jewish writer. Compared with others, I enjoyed great privileges. First, because I had a passport. Second, because I was a member of a writers union and had a practical way of getting food and, third, perhaps the greatest privilege was this: I was not drafted to fight at the front.

RIBALOW: You mean during the actual War?

GRADE: Yes, yes. A writer was not drafted into the Army. Since I left Russia, as you must know, I have been an enemy of Soviet Russia, and yet I continue to think if I would like a system where all are equal and a writer has no privileges compared with others—or do I prefer a system where a writer *is* privileged, where he isn't required to serve in the Army in wartime and isn't in danger of losing his life?

RIBALOW: You know, in Ireland, writers and other artists are exempt from paying taxes.

GRADE: *I like that!* Let me tell you what prevailed among the thieves of Vilna. I've written about it in one of my poems: you steal from everyone except from artists and rabbis.

RIBALOW: Then you got to Poland in 1946.

GRADE: Right. We went to Lodz for half a year. Then to Paris for two years.

RIBALOW: Who was the "we"?

GRADE: A group of Yiddish writers. After two years in Paris, we came to America.

RIBALOW: I understand that you were the leader of the Jewish cultural group in Paris.

GRADE: That's true. I was the chairman of the Writers Union. I might as well say it as it already has been published and reported. Then I came to America.

RIBALOW: Why?

GRADE: It was an accidental thing. There was a Cultural Congress in America. And first of all, we didn't want to remain in Paris. After all, we *were* strangers. We needed official documents and we had to renew our papers every single month. So we began to think of where to go. So this Congress came along. The organizers said they needed us, the writers living in Paris. Mainly, they wanted me to come. I told them I wouldn't travel without my wife. I had done this once before, this *kunts,* leaving my wife in Vilna, and I never saw her again. So the officials in New York cooperated and sent papers, the proper papers, for both of us. And other writers joined us. Arriving here, we didn't think of going back.

RIBALOW: Did you know of the declining state of Yiddish in America: the disappearance of newspapers, the decline of the theater, and so on?

GRADE: No. No. You don't understand. You can't compare America when we came in '48 with America today. Everything is relative. There were then in America all the Yiddish writers who have since passed away. Beginning with Abraham Reisin, who lived, I think, another ten years after our arrival. Boraisha was still working. Mani Leib. Leivick. Auerbach. All the Yiddish writers. And they all received us warmly. Secondly, when you leave a country for another, this isn't the only measure. The role of Yiddish journalism didn't affect me personally, anyway. I was a poet and I started prose later.

RIBALOW: I did want to ask you about your prose writing. But first let me ask you about the way you earn your living. Surely it is almost impossible to earn a living as a poet in Yiddish, just as it is in other languages. I have heard that you lecture and are a pedagogue.

GRADE: Not a pedagogue, a lecturer. I'm a bad pedagogue.

RIBALOW: What do you lecture about? Your own work?

GRADE: No, no. No! No! Never! Nothing about myself. Come on. One second. Let me show you my library. . . . My own books are buried on the last bottom row on a back bookcase. No, I lecture on other subjects only. To my regret, to my very deep regret, I've always earned my living by lecturing. And I've always had to devote a great deal of time to the preparation of my lectures.

RIBALOW: Do you read your lectures from a manuscript?

GRADE: In the beginning they were extemporaneous. Then I decided it better to read from a prepared script, or manuscript. I think I told you—before this tape machine started to run—that I delivered one lecture for almost three hours, two hours and forty-five minutes, in Buenos Aires. I talked on the same subject the same amount of time in Tel Aviv. Standing room only. There weren't enough seats for the number of people who wanted to join the audience.

RIBALOW: In Hebrew or Yiddish?

GRADE: Yiddish. And also two hours and forty-five minutes in Johannesburg. The lecture was on "My Meetings with Soviet Yiddish Writers." It must have been an interesting lecture for people to stand for nearly three hours. But when I wrote it out and read, it really ran only an hour. Except that I continue to extemporize.

RIBALOW: Apparently, you're a good lecturer.

GRADE: So I'm told. I do read well. People think I'm talking extemporaneously.

RIBALOW: Where do you lecture?

GRADE: Everywhere. Across America. South America. Johannesburg. Buenos Aires. Chile. But these are not short trips. I go for six weeks. I've also been in Northern and in Southern Rhodesia. At least that's what I used to do some years ago. I don't travel such distances any longer. But I've visited Miami some twenty-five times—the same with Chicago and Detroit. My trips have been cut with the years.

RIBALOW: I assume these are the Yiddish circles.

GRADE: Of course. When I first came to America, these cities had large Yiddish centers and I was asked back year after year. But as the audiences weren't in the hundreds. . . . You know, an English-language lecturer can prepare four-five lectures and use them all his life, traveling about the land. But a Yiddish lecturer doesn't have access to hundreds of Jewish centers—as you would—and so he returns again and again to the few cities where there are Yiddish readers. And he cannot repeat himself.

RIBALOW: What are your themes, your subjects?

GRADE: The themes are on historical subjects. I prepare a suggested list and they choose. The list includes Jewish history, Graetz's ideas. Yehuda Halevi. Moses ibn Ezra. Rambam. All in a popular way, of course. And I talk about Jewish writers, literature. When I talk about Yehuda Halevi, or the Rambam, I don't pretend to say new things. First, I can't. I'm not a specialist. Nor does the audience want anything new. It's enough if I acquaint them with what they don't know. If a professor sat in the hall, he wouldn't feel too good about it all. He'll know better. But I do prepare well. Bialik is a subject of mine. I spoke on Bialik at the Hebrew University and it made an impression. I don't apologize for that one. Bialik himself could have sat there.

RIBALOW: In 1950, you first began to write prose. "My Quarrel With Hersh Rasseyner," reprinted in *The Treasury of Yiddish Stories*.

GRADE: Right. But it was originally published in the *Yiddisher Kemfer*.

RIBALOW: Why did you decide to write prose, after your years of being a poet?

GRADE: It wasn't a matter of "deciding" to write prose. I had published a volume of poetry and an evening was planned in my honor. The book was *Die Mamma's Tzavuah (The Mother's Will)*, not *Der Mamma's Shabosim (My Mother's Sabbaths)*. I knew it was to be an important evening and that I would be required to speak. So I began to write my speech, about Vilna. As I wrote, I thought I'd tell about my life and that it would be appropriate to describe a meeting between myself and a Mussarnik [a follower of the Mussar movement, a religious movement]. So in my prepared remarks, I included three pages on "My Quarrel With Hersh Rasseyner." There was a very large audience and I noticed that of my entire speech, on literature, on Vilna, the audience was entranced by these three pages. Aha, I said to myself! If that's the case—wait a minute! I rode home by subway and made a few notes. That was the start. It took me a few months, but the result was an essay which became "My Quarrel," and published it in the *Kemfer*. It made a great impression in our Yiddish circles.

RIBALOW: It *is* a remarkable story.

GRADE: But this really wasn't the beginning of my prose writing.

RIBALOW: It wasn't?

GRADE: No, to me "My Quarrel" was an essay, not a story, not fiction. My real start came a few years later. One day I sat down to my desk and wrote a story, "Shifrele." To my way of thinking, this was simply a short story for a popular audience. At this time, I also was invited to join the staff of the Yiddish *Morning-Journal*. The story was read by various editors, of other papers as well, who also saw some other stories I had written. Later, they appeared in *Der Mamma's Shabosim*. David Meckler, the editor of the *Morning-Journal,* was especially pleased by the stories. He said, "You're a poet and you now have written a group of good stories. But let's not publish 'Shifrele' first. Begin with a chapter from *Der Mamma's Shabosim*. These are more characteristic of you." He had already published some of my poetry. He wanted a story a week from *Der Mamma's*

Shabosim, so each week I wrote another one, and that's how the book came into being.

RIBALOW: So this was your first book of prose?

GRADE: Yes. And the Mamma is the heroine of the entire book. Then "Shifrele" was published in a later issue of the newspaper and I joined the *Morning-Journal,* which merged with the *Day.* And then I started *The Agunah.* That's how it began.

RIBALOW: What's the basic difference between your poetry and your prose?

GRADE: I'll tell you, but first I want to say that I believe there was a transition from my poetry to my prose. The key here is that the bridge is from lyric poetry to epic poetry, poetry that tells a story. For example, I had written, or was engaged in writing, one single poem for twenty years. From 1942 in Russia, and in Asia, and through the years in America. It was published in the *Kemfer.* Incidentally, I never published these narrative poems in a book. About 5,000 lines appeared in various magazines and journals, but not in book form. So this was the bridge to my prose. I've published ten books of poetry and six volumes of prose, and there are three more that have been completed. Maybe four. I want to tell you something else: I wrote stories in prose which are more poetic than poems. In 1973 I published a book, *Die Klaus un die Gass (The Synagogue and the Street).* There is a story there, the first one. . . . Those who look for a plot might ask: What happens here? It's called *Zaydes un Einichlach.* But Abraham Sutzkever, you know, the great Yiddish poet, wrote to me, saying it is the most beautiful thing I have written: "Rembrandtish." He believes it is a poem that is flawless. But it is prose. . . . See? And there are other stories somewhat like that. They are about Israel, about the United States. I'll tell you the truth: One reason I don't publish my very long poem, the one I've been writing twenty years, is that I find it contains too much prose in rhyme. I've reworked it a great deal but it remains difficult to cut out all the prose. Don't think that because something is written in verse, it necessarily is more poetic than that which is written in prose. It may actually be the reverse. It was like that with me. More than once.

RIBALOW: You've talked a long time. Tell me, are there other differences between your poetry and your prose?

GRADE: Of course. A deeper difference is that I have a special complex, something I myself cannot explain. I am a generally "human" or "humane" writer in poetry. I write of love, and even more about nature. I have whole books about nature. Naturally, too, I have written lyrical, *menschlich,* poems. And, more than anything else, about the *Churban,* the Holocaust. Also, on my mother, a great deal about my mother, the *Churban,* the yeshiva, and on themes relating to man. In prose, I confess, I cannot get out of the synagogue courtyard. Not that I don't desire to.

RIBALOW: You can't escape?

GRADE: I *cannot,* although I have written a few "worldly" things.

RIBALOW: You are saying that you are parochial in your novels and universal in your poetry?

GRADE: Yes.

RIBALOW: Let's talk a bit about your books, those published, and the stories that have appeared in magazines but remain unpublished in book form. For example: *Die Klaus un die Gass*—what is it, a collection of stories or a novel?

GRADE: There are four long stories—novellas—in that volume.

RIBALOW: What are they about?

GRADE: One is called "Himmel un Erd," "Heaven and Earth." And then there is "Die Rebbitsin," which created a great stir. Then there's *"Zaydes un Einichlach."* This is a gentle, subtle story. If you couldn't read it in Yiddish, you couldn't really appreciate it. I've got other long tales as well.

RIBALOW: What are they?

GRADE: One is "Alte Bochurim," or "Bachelors." It has had only magazine publication. It is long, four hundred pages. And then "Froyen fun Ghetto," "Women of the Ghetto." It's about Jewish women who, after the War, after surviving, commence living new lives. I don't know about these. . . . My readers are used to my traditional stories. They didn't care much for "Alte Bochurim." Still, some thought it my best work. . . . You never really know. Up until now, I haven't really thought of doing anything else with it.

RIBALOW: Where are your stories set? In Europe?

GRADE: Everything is in Europe. I'm not at home really in America and I don't write about America. Only one thing do I write about America: nature.

RIBALOW: I understand you live in the Adirondacks five months of the year.

GRADE: I was in other parts of the United States, too. Yosemite, Grand Canyon, Zion Park, Yellowstone Park, the Mormon Tabernacle. And I wrote poems about all these places.

RIBALOW: You say that your poetry is universal, about nature and the Holocaust, and in your fiction, you don't get out of the synagogue center and the shul. Tell me a little about "Die Rebbitsin," which you say raised a storm.

GRADE: This girl was engaged to a boy. She herself was the daughter of a famous rabbi. But the young man to whom she was now engaged wasn't too appealing. He *phumphk'd,* that is, he sort of talked under his nose—which was a long nose. He didn't speak well and wasn't good-looking. But he was a *gaon,* a great scholar. Yet in the end it was *he* who rejected *her.* He didn't want her. Why? Because he sensed that she didn't have a good, a warm, an understanding heart. In fact, if the truth be known, he thought her hard-hearted. So she went away and married another rabbi, a decent man, a "guter Yid," a fine speaker, but not a *gaon!* This husband was fated to remain a small-town rabbi. But the *gaon,* he had a different life cut out for him. He married a woman in Grodno and he became the *gaon* of his generation, and not only of his city. So the woman he had rejected now regrets that she married the wrong man. Don't misunderstand. She loves her husband and has had children with him. But she decided to go to the town where the *gaon* is the rabbi. This is the heart of the story. She and her husband go to Grodno, where their children now live and she pushes her husband higher and higher, further and further, to get him to assume the position of the *gaon,* to push the *gaon* out. This is all based on a true story—but not about a rabbi and a rebbetsin, but about a writer and his wife. I altered the people. I put beards on the men, so to speak. One rabbi guessed I was writing about another rabbi, the *Vilna Gaon,* and in a sense I was, but behind it all I drew from a real situation of a writer and his wife. So you see how I change and alter my characters? There are people in this story who are modelled after people I know in, say, Detroit. But where do I bring them? To a city in Poland! Understand?

RIBALOW: So this is one work of fiction and *The Well* is another. What are your books, by name and in some detail?

GRADE: I'll tell you. In prose and in poetry. First, the prose: *Der Mamma's Shabosim.* The second one was *The Agunah* and the third *The Synagogue Courtyard.* Two volumes of *Zemach Atlas* and *Die Klaus un die Gass.*

RIBALOW: That's five.

GRADE: Six. *Zemach Atlas* is in two volumes. [Eventually published as *The Yeshiva*]. Now I'm writing another novel in two volumes. I hope to live to see them published. The work is running serially every Sunday in the *Forward.* It's called *Bais HaRav, The Rabbi's House.*

RIBALOW: What happens with the novel, or novels, after newspaper publication?

GRADE: I rework it four or five times.

RIBALOW: Who then publishes the book?

GRADE: The writer himself. That's the way it works in Yiddish writing. Some friends help in its publication and I also invest my own money. My traveling around America has a disadvantage in that I am obliged to be a public speaker. But it also has an advantage. During these past twenty-five years of traveling around I have developed many personal friendships. Some people have helped in financing my books. Secondly, they play a part in disseminating them.

RIBALOW: I have another question. There were seven years between the publication in English of *The Well* and *The Agunah*. And it was quite accidental, first, that they were translated and, second, that they were published as they were, with regard to the order in which you wrote your books. At the moment, I suppose you have no idea of what will next appear in English?

GRADE: No, I have nothing else translated.

RIBALOW: What has been published in Hebrew?

GRADE: In Hebrew, it's better. *Der Mamma's Shabosim; The Agunah;* then *Zemach Atlas*, both volumes. *The Agunah* and *Zemach Atlas* have been published by Am Oved. Also, a book of poetry.

RIBALOW: Any other languages?

GRADE: One. In Portuguese. Now to the poetry. In Vilna, I published *Yah, Yes,* in 1936. My first book. Then, the second book *Mussarnikes.* This was an overture to *Zemach Atlas*. The poetry came out in 1937. In 1938 it went into a second printing. Two printings for a poet in Vilna was an achievement. After the outbreak of the War, when I went to Russia, I published nothing at all. But while I was in Russia, a book of mine called *Doyras, Generations,* was issued in the United States. It included poems, early and later ones, that had appeared in journals in various countries. After that, when I already had left Russia, I published a small book in Warsaw called *Auf die Churvas, On the Ruins.* Then, in Paris, I published a book in Argentina, *Playtim, Refugees.* Then a second book in Argentina, *Shine fun Varloshene Shtern,* more poetry. Then I came to America and published *Die Mamma's Tzavuah, The Mother's Will.* Years later, I published *Mensch fun Fire.* Then—*Auf Mein Veg Tzu Dir, On My Way to You.* In between, I seem to have forgotten another title published in Paris: *Farvokseneh Vegn, Overgrown Paths.* Also poems. There! I have ten volumes of poetry.

RIBALOW: You also have won many literary prizes, haven't you?

GRADE: Yes, sixteen, but I don't want to linger on this. It may be a sign that I'm a bad writer. A good one doesn't win prizes.

RIBALOW: Many writers don't read other writers. Some well-known novelists say they have no time to read others because they themselves are too busy writing their own work. But I see that you have a large and impressive library, in what, five languages? I see *you* read. Do you read any American-Jewish writers? Bellow? Malamud?

GRADE: I've read Bellow. He's a good writer, Saul Bellow. I plan to read many other American writers, but I have a long way to go, a long way.

RIBALOW: Is it the language barrier?

GRADE: Two things. Let me tell you a secret. I write ten percent of the time and read ninety percent. If you were to divide my time, I would say that I read almost all my free time. I haven't yet met my deadline for the *Forward* for the next section of my novel. I haven't begun it yet. What have I done? If I were to tell you what I've read, you wouldn't believe me: Orations! Speeches! Look at the subjects that interest me! At the last moment, when I no longer have any choice, I write my chapter and, as soon as I'm done, I get back to my books. But no matter what else I'm doing, somewhere within me I'm busy with my writing. Even when I'm reading, I'm working. Deep at the core, the most important thing is the writer within me. Whatever I read, I ask myself, How can I use this? There is a controlling factor within me that permits me to read only that which allows me to draw juice and honey for my writing. So as I don't write about America, I don't read Americana. I read philosophy. I read Judaica. And I read a great deal of history. I do read a little literature, a little fiction. Unconsciously there is working within me something that seeks out philosophical themes; the war between the world and the Jew. See! I have a *shas* there.

RIBALOW: You are crowded in, hemmed in by your books. Harry Wolfson of Harvard piled up his books everywhere: in closets, even in the bathroom. When my books overwhelm me, I give them away, sell them off. . . .

GRADE: You think I don't do it? I give away hundreds of books. Hundreds! How do I get them? They are sent to me by publishers, by writers. So I read a great deal and write very little.

RIBALOW: It can't be quite accurate because you've produced a lot.

GRADE: Yes . . . Yes. I'll tell you another thing. As I studied in a yeshiva until I was in my twenties, I've got certain kinds of books. I'm not a formal scholar . . . but I do study and have studied. So I collect books. And I say to the books, "Wait awhile; I've already looked into your pages." Then, for the time being, I occupy myself with worldly books, perhaps because I want to tear myself away from the world of the *bais medrash*—and I can't. So I become exhausted from the effort. Finally, I see that I won't become a worldly man. I won't get away from the grip of the *bais medrash*, and I tried in vain. I'm too deeply rooted in the *bais medrash*. For twenty years, I learned there and for forty years I've been out of it. These twenty years—these accursed twenty years—don't let me break free. So I return to the ancient books and I ask myself, Why did I go away? Where did I go? I ask these questions and return to the Jewish book shelves. Then, again, I turn to the *goyish* side. But then I'm back to the Jewish shelves. See . . . here's Graetz's history . . . and Dubnow's history . . . and the religious Jewish history by Yawitz, in Hebrew. Ahah! here's Raphael Mahler's Marxist version of Jewish history, in four-five volumes. And, see, here's Dinur's modern history, full of good material. I read them till I "overeat," till I'm overtired and then go back to the worldly shelves of books. And once in a while, I turn to an old love of thirty years—Spinoza. He couldn't get away from the Jews either.

RIBALOW: What about your major novel, *Zemach Atlas*? It hasn't yet appeared in English, although it has been translated into Hebrew. I know it is difficult to get some of your work translated, so will you give me some idea of what it is about?

GRADE: Zemach Atlas is a bearded Jew, A Rosh Yeshiva, a head of a yeshiva, who believed in the moral teachings of the Torah, but wasn't sure that there was a God who gave the Torah. No matter how much he told himself, "Ani Maamin . . . ! I Believe!—he believed the Torah was true, that man should care for his brother, for he was a Mussarnik, or Mussarite, but he was unsure there was a God who gave the Torah. This was one tragedy. Then he experienced a second tragedy: He always spoke out clearly and said precisely what he believed. To the English-language reader, the American reader, this may not be a particularly exciting subject. If you write about women, all right, he's interested. But if you begin a story, a long story, about a pious man who isn't sure there is a God, will he read on? I don't know. The subject may not interest him altogether. Is there enough conflict in a hero who doubts the existence of God? What kind of a hero is that?

RIBALOW: It isn't a matter of your material, I'm sure. It is how it is handled. There are many unlikely subjects that attract readers. But let me ask you now, what is the main theme of your work, in prose and in poetry? It seems to me you are deeply interested in religious issues.

GRADE: This is what I'm interested in: in traditional Jews. This, of course, leads to theological matters. *The Well*, for example, is concerned with both. I describe a rabbinical home, and also a rabbi who talks from a pulpit. He has an audience, but the Jews don't really want to listen. They react by banging their fingers on the table. I describe the fingers . . . for almost a full chapter. I tell the history of their lives through their fingers. Fingers that pound their breasts in the prayer of "Al Chet." Fingers that spread themselves in blessing a grandchild. I continue to describe all sorts. . . .

RIBALOW: Of Jewish images.

GRADE: Yes, images. And fingers that pinch a little boy who doesn't know the Sedra; fingers that smell of tobacco stains; fingers . . . all used in activities for which a Jew used his fingers. Both the pious and the worldly. How can this be translated and transposed to another *milieu*, another culture? You see, I can't escape my origins. My heroes are traditional Jews in conflict with the secular world, or in conflict with themselves as they are drawn to the outer world. Understand? Either in conflict with the outside world, because that world doesn't attract them. Or in conflict with themselves as they are drawn to that world, as in the case of Chaim Grade, under the various names of the heroes of his books, like Zemach Atlas. What is *The Agunah?* It is a fight with the law. Zemach Atlas is at war with himself, with the worldly man deep within him. You understand? In *Zemach Atlas* there are no legal issues. Yet it is a book full of moral battles.

RIBALOW: How do you show this?

GRADE: I'll give you an example. Zemach Atlas has a nephew, his wife's nephew, who has impregnated a servant girl in his own father's house. This sort of thing happened often, in almost every town, in almost every home. What happened with such an unfortunate girl, who became pregnant by a respectable, rich young man? Why, she was sent away. And if she had the child, they sent her to live in a village, among Jews of course. Zemach Atlas, the rabbi, the Mussarnik, says, "What! She's pregnant by him? He must marry her, of course." The young man's parents exclaim, "What, our son marry a servant girl!" Zemach Atlas replies, "Naturally, he's the father of her child!" This is the war between moral law and society. You see, I've taken my major hero who believes in the Torah but isn't sure about his belief in God. This, by the way, was a major sickness in many yeshivas. It *was* a problem. Zemach Atlas was not alone. He believed in morality but he was not certain about God. . . . This is an important theme in my work. But, of course, as you must know, all art is imagination and, so, how true is it all anyway?

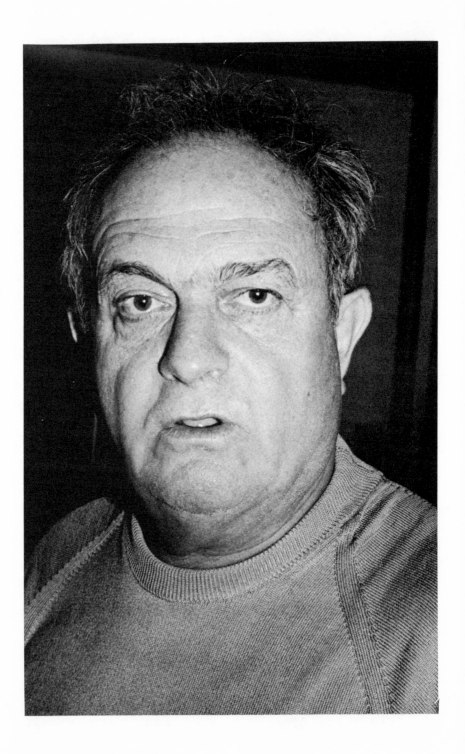

A Conversation with

Meyer Levin

Meyer Levin's opening sentence in his remarkable autobiography *In Search,* first published in 1950, is "This is a book about being a Jew." His entire career, as a novelist, playwright, folklorist, memoirist, film producer, educator, lecturer, and journalist, has revolved "about being a Jew." Some of his books, like *The Old Bunch* and *In Search*, have become American-Jewish classics.

Levin remains a modest man, constantly seeking his "audience," always aware that each new novel requires a "new breakthrough." The author of many notable books, he finds few are in print. In spite of his constant productivity, Levin has not had the major best seller, which would allow him the luxury of financial security earned by lesser writers.

Over seventy years of age, Levin is youthful, full of stamina, ideas and energy, and as open and candid as when I first met him almost forty years ago. He fights the Literary Establishment, sometimes tilts windmills, but remains a fighter for principles. He is a valuable man.

We talked on December 1, 1974, in what was then his New York City home, a brownstone on the West Side. The study was small, almost claustrophobic. The room was dominated by a large desk, which was heavily laden with papers and books. Of course there was a typewriter in the room, a few small chairs and files, which, he cheerfully admitted, were not too well organized. I suspect the reason for this is that he is often on the road and rooted on two continents, thousands of miles apart. A few years after we talked, he sold the house.

RIBALOW: You've been writing for fifty years—are matters worse or better for Jewish writers since you began to write?

LEVIN: For really Jewish writers, I would say they're worse. For Jewish writers who are advertised—or who get known as Jewish writers—but are really anti-Jewish writers, they're better. At the present time, there's a kind of a pause in which way its going and this pause comes largely from the peculiar spread of the word "ethnic." If you noticed, about three-four years ago, ethnic began to be applied very widely in the arts—also in literature.

RIBALOW: But they didn't mean Jews.

LEVIN: They didn't, but they did. The Jews have sort of accepted themselves—
the assimilationist Jews, let's say, or the unsure Jews. They have accepted
the word ethnic as explaining them, too. The Jews get included very much
in the use of the word.

RIBALOW: Isn't ethnic a catch word?

LEVIN: Yes, but like all catch phrases and all catch words, this caught on and I
think it has made a strong difference in how a certain area of Jews,
particularly among the young people, think of themselves. To a degree,
it helps dissolve away Jewish identity because it belittles it. There's in
ethnic both a recognition and a belittlement; in the word itself. And I
think that the quality of the word, to include ourselves among ethnic
groups, gives Jews a grouping nevertheless. It diminishes the particu-
larism of the Jew, which is of course the central question in Jewishness. So
that I would say at the present time there is a stronger tendency than ever
to assimilation, that ethnicity helps the conscience of the assimilant and
that to counterbalance that, the hard core of Jews who are seriously
studying Judaism in the colleges, and those who center their lives on
being Jewish—this hard-core group is better than ever in its clarity, in its
determination and in the reward it gets from what it does. But it's
shrinking.

RIBALOW: How does this relate to the Jewish writer. Is it a matter of who is the
audience?

LEVIN: Who's the audience, right. The audience for writers like Philip Roth
and Bellow and Malamud was a Jewish-based but general audience. I
believe that it flared up and responded not only to their quality as writers
but to a kind of hidden assimilationist quality in their work. None of
them, in their fiction, pictured the inside of the living American Jewish
community. That is, in none of their novels will you find characters who
are intensely involved with Israel, or are part of the structure of the
community.

RIBALOW: They may not know it.

LEVIN: They don't know a thing about it. They're totally alienated from it.
They *were* called the novels of alienation. Only Malamud offered some
sort of connection with the past. The nostalgia element was always
admitted, even cherished, because the nostalgia element enforced the
idea of something that is no longer here, that is gone, that we don't have
to deal with in our actual living lives. So that this phase in American

Jewish writing was due to this curious balance of identifying by reading and praising an author who was a Jew and at the same time accepting an alienated interpretation of the Jew in the American world. Today I think we have passed that phase. The coming generation of American Jewish writers, I believe, will be young writers who will have been to Israel or will be involved with the revival of Jewish studies. They will be trying to see themselves in the light of this material as real Jews. There may be a few more popular novels making jokes of the Jewish life of the past, or being critical of it, or satiric of it.

RIBALOW: That seems to be fading.

LEVIN: Yes, we may have a few more but I think that phase is over. What I said about the serious work means a more limited audience unless of course there's the writer who, by great power or strength, crashes through to public attention no matter what he writes about. People always mention Chaim Potok as a popular writer who nevertheless has certain real qualities in his work and who writes about Jews. But again, you have an example of an attachment to the past, the problems of the past. He presents them as the problems of today. The Jew who has little knowledge of Jewish life or the Jewish world doesn't notice the absence of the real problems of today. Of course, his last book, *My Name is Asher Lev,* has brought in very strongly the theme of the Russian Jews. It was a kind of a private movement that his father was engaged in, bringing them out secretly and we never really learned very much about it so that it seems sort of imaginary. Yet we know that in the forefront of Jewish activity is a very complex and open movement on the subject. *That* he doesn't touch. Another example. He engages his artist in the theme of shall-a-Jew-portray-living-beings-in-his-art? as a basic problem. This is something that we dealt with eighty-ninety years ago. So that it seemed to me that he was either by sleight-of-hand avoiding engagement with the present scene, or trying to make us believe that the questions he raised were still very strong among us in relation to art, which of course is not true. Or else it was just the gripping ability that he has of involving the reader in the story. I certainly applaud him up to that point but it still is not representative writing for the Jewish community of today.

RIBALOW: Charles Angoff has said that you will be remembered as the most important interpreter of Jewish life and that you will be studied in years to come but that generally you are more pessimistic than he is. What of your work—do you think it will survive? Angoff added, by the way, that when anyone will want to know anything about American Jewish life, he will have to read you.

LEVIN: Well, I can return the compliment. They will also have to read Angoff.
... What I think will survive of the whole range of American Jewish
writing today?

RIBALOW: *Your* work. What do you find now is most lasting in your work? *The
Old Bunch*?

LEVIN: *The Old Bunch,* which was published in 1937, is still current. There is
still a paperback edition, although it is very hard to find, but it can be
obtained from the publishers. There was a hardback edition fairly
recently, issued by Simon and Schuster, ten years or so ago, but not any
longer. I'd be content to have the books I wrote in paperback as long as
they are around. The difficult factor is that paperbacks, too, are judged
by volume of sale and there's great difficulty in maintaining a paperback
for sale. *The Old Bunch,* as I said, is around and it's on quite a few reading
lists in college—as collateral reading in such subjects as Urban Life in
America, in American Civilization and sometimes in Literature. Of course
now there are many colleges that have courses in Jewish studies and it's
almost always there. That gives it a continued existence. I think the two
autobiographies may survive, certainly as long as *The Old Bunch* or
longer. That is, *In Search* and the new one, *The Obsession*, although *The
Obsession* still hasn't gotten into paperback. Somehow the content of a
book can bring it back or cause it to survive. That was the experience with
In Search.

RIBALOW: *In Search* made a profound impression on me when it was published in 1950. Now that it is available in paperback, do you get much of a
response to it from a new generation of readers?

LEVIN: Yes. I get fan letters now. *In Search* is a good example of what I mean
about a book finding itself. When I first wrote it, in 1947, I took it to my
friend, Elliot Cohen, who had then started *Commentary.* He asked me
to take it to Alfred Kazin to read. I was then living in Paris and had come
here for only a few weeks to try to place the book. Kazin read it and I
came eagerly to his door the next day. He came to the door—I didn't even
get inside the house. He just shook his head sadly and said, "No, No, No,
this isn't it," and gave me back the manuscript. That was the verdict.

RIBALOW: Was Kazin a reader for any publisher?

LEVIN: He was already, you know, a *mavin,* the important critic in that area.
Well, then there were a succession of peculiar disappointments. One
publisher took it and then returned the contract and so on. I wound up
getting so angry that—since printing was very cheap in Paris—I used my
last few dollars and went back to Paris to get the book printed. I had that

crazy idea that every writer seems to get once in a while that he'll be able to sell his book on his own. Of course, I couldn't. I went around with two satchels and went on lectures for the next three years getting rid of those thousand books. Meanwhile, a very small American house, Horizon Press, put out a hardcover edition and that lasted for half a year or so and the book disappeared. Well, recently a friend of mine, who is a member of the Literary Establishment, said she was at a party and got talking to Kazin and my name came up. He said he had just been rereading *In Search* and that this was a great book and that I had been under-evaluated as a writer. And here's the man who very nearly broke me in a literary way! So that there is sometimes truth in the axiom that if it is good, it will live. Somehow, *In Search* was republished. Basically, it happened because at that time another book of mine, *The Settlers,* was doing pretty well—you know, that's when publishers will take up some of your old books and put them out again. But *In Search* is getting a new audience and I get strong reactions from young people because . . .

RIBALOW: Because there's so much in it they never knew.

LEVIN: So much in it they never knew. Now I have the precise trouble with its continuation, with *The Obsession.* I had a hard time getting it published; my publisher brought it out with a certain reluctance. It then received brutal treatment in the *Times.* It is a book that was rejected in a great part of the Literary Establishment, the part that is precisely dominated by Jews who don't want to be Jews, by self-hating Jews. This circle saw to it that *The Obsession* got what was called "the treatment," and at least five interviews with me with important periodicals were held up and never appeared in the press. The hush-up has been so strong that the book is not to be found anywhere in a bookstore that I know of only six months after publication and I am unable to get it into paperback. Now, I don't think I'll be around another twenty years to see if the pattern of *In Search* happens. But I do get resonances from it. From the personal responses I get, I know that this is perhaps the best thing I've written. Certainly as good as other books that have been very highly praised. But it's virtually been snuffed out by antagonism from the politically anti-Jewish scene, the anti-Israel scene. It is the same fight I described in *The Obsession*, the same fight that has been going on for nearly twenty-two years, which started over the censorship of the Jewish material in the Anne Frank story on the stage. For that reason I think it's difficult to make an assessment of my work without getting prejudiced on one side or the other.

RIBALOW: *The Obsession* was published earlier this year, 1974, and *The Fanatic* some ten years ago. In a sense they both deal with the Anne Frank confrontation. Are you now, in any way, going to continue to treat that subject? Frankly, I'm a little surprised. When you wrote *The Settlers,* I was expecting the next book, its sequel. But you wrote *The Obsession* next. And then *The Spell of Time.* I know a number of people who read *The Settlers* and discovered that the history in it was all news to them, because it dealt entirely with the pre-Israel period in what was Palestine. They are waiting for the next book in the series—a sort of "what happens next?" mood.

LEVIN: I have been working on the continuation of *The Settlers* and have made quite a bit of progress. I hope to finish it in the not too distant future. [*The Harvest* was published in 1978.]

RIBALOW: So what happened in between the books in this project?

LEVIN: Just as *The Settlers* was a body of material which I felt I would continue, *In Search* was a body of autobiographical material which had to be continued because the theme of it around the Jewish question *did* continue and continued most dramatically in an autobiographical way, which I related in *The Obsession.*

RIBALOW: And *The Fanatic*?

LEVIN: Now *The Fanatic* was an attempt to deal with the—not the Anne Frank subject so much—but more with the Holocaust itself, using my Anne Frank experience as the background for the novel. Nevertheless, *The Fanatic* differs from *The Obsession*, which was a personal and factual relation of the whole thing, whereas *The Fanatic* does with the material what a novelist would do, that is, changes it considerably, goes afield from it at times, in order to make it into a novel. I had hoped I would get it out of my system with *The Fanatic*, but since the condition itself, the suppression which is at the bottom of these books, continued, the autobiographical experience continued to the point where I felt I had to do *The Obsession.* Actually, I had planned this along with *The Settlers.* It was even in my book contract that, after *The Settlers,* I would do *The Obsession.*

RIBALOW: What about *The Spell of Time*? I notice it was issued by another publisher, Praeger. In my own review of it I have made a point of your versatility. You've done screen work, many family chronicles in your novels, autobiographies, short stories, Jewish histories for young readers, a Haggadah, film documentaries. . . . This book, this new one, really is a novella. Also, I remember how different from your usual work *Gore and Igor* was. How do you get moved to do so many things in so many styles?

LEVIN: A writer or a painter should vary his work. If you get stuck and rewrite the same kind of work or write the same novel all your life, I don't think you can develop very much as an artist, although there are examples that disprove every generalization, including the one I've just made. The impulse of writing with me has always been stimulated by the challenge of a difficult form, a different style, a different kind of expression to undertake from the stage to the screen, from the long novel to the short novel, the documentary novel to the totally imaginary novel. Because only a few of my novels have attained a wide audience, I am typed in peoples' minds as the guy with the big, heavy documentary book. Particularly this happened with *Compulsion*. Because of *Compulsion*, most readers—for every one who has read anything else, there are five who have read *Compulsion*—most readers ask about that book. So I am most connected with it. If they read *The Old Bunch*, they think of me as the man who writes enormous books only with a social background. If its *The Settlers*, they also see it is a big book, with a social-historical background. But I have always tried to do things that are entirely different. *Gore and Igor*, of course, is a black humor novel.

RIBALOW: I was rather taken with that one. People I know, who also know you, have asked me, "How did he get to write something like that?"

LEVIN: I've heard that question, even with disapprobation. I get accused of having departed from what I'm supposed to write and, of course, there have been many people delighted with *Gore and Igor*. It's the same with *The Spell of Time*. People completely forget that I more or less introduced Hasidic folklore into the English language with *The Golden Mountain* way back in 1932. This story is simply an attempt for a modern writer to make a wedding between present-day characters and a theme in the stream of Hasidic ideas and beliefs, so that the theme of the story weaves together the present-day curiosity about mysticism and about the expansion of mind-blowing drugs. These somehow do go together and there's a great vogue at the moment for mystical experience, which I hope wasn't stimulated by the vogue, because this story was conceived and written five or six years ago, so it wasn't a response to a vogue. It was really a prediction of it. It was done as a kind of vacation or separation from the heavier works. While I don't think it's light except in terms of length—it's physically light—the themes in it are as serious and profound as any others I've ever dealt with. How far I've succeeded is another question. But the questions that are aroused are those of predestination, predestination and love, which are themes that people wonder about even in a sophisticated age. It's also about the identity of the soul itself: what sort of an entity it is and whether character expresses the soul. All these things are involved in what I hope was simply constructed as a tale. The tale is virtually the origin of literature. The Biblical tale I had in mind, and the tales of all folk literatures . . . and I tried to reach back to that to get the form for this story.

RIBALOW: Recently I was told by a novelist that all fiction, like all history, is false. Fiction, he said, comes totally out of the life and the imagination of the author. He quoted Flaubert as saying that not only Madame Bovary, but also her dog, is myself. Novels, therefore, are not to be believed. You are in all your novels—the argument runs—and so what they are is a reflection of the individual who is doing the writing.

LEVIN: Well, this is comparable to the metaphysical question of: Do we exist or are we all a figment of some great imagination? Of course, since the characters come out of the writer, he is in all of them. Nevertheless, in the kind of novels for which I am habitually known, not the totally imaginary ones like *The Spell of Time*, the sources are in known events or from known historical personages or, as in *The Settlers,* from memoirs and from personal recitations to me. Now, when I come to take these events and interpret them into my writing, I can only do what my imagination comprehends and meets with, so it comes out that the characters—all of them—are partly me. This was perhaps more true earlier, as in *The Old Bunch,* but nevertheless they were drawn just as strongly from people around me whom I knew and whom I combined or transposed a little bit, but the *me-ness* of it, the fact that all the characters that any writer writes really partake of himself, is an oversimplification. I could say, for instance, in *The Fanatic,* that the characters were much more myself than objective characters from other people. But even so, they wouldn't be exactly me.

RIBALOW: As I hear you talk about your work, a question comes to mind. I can't help thinking of some other writers with whom I've recently talked. Charles Angoff told me that he draws on his memory: he has "total recall," as he puts it, and on his experiences, which he rewrites as fiction. The Yiddish poet and novelist Chaim Grade works along another path. He has an enormous library, a library in Yiddish, Hebrew, English, French, and Russian, history books, art volumes, and the basic religious books, like the Talmud. So he draws a great deal from books. What about you? And are you a fast writer, a slow writer? Like Georges Simenon, who can write a book in three weeks, or like Joseph Heller, who writes his books more than a decade apart?

LEVIN: That's just a gag of course. Heller was obviously blocked and his publisher made a virtue out of a difficulty. There's no sin in being blocked. But for advertising publicity, they made the public believe he's working every day for fifteen years. He struggled with a block. No, I'm not like Simenon. I'm a middling type of writer, I guess, in terms of speed. When I work, I try to work consistently.

RIBALOW: If Angoff draws from his experiences and Grade works in part from books, I imagine that you, too, also do some research, as I think back on novels like *The Settlers.*

LEVIN: I do an enormous amount of research on some books, not on all of them. On *The Settlers* I did years of research. I'm still doing research on certain aspects of the continuation [*The Harvest*]. *Citizens* was a novel describing a steel strike. I very specifically used what today is called the documentary novel method, as again I did in *Compulsion.* I don't claim to have invented it. Dreiser used it in *An American Tragedy.* Various approaches to this method have been used in literature virtually since the beginning of the novel. But each time it can be used more consciously and more meticulously. In *Citizens,* in 1940, I was using it the way Capote and others claim to have discovered the use of it today. That is, I was using actual events in such a way that nothing in the novel violated the incidents that took place. As for the inner interpretation, that had to come from me. The same was true in *Compulsion* where I explained carefully to the reader—and I did the same in a preface to *Citizens*—that the events were as recorded in order to give me, the author, a stronger sense of verity. In other words, since these things actually had happened, any explanation I made of them as a novelist had to be closer to the truth than if it were merely an imagined circumstance that I then explained psychologically in terms of the people in that circumstance. Now, another form of criticism would take the attitude that this is puny and confined to a kind of realism that doesn't permit the development of the human imagination or whatever are the terms they use in criticizing this attitude. They can say it's too confining for art to proceed that way. These are the two poles of artistic creation: where you demand complete freedom or you say I will bind myself to what seems to be the reality and yet I will find some imaginative, universal essence within that precise reality that I am confining myself to. This is the case for certain kinds of magic realism in painting, where the same thing happens. The painter does not deviate. He tries to reproduce what is before his eye but at the same time infuse it with a magic quality of a spirit that comes from himself.

RIBALOW: How does this all relate to *Compulsion* or your other novels?

LEVIN: In *Compulsion*, while never ever departing from the psychiatric reports of the boys, I constructed what may be a weak or wrong psychoanalytic interpretation from the studies that have been made of them, not from my own imagination of what their fantasies were but from the actual fantasies as written down by examining analysts at the time. Now, it held water, what I constructed. So well, that many psychiatrists and analysts agreed with me that what I had evolved is a plausible hypothesis for their troubles. There, too, you may ask, "Is that the function of a writer of fiction?" I think the artist invades all kinds of areas. Maybe the professionals think he is an intruder, but if it contributes to what he needs, to bring out what he wants to show or say, then that's his privilege.

RIBALOW: We had talked about *The Old Bunch* being almost from the outset, and then again in retrospect—a classic of American-Jewish fiction. But recently I've noticed you haven't been writing about Jewish life in this country. Is there any particular reason for this? I was struck by this development when I read *The Spell of Time* and *The Settlers*.

LEVIN: No. It's in no way deliberate. What happened essentially is that I was so overwhelmed by the Holocaust that almost everything I have written since then has been in relationship to it, with the exception of *Compulsion*, which is about American-Jewish life. I felt drawn into the area of the entire Jewish experience of our time. In a sense I had already set down the American-Jewish *milieu* as I grew up in it. Then the Holocaust happened and I felt that Israel, the Palestine Jewish experience, and the Holocaust are part of the American-Jewish experience. So that this is what absorbed me. Meanwhile, I seem to have neglected the American-Jewish scene.

RIBALOW: Is it possible also that this happened because you live in Israel as well as in the United States?

LEVIN: Oh, no. I've been living here enough during that period to have picked up material, but it just worked out that those things seemed more important to me to write about at the time—*as* an American Jew. What I did with them was written from the *inner* viewpoint of my total experience.

RIBALOW: How important are reviews to a well-established writer like yourself? I would imagine, in part, that you have a following. After all, you have been writing for fifty years and now you have a new novel issued. In the movie field, people go to a film whether the reviews are good or bad. Don't you have a following so that just the knowledge that the book is out should be enough, regardless of reviews?

LEVIN: True, but only to the smallest extent. Much less than people imagine. At least for me. There are certain writers of other categories where reviews don't matter. They have an enormous following and that's it. You have to proceed upwards from the level of the just plain adventure and sex writer, who sometimes doesn't even rate reviews but ... Harold Robbins ... you know writers whose readers are waiting for any book of theirs. So you must count that out because that's really a different field. Then you get into the intellectual field where reviews do count to a great extent but where a following for a writer—like Nabokov—will nevertheless buy to a certain extent any of his books no matter what the reviews say. And then it depends on word-of-mouth. Is this a good Nabokov or not? Basically, reviews affect such writers, too. Since I am now in what has been declared a special field—"writing about Jews"—I am regarded not as a writer, for example, like Isaac Bashevis Singer, or Elie Wiesel, about Jews—who do have such a following. Here, reviews may not be of great importance. Nevertheless, these writers will receive important reviews. My current book, *The Spell of Time,* is an example. It has been out about a month now and I have had practically no reviews in the magazines. The same was true of *The Obsession* and of *The Settlers.*

RIBALOW: You frequently are critical of "Jewish" writers who really aren't very Jewish. Who are the truly Jewish writers, in your judgment, who write like, say, Angoff and yourself? Not, of course, in your styles, but your outlook.

LEVIN: We have very few people who have taken the position in writing in English that Angoff and I have. Of course, Myron Kaufmann wrote an excellent novel, *Remember Me to God.* He's definitely trying to work in this field, both in his first novel and his second *Thy Daughter's Nakedness,* but it is difficult. We don't always write the same quality, neither I, nor Angoff or anybody. But Kaufmann at least has the point of view of a writer who wants to write from within what's happening in the Jewish community, the total Jewish community, not merely the American-Jewish community.

RIBALOW: Whom else would you list and recommend?

LEVIN: Very, very few. There may be some I haven't read or heard of. Cynthia Ozick, I think, is trying to do this and is a brilliant writer who has yet to write her big novel. But it would be from that point of view when it happens, I'm sure.

RIBALOW: The last time we met, you were reading the galleys of *Anya* by Susan Fromberg Schaeffer.

LEVIN: I'll get to her in a moment, but first I'd like to mention Hugh Nissenson. He writes so little, but he certainly is qualified. Herbert Gold may surprise us with a big novel. The more he gets banged on the head for declaring himself a Jewish personality in the literary world, the more likely he is to respond by writing an important novel of the kind we are talking about. He surely has the quality as a writer and one of his early novels, *The Prospect Before Us,* and *Fathers,* indicate that he had that feeling. As to *Anya,* I noticed an interview with Schaeffer in which she said, I don't want to be typed a Jewish writer. What she did was something similar to what I did in *Eva.* She listened to a survivor and put into form what this woman had told her. But I think it's curious, to say the least, that a woman who is writing so strongly out of the Jewish experience, should make the kind of remark she did.

RIBALOW: How do you account for the popularity of some of the Yiddish writers?

LEVIN: This is a built-up thing that has to do with Jewish identity, with a nostalgic quality. In other words, it's an out; it's an escape hatch as much as anything else. It's popular and even "cultured" to enlarge on the quality of Yiddish writing and this shows that you are "not ashamed of being Jewish" even while you are alienated from current Jewish life. Then there is also, among people who are in Jewish life, a genuine feeling of enlarging their experience of Jewish life through the generations that went before.

RIBALOW: Looking back, are you satisfied to have written so many books about Jews or would you, like so many Jewish writers, have done otherwise?

LEVIN: I am satisfied. Each book is written out of a sense of pressure within one's self to deal with that material or that story. There isn't very much choice about it.

RIBALOW: There are writers, however, who select options for themselves. They go to Hollywood, or they write about Jews and alter their names and so on.

LEVIN: I went to Hollywood. For making a living, so to speak, I had to do a lot of things, and I've earned money doing many things. But what I wrote in what I considered my serious efforts had to be what demanded in me to be written. If it was Jewish material, then it had to be Jewish material.

RIBALOW: How do you see your role as a Jewish writer? A *maggid,* an educator, an entertainer?

LEVIN: Well, I'm something of all of those. As you know, I've tried even formally to be an educator with some books that I collaborated on, some I wrote, for younger people. They're used in ninth, tenth, eleventh, and twelfth grades. I've also produced an Israeli Haggadah, which is a very important document to me because I feel that the celebration of the Seder in the home is perhaps the last significant occasion for even the nonreligious Jew to interpret for himself and assert his Jewish being. I have made some films that are educational about the Falashas, the path of Moses through the desert; and of course, *The Illegals*, about the escape of the survivors from Europe. So that you also can say is educational, but none of these things definitely separate out into categories. I would, if I were more confident of the quality of my work, say that what is basically of importance is whatever I have achieved in a belletristic sense. But I have been slammed over the head for so long by the intellectuals and the intellectual Establishment critics, that I wouldn't dare make any assertions in that regard and I have to leave that to others. I can only say that certain literary works or efforts at literary works have been done out of what was to me the literary impulse, while certain others have had an educational impulse as well. The literary impulse is of course to me the most important.

RIBALOW: What, if anything, do you think will last?

LEVIN: If any of my books last, if they have quality, then it would be very gratifying to know that I did have that genuine impulse and I had the talent to realize on the page what I felt I was doing. There's a distance in writers, for each one thinks he is really writing something good, even some of the most popular ones. You *have* to believe in what you are writing. So the final judgment is not in your hands. But it's been at least gratifying to me that some of these books have lasted thirty years and more and that they do maintain for quite a body of people a literary status. Maybe when the prejudice against Jewish subjects among the literary elite is reduced, it will be found, let us say, that *The Settlers* stands as well as they think *The Old Bunch* stands as a work of literature. I don't know. As far as from within myself, it comes from the same source and I gave it the same unstinted effort and I did it as well as I could, so I hope it will stand. I think that I also did good things in *In Search* and particularly in *The Obsession*. The rest is up to the future.

A Conversation with
Susan Fromberg Schaeffer

Susan Fromberg Schaeffer is a sweet-faced wife and mother who happens also to be a prolific, successful, and very good novelist and poet. By profession an academic, she somehow manages to publish frequently in a wide range of periodicals both in the United States and England.

Her first novel, *Falling* (1973), and *Anya* (issued a year later) were well received and were commercial successes as well. Her most ambitious work of fiction, *Time in Its Flight* (1978) was a major book club selection. All of her novels were reissued in paperback. She has, at the same time, continued to produce sensitive and fine poetry. Her volumes are *The Witch and the Weather Report* (1972), *Granite Lady* (1974), *Rhymes and Runes of the Toad* (1974), *Alphabet for the Lost Years* (1976), *The Bible of the Beasts of the Little Field* (1980). She also has published a collection of stories, *The Queen of Egypt* (1980). Her next novel, *Love*, has been scheduled for publication.

A Brooklynite educated at the University of Chicago, Mrs. Schaeffer lives with her husband Neil—she is an associate and he is an assistant professor of English at Brooklyn College—and their two children in a spacious old-fashioned wood-framed private house in Brooklyn close by the campus where she and her husband teach. Like her, the house is *haimisch*, warm and comfortable. They also have a summer home in Vermont.

Unaccustomed to public acclaim, requests for personal appearances and invasions on her privacy by well-wishers, Mrs. Schaeffer nevertheless manages with grace to handle her new "problems." She laughs easily and musically and talks with candor about her work, her obsessive drive to write, and her ideas of being Jewish and how Jewishness does, or does not, affect her work.

77

This conversation took place at the Schaeffer home, in a comfortable corner of a living room full of Edwardian, carved oak furniture, on December 15, 1974.

RIBALOW: *Falling* was a first novel and was called one of the ten best of the year by *Time* magazine, and it received other favorable notices. In a recent issue of the *Saturday Review,* you were named as a "young hopeful" of 1974. Are you surprised by all this attention and praise?

SCHAEFFER: Yes, I was. With the second novel you kind of get used to things a little bit, at least you get used to the unpredictability of things. With *Falling,* I expected everything to be predictable. Everything to be bad.

RIBALOW: Was that the first book you attempted to write?

SCHAEFFER: That was the first novel I wrote. I thought about it on and off for eight years because I remember mentioning how I was going to put it together to someone in Chicago and he said you have to have more than a collection of imagistic patterns to put a novel together. So I forgot about it, and then I kept thinking about it and then I started to write it. I just wrote the whole thing through and I expected nothing but evil to come of it. When it came to having the final copy typed up—it was about three hundred seventy-five pages long—my husband said I could have my choice between having it typed professionally or buying a couch. I decided that, given what was likely to happen to the novel, I'd be better off spending the money on the couch. So I typed it myself and we got the couch.

RIBALOW: How do you actually work? Do you write longhand; type, and edit much?

SCHAEFFER: I type.

RIBALOW: I ask for a reason. It seems that both of the books, I read *Anya* before *Falling,* have the same sort of flow—long paragraphs; you don't break up the page much. It all has a very old-fashioned look, as though you are not worrying whether the reader is going to turn away from you.

SCHAEFFER: I don't think about the reader at all when I'm writing a book. I really don't care about the reader a bit. I think of myself as writing to other people I'd like to write letters to, to those who have a sort of kinship with me. What happens is, my schedule is so busy—I teach full time at Brooklyn College and I have a house to run and I write poetry full time also—that I memorize everything in my head. I commit it all to memory during the day.

RIBALOW: Then you put it down?

SCHAEFFER: Well, then I edit it in my head as well. Only then do I put it down. And then I *do* go over it.

RIBALOW: It's like somebody being in jail, trying to have the days pass quickly and doing problems in his head.

SCHAEFFER: Yes. As soon as I can, I get near the typewriter and write it down. I go over what I've just written, which is the first editing. I then go on to the next section. When I finish the whole thing, I reedit it all, from beginning to end. That is, as I retype it, the final draft and the final editing are done at the same time.

RIBALOW: Now that I've read *Falling,* I find that it is, in a sense, a "Jewish" novel. Your heroine, Elizabeth, is a neurotic with a love-hate relationship with her parents. . . . But I assume you don't consider this a "Jewish" book, do you?

SCHAEFFER: No, I don't but then I have very complicated problems with thinking about these issues. This has only become clear to me since *Anya,* which is on a specifically Jewish subject, the Holocaust. I tend to think of books which we call "Jewish books" as books written by people usually in Yiddish and then translated into English. I also tend to think of a book written by an assimilated Jew as being not a really Jewish book; it's an American-Jewish book, somehow diluted. But I suspect I'm the only one who thinks of things this way. I guess *Falling* could be considered a Jewish book, if you look at it from the point of view of the presiding sensibility; after all, it's about a definitely Jewish family. . . .

RIBALOW: That's right. Your Elizabeth is constantly tortured by her mother, who is drawn as a classically possessive mother. You have a scene early on where the girl has a horrible experience. Her mother insists that Elizabeth get her hair cut. It may be a minor matter to many people, but to the mother it is major and she is adamant about it. The girl is hysterical and she runs and hides in the bathroom. When she finally emerges, her mother beats her badly. There is real hate between the two. To me, that hatred is never really or totally dissipated or dissolved throughout all the years the book encompasses.

SCHAEFFER: Especially since in the book the grandmother is permitted to have her hair as long as she wants. So to the child it seems extremely unfair. The grandmother and the mother have never gotten rid of their possessive relationship to each other and it extends to the third generation, though the coupling is a little weaker between the second and the third generation. As far as my experience with non-Jewish families goes, you *never* find this maniacal concern with every little detail over children.

RIBALOW: Yes. I've got a friend who can't understand why you are constantly in touch with members of your family.

SCHAEFFER: No, my friends don't understand it, either. My brother tends to stay over at the house once a week, now that he's living close by. My other brother is in California and we talk to him once a week and I talk to my mother every day.

RIBALOW: It's a perfectly natural thing.

SCHAEFFER: If I didn't—if she's not home when I call at a certain hour, I assume she's died. And if I'm not home at a certain hour, she calls my brother. To me this seems absolutely normal and then I find out there are people who haven't talked to their brothers or sisters in five years and they don't care if they don't talk to them at all.

RIBALOW: Let's switch to some of your background. I know you attended the University of Chicago, at least *Falling* is set largely in Chicago. You taught there and you are presently an associate professor of English at Brooklyn College. You've written four books of poetry, the latest being *Granite Lady*.

SCHAEFFER: *Granite Lady* was published simultaneously with *Anya* by Macmillan.

RIBALOW: Who published the other poetry?

SCHAEFFER: The first book, *The Witch and the Weather Report,* was published by a little press, called Seven Woods Press. In September, Macmillan is issuing *Rhymes and Runes of the Toad.* It's illustrated and has one story in it. It's really a grown-up book but it's got pictures, which makes me happy. I never understood why grown-up books couldn't have pictures. There's a fourth one called *Asylum,* which is a poetry sequence which forms a novel of one person's experience. I don't know how else to describe it. It's about a person who is schizophrenic, but at the beginning of the book, that isn't so clear. The illness runs its course and at the end of the book there are indications that matters are improving but the whole problem isn't resolved. This all came about from my getting into an argument about whether Sylvia Plath was or was not schizophrenic. With my obsessive way of doing things, I started reading all the medical books. To be even more obsessive than normal, I took the first book on schizophrenia there is, Ernest Bleuler's *Dementia Praecox and the Other Schizophrenias.* I still think that's about the best book on the subject, even though it's the first. I worked my way up to all the contemporary writers on schizophrenia.

RIBALOW: *Asylum* for a moment. What does it deal with? Schizophrenia?

SCHAEFFER: What it really is is an attempt to find out what this extreme experience is like through the imagination rather than through experience. There's been this whole school of thought that started gaining momentum after Sylvia Plath's suicide and after A. Alvarez started writing articles about it—whether her suicide was intended or not, whether the only way to write good art is to live on the edge of the razor blade. I'm dead against the idea that the only way somebody can develop a large talent is by losing their mind. It is setting a disastrous precedent for really young writers who are very impressionable when they are in college. One of my students said to me that he thought maybe the problem with his poetry is that he wasn't neurotic enough. I thought I had a nut in my class but Denise Levertov wrote an article saying that she had been hearing the same sort of thing from her students, that they were beginning to get the notion that if you hadn't had at least one psychotic collapse, you were not destined for greatness. I don't approve of this suicide celebration.

RIBALOW: So even though you write about schizophrenia and nervous and neurotic people, you look at it from a "healthy" point of view.

SCHAEFFER: I'm very interested in it, but not enough to want to have to go through it myself. I do want to understand it, but not to the extent of wanting to take LSD to find out at firsthand what that life actually is like. I would not like to spend a month staring at palm trees growing on my wall if I was trying to finish a novel.

RIBALOW: To return to your work. This question strikes me: *Falling,* from what I've learned and read about you, is based on your own background: teaching, some of your observations on grading papers, analyzing the poetry of Dylan Thomas, going for interviews for teaching jobs, coming to and from New York City.

SCHAEFFER: Some of *Falling* is definitely based on fact but then I have this tendency to take what is the seed of a normal incident and to turn it into some kind of unrecognizable burlesque of itself.

RIBALOW: You know, the Yiddish poet and novelist Chaim Grade says that half of the people in his untranslated novel *Zemach Atlas,* about the head of a yeshiva in Lithuania, are drawn from individuals he met in Detroit. But he brings them to Vilna, shifting his characters from one continent to another.

SCHAEFFER: My students complain that I tend to do the same thing in class. I take a single thing that somebody has said and I make an elaborate crystal palace out of it, usually with sinister overtones.

RIBALOW: So here you are: You've written these two published novels, *Falling* and *Anya; Asylum* is done. Is it being published?

SCHAEFFER: It's going to be published simultaneously with my third novel, called *Time in Its Flight.*

RIBALOW: Is that a conventional novel as compared with *Asylum?*

SCHAEFFER: Yes, yes. It's more like *Anya* in form than like *Falling.*

RIBALOW: You say two books will be published simultaneously?

SCHAEFFER: Yes, officially one, *Asylum,* will be a book of poetry and the other a novel. They'll have related themes because *Time in Its Flight* deals tangentially with insanity. It's about life in rural New England in the nineteenth century, from 1830 to 1900.

RIBALOW: You've had to do research on that, no doubt.

SCHAEFFER: I've gotten started now and it's fascinating.

RIBALOW: Where in New England are you placing it?

SCHAEFFER: Vermont. We've lived there for five years in the summers, in a little town called Harmonyville, outside of Brattleboro. The town has about ten families. What I did—although the material actually comes from all over the country—was to collect old diaries, old letters, old pictures, etiquette books. . . .

RIBALOW: Isn't that a change for you? *Falling* was written from within yourself.

SCHAEFFER: I often wish I would do another novel like *Falling* because with something contemporary that takes place in a neighborhood you are familiar with, all you have to do is think of what you want to do with your people and move them like pieces on a chessboard. But if you don't know what the people are really like, or what the terrain is like, or the state of affairs at a given time and place, then you've got your problems! I had a lot of medical books up there and did research. I studied the medical books that the doctors had at the time. Some are amazingly sophisticated, yet there was an awful lot those doctors couldn't know.

RIBALOW: With a husband, a year-old son and a full teaching program, how do you manage to do all that you do? After all, you are a very prolific writer.

SCHAEFFER: I work very hard. It's a disposition that seems to run in our family which no one has tried to inculcate in another. I sometimes wonder if it's genetic, like arthritis, which also runs in our family. But— two days before we were having a party—there were lots of things that had to be done. Then I decided the living room could not remain un-painted for another second, so I started painting it two nights ago and I was painting until three in the morning, which is why it's pink now. Once that obsession begins with writing, I'll put the baby to bed and I'll go to bed for two hours and I'll work to four in the morning and get up again at eight o'clock, work all day and go back to bed for three hours. When I finish, I collapse entirely. In the meantime, once I do get started, I feel like the sorcerer's apprentice. I can't stop easily.

RIBALOW: Let me turn to *Anya* for a while. I'm going to base many of my questions on the basis of a formal talk of yours that I heard a month or so ago at the Park Avenue Synagogue. You said, at one point, that as a child you were constantly terrified by tales about the Nazis, that you are part of a huge family and that everyone worried about the plight and the fate of the European Jews and the possibility of Hitler overwhelming the world.

SCHAEFFER: It wasn't the first generation of Jews in this country who carried on like that. It was the second generation, which my mother and father represented, who were always talking about how at any moment the same thing could happen again and this—I never understood it; I don't under-stand it to this day—why my grandfather wasn't always talking about the horrors of the war, whereas my parents, who never had any direct expe-rience with it, were constantly anxious about it. After all, my grandfather foresaw it all coming and arrived in this country by a circuitous route and brought all his relations here; it cost him a lot of money to bring them. Yet he didn't have this obsession. My parents somehow must have felt that if you didn't think about the second World War and the Holocaust, you somehow would lose an important aspect of your Jewishness. My grand-parents seemed to take it for granted that anybody who was Jewish would understand there were pogroms and dangers and that people should have passports and they should be ready to leave. . . .

RIBALOW: Do you have a passport at all times?

SCHAEFFER: I want to now. I never used to feel that way, but after writing *Anya*, I do. After writing this book and after talking to people and finding out how people were so unaware and so accepting and so sure that everything would be all right if they remained where they were, it began to dawn on me that—anti-Semitism apart—the world was just the most unsafe place one could hope to be. It's not anything I worry about every day, but it strikes me, to be practical, you should be as mobile as possible.

RIBALOW: You also said that an accidental meeting with a woman who spoke a foreign language, you never did say which language. . . .

SCHAEFFER: Russian.

RIBALOW: Telling the story of how a mother died, or was killed, so that her child might survive, led you to the first glimmerings of *Anya* and that the word "holocaust." . . .

SCHAEFFER: I had never heard of it before.

RIBALOW: Yes, that's what you said. I'm now getting used to this concept—the realization that there are people who never knew about, say, Hitler. I force myself to realize that it's a great many years ago and a lot of people have come and gone since then. Unless they are taught formally, unless they hear it in their homes, how would they know it? But then when you said you had never heard the word "holocaust" before, either—a writer, a poet, a teacher—and having said earlier that the family was involved in and concerned about these things, that also surprised me.

SCHAEFFER: My family always talked in terms of the personalities. We thought of it all in terms of the people—Hitler, and Goebbels, and Eichmann—and the event as part of the war. The word "holocaust" seemed, when I did hear it, oversimplified to me. It made it sound like a kind of firestorm. Really, I think my major acquaintance with the whole period and my first interest in it does come from Meyer Levin and *The Diary of Anne Frank*. We read it in high school and then we were all marched off to see the performance of the play. I found that a shattering, shaky experience. *The Diary of Anne Frank,* that is. It confirmed my tendency to think about events in terms of people. The Holocaust subsumed the people, made the people disappear into the symbol, *which I was objecting to* because I knew it was people that went through it, not this kind of gold label which is what the Holocaust had sounded like, a flaming coin. The people had seemed somehow to have disappeared.

RIBALOW: How many printings has *Anya* had?

SCHAEFFER: It's about at the end of its first printing now, about 22,000 copies.

RIBALOW: You did indicate it's been sold to a paperback house?

SCHAEFFER: Yes, to Avon. It's been a best-seller for six weeks in Chicago and it's been an alternate selection of the Book-of-the-Month-Club. I have no idea what the total sales are. It's also a Woman's Today Book Club Selection and we don't know what they've sold of it, either.

RIBALOW: How do you account for the popular reception of *Anya?* You had said you were amazed and had expected nothing special from *Falling.* After *Falling,* you had won some recognition, acceptance, a "name."

SCHAEFFER: Having written *Falling,* I was more aware of how unpredictable everything was. I thought that in a way *Anya* was a much more dangerous book to write. For some reason I had got it into my head that the only acceptable type of book to write about the Second World War and the Holocaust was one which was very declamatory in style and very condemning of everybody who was not Jewish. I expected that Jewish readers would be upset by *Anya* for it was, for the most part, nonhysterical and spent a good deal of time on events before the ghettoes and the concentration camps. On top of that, I had picked someone whose experiences were not of the worst sort.

RIBALOW: Let me stay with that for a moment. Is *Anya* based on the life of a real person, or persons, or a group of people? The details are very dense; it's all quite vivid and the later part of the novel is so flowing with detail that you make it extraordinarily credible for a writer who wasn't there.

SCHAEFFER: I worked primarily with one person. What I wanted to do and what people I talked to wanted to do were poles apart. I wanted to write a book which began with a normal life which was interrupted by history when history collided with it. But people who have survived the war want to start to talk about their experiences when they really became dreadful, beginning with the ghetto.

RIBALOW: You deliberately selected a situation where the person, in this case Anya, was not in one of the "bad" camps, but in one of the "better" ones.

SCHAEFFER: Well, it was a labor camp rather than a concentration camp. What it had in common with a concentration camp was the "selections," that at any moment a certain number of people would be selected from the people in the camp so that the German quota for dead Jews could be met. If that had not been part of the life in that particular camp, it would not have been any worse than the Russian labor camps. But it was living with the notion that even when you had gotten finished with the day's work, somebody would come in in the middle of your eating whatever they were giving you for supper and drag you off—that gave it its nightmarish quality.

RIBALOW: To pursue some of your observations at your Park Avenue Synagogue lecture. I made notes at the time, hoping to ask you some questions I'd like cleared up. Among other things, you stated that the Holocaust can become "a graven image" to the Jews. What did you mean to convey when you said that?

SCHAEFFER: I was thinking of the story in the Bible of Gideon and his victory over the Midianites. It's not terribly clear in the Bible, really—I've looked at the passage many, many times—what exactly his intentions were when he melted down the pendants and the earrings and the jewelry from the Midianites and made the monument or the ephod. The ephod was supposed to commemorate the victory but instead the Israelites fell to worshiping. After that, the only things told about them is that Yahweh withdrew from them. They did not prosper. And a great many people I heard from immediately after the interview I had given to the New York *Post* seemed to feel that the Holocaust belonged absolutely to the Jews and were talking about it in a proprietary way as if it were a pair of shoes you could own; it belonged to the Jews the way a house belongs to someone and nobody else can trespass upon it. Not only that: their way was the only way of looking at it. It became clear to me that there were many people who did nothing most of the day but think about the Holocaust and all the terrible things done to the Jews during this period called the Holocaust. This did not seem to me desirable. It didn't even seem in accord with the Jewish faith, which doesn't believe in making a religion out of suffering.

RIBALOW: To follow up. If the Holocaust is "hugged by the Jews," as you said, it is to blaspheme against life. What do you mean by that?

SCHAEFFER: It did seem to me that way; that if you make a religion out of suffering, if you hug it to yourself, if you exclude all the other things from your sight, you commit the sin, which—when it was first explained to me —made a terrible impression on me, because I tend to it. According to a writer who once spoke to me about it, it is called "zindig"; that is, you always manage to look on the dark side of everything and hence blacken God's creation in a way that He doesn't approve of. A great deal of sinning was being committed in the name of love for one's people. It seemed to me that there were those who were alive and in need of help now. They could use a lot more thought than those who were now dead and beyond help. I certainly didn't imply anyone should forget about the Holocaust.

RIBALOW: You had another line somewhere: "It is irresponsible and immoral to keep the Holocaust alive for Jews alone."

SCHAEFFER: I think it is. First of all, one of the problems is that the Jews of this generation are doing their best to forget it. Most people my age, and especially younger people, would rather not hear about the Holocaust. Right after that I said that, *Present Tense,* the new Jewish magazine, came out with an article which said the same thing.

RIBALOW: You've also observed that Jews have been "cherishing" the Holocaust.

SCHAEFFER: Some. I didn't mean everybody, but an influential part of the intellectual Jewish Establishment. I know my own first reaction, when I started giving lectures, was to feel extremely guilty that I wasn't spending more time brooding and putting my whole life in the framework of what had happened. History just isn't static.

RIBALOW: Life isn't static either. You say also that the "assimilated Jews live with a legacy of fear."

SCHAEFFER: I think that's true.

RIBALOW: As against which kind of Jews? Which Jews *don't* live with a legacy of fear? Golda Meir frequently talks about the charge that she mentions too frequently "the Masada complex," and she says, "I'm guilty. I have that complex." In view of what has happened on the world scene *vis à vis* Israel in the last couple of months, it seems there's pretty good reason to have such a complex.

SCHAEFFER: It's nice to know that someone like Golda Meir says that she has complexes. Right now, I think, in particular with all these threats to Israel and to its existence, I don't believe there's a sensible Jew in this world who doesn't worry about what may happen.

RIBALOW: We haven't got around to the assimilated Jew yet, in all his ramifications. I have here a note of mine, again taken during your lecture. Correct me if I'm wrong. But here it is: "Why do assimilated Jews understand the Holocaust more than others?"

SCHAEFFER: I don't know if they do.

RIBALOW: Maybe I took it down wrong.

SCHAEFFER: I was hoping they would *get* to understand the Holocaust on an emotional level. I've met a lot of people, for instance, who teach with me and even know all the facts about Auschwitz, its physical layout, Dachau, and the other camps—yet they're detached from it all. It's like someone saying he doesn't have to have children because he can imagine what it's like.

RIBALOW: But they can't, can they?

SCHAEFFER: No, they can't. I had delusions of that sort before I had a child. I thought, well, I was a child once, and I have total recall and I remember everything, much to everybody's horror. Twenty years later, I'll remind someone of an argument they had with people, even quoting names and dates. It's awful. Nobody likes me for this particular talent.... What did I start out to say?

RIBALOW: We were talking about the assimilated Jews and hoping they would become more emotionally involved with the Holocaust.

SCHAEFFER: Oh. But I don't think they do understand it. ... It's a different thing to try to get some kind of emotional nerve endings connected with something than just to be able to recite information. Also, the pictures and the facts are so overwhelming that when they're given to you in large doses they create a numbing effect. Especially pictures. I remember there was one person I was talking to. He brought out some pictures he had taken right after Auschwitz was liberated, pictures of thousands of bodies. When I talked to him, I was capable of following his story— emotionally, that is. But the pictures made it all too much. It was just unimaginable. I couldn't believe they were real pictures. Of course they were. But somehow there was no human intelligence or human sensibility acting as an intermediary. It was so alien, it was something I just rejected.

RIBALOW: You had an image that struck me, but I'm afraid I didn't get it down too well, but it made an impression on me. You said that the Red Sea had parted and the Jews were walking on sort of a trail. There were waves on either side and those who linger, or are uncertain about the path they take —right behind them, other people are drowning. So at all times, Jews are walking where there's danger on either side and behind them. The best they can do is go steadily forward.

SCHAEFFER: Yes. That was part of my attempt to explain why I thought it was necessary for Jews to share the Holocaust, or at least try to have people who are not Jewish understand what had happened. In this way there could be a sympathetic or an emotional kind of communication. I used that image of the Red Sea because it was an image from the Bible, which is an image of the whole history of the Jews: that they are always fleeing down this path in the Red Sea, that the two halves of the Red Sea are always the hostile nations that are surrounding the Israelites the same way that Israel is surrounded by hostile nations right now; the Red Sea is always in danger of closing behind them if they don't somehow move fast enough; that even if some of their enemies are drowned—as was true of Moses when he led the Jews through the Red Sea—the losses to the Jews are still enormous. Unless there can be a more stable path, a solid foothold that's more permanent, there's always going to be this Red Sea existence. There *has* to be some kind of communication between Jews and non-Jews, a less antagonistic relationship between the Jewish nation and other nations. And I have absolutely no idea of where one begins.

RIBALOW: You did say at one time that many children don't want to know about their Jewishness because of the Holocaust. How do you know this?

SCHAEFFER: From pure experience with my students and myself and friends. I know from my own experience, which I thought was possibly unique, that I was so petrified of all this that I avoided Jewish things, or tended to. But of course there were other complicating factors. For instance, the Hebrew school I went to as a child. It was Orthodox and I loved it.

RIBALOW: Around here, in Brooklyn?

SCHAEFFER: Yes, on Avenue U above a shoe store. It was dark and serious. The Hebrew letters were like a code; to me, it was a magic place. Then we moved to Long Island and I went to a Hebrew school in a Temple, built like Grand Central Station, marble all over. And who was teaching in that school? Not these learned old men but friends of my mother's! It struck me as sacrilegious. And what were the students doing? They were painting their fingernails while the teacher talked, and throwing balls of paper at the teacher when she turned her back to them and faced the blackboard. I was so horrified that I didn't want to go and explained the reason to my mother. It was a desecration of the Temple, I said. I had just come from this tiny school where everybody worked very hard. She didn't believe me. She was sure no one was painting nails in class. I insisted that everyone is painting her nails in class. Not only that, they kiss each other behind books and everyone makes arrangements to go to parties and movies and that's not my idea of a Hebrew school. She said only, You're going. You're Jewish and you're going! I swore that if she made me go, I'd never enter a Temple again. It was ten years before I broke that promise. I was so thunderstruck at what I thought was becoming of the Jewish religion, that I wanted nothing further to do with it.

RIBALOW: It sounds extreme.

SCHAEFFER: I had had a very odd background as a child. My grandfather and grandmother were Orthodox and I don't know what got into my grandfather one Yom Kippur. I was his favorite, his eldest grandchild, and he decided to take me into the men's section of the synagogue. He dressed me up in my brother's suit and put a little hat on my head. I was told not to say a word because I had a high voice and I wasn't supposed to look at anybody or anything. I was *so* impressed. Of course I had no idea of what was going on. Everyone was praying in Hebrew and rocking back and forth and I thought that this was where all the secrets were. That's why I got so totally dedicated in Hebrew school. Then, after this, to go to this ludicrous synagogue was too much for me.

RIBALOW: You cut yourself away from it.

SCHAEFFER: You see, a lot of people that I knew felt their parents were just mouthing things about religion, saying it was important to be Jewish but they themselves were not going near the synagogue. If they did go, the synagogues didn't seem worthy of going to in the first place. Then there have been endless numbers of students that I knew, and people I went to high school with, who have been so thoroughly petrified by what they've heard of what might happen to them, that it was like the cancer reaction—they didn't want to hear about it.

RIBALOW: When I talked with Meyer Levin, he told me that he had read somewhere that you don't think of yourself as a "Jewish" writer, which he found very difficult to understand in view of the subject and the care and the devotion you gave *Anya,* which he liked very much.

SCHAEFFER: When I say I don't consider myself a Jewish writer, which means to me Isaac Bashevis Singer, people think I mean I don't consider myself a Jewish person, which is quite untrue. I'm a little *too* pleased with myself for being Jewish. That was also part of the family tradition: it was a wonderful thing to be Jewish. As far as I was concerned, the word "Jewish" and the word "family" were synonymous. Mine is a very close family and I'm extremely fortunate to have it. To me family life and Jewish life are indistinguishable, so of course I think of myself as Jewish.

RIBALOW: What about your books? Your first two novels have Jewish themes. What of the next one?

SCHAEFFER: That one won't. Partly the reason I wouldn't call myself a Jewish writer is because I'm not trying deliberately to write on Jewish themes— and I don't try deliberately to write on anything. Whatever turns out to be the obsession which hooks into writing something that is a book is what I'm going to write about. It turned out the first novel was about a Jewish family and the second one also was about a Jewish family under circumstances which are particularly identified with the Jews. This third novel became an obsession when someone told me of a diary they had of a woman who had moved from Boston to Vermont. The diary was entirely about her loneliness. Partly because I lived in Vermont in the summer and gotten attached to the people and the surroundings, the whole thing became very obsessive. Of course, if you're going to write about Vermont in the 1800s, you can't introduce a rabbi into the story.

RIBALOW: What do you see yourself writing in the next few years.

SCHAEFFER: Well, I'm going to write this novel, *Time in Its Flight*. I keep writing poetry all the time. One night I woke up in the middle of the night and wrote down a poem, folded it carefully, put it in my jewel box and the next night at eight in the evening, while talking to my best friend, one to whom I read everything, I said, "Wait a minute. I wrote a poem yesterday. Let me go get it." I had forgotten completely that I had written it. It was like in a dream. I went to the jewel box and, sure enough, it was there. I read it to her on the phone and she said, "That's very good!"

RIBALOW: Do you write short stories, too?

SCHAEFFER: Yes. Short stories are my playground. You don't have to live with the characters for 500 pages and you can do all kinds of experimental things. I have a wonderful time making dreadful mischievous things happen to the characters.

RIBALOW: What does your husband do when you write?

SCHAEFFER: He writes also, mostly scholarly articles and he publishes short stories, but when I'm writing a novel he mostly waits for it to end. He leaves me alone because once I get started I can't stop so it ends quickly. He thinks this is the best way because then it's over with, like German measles.

RIBALOW: Like a disease.

SCHAEFFER: My fever will be coming down.

RIBALOW: Georges Simenon writes his books in intensive three-week bursts. When he's done, he visits his doctor, has his blood pressure taken and then goes fishing, or whatever he does to relax.

SCHAEFFER: I see a doctor before I start. I consider writing like going into training.

RIBALOW: How long did it take you to write *Anya*?

SCHAEFFER: About five months, but that novel was written by my writing almost around the clock. Before that I walked around the house all the time with the tape recorder or with notes and hearing things over and over and over again.

RIBALOW: So when you sat down to write, you had in effect lived the story of Anya.

SCHAEFFER: Yes. But *Falling* took six weeks. That was a maniacal performance. I wouldn't even take off my coat when I came home from school. I'd start in right away. I used an electric typewriter so I didn't even have to wait for my fingers to warm up.

RIBALOW: What do you think of your reviewers?

SCHAEFFER: It's an eerie thing; I don't know if it's true of other writers—reviewers have often anticipated what I'll be writing about next. They don't do it deliberately, but they'll say the central theme of *Anya* is "time." That happened in *Time* magazine's review of *Anya*. Sure enough, about a month later I realized time *was* the subject I was interested in. I had always known the next book was going to be called *Time in Its Flight*. The same thing happened with *Falling*; somebody wrote something about the type of mind I had and more or less predicted what the next novel was going to be about. It's a help in some ways. It kind of speeds up the process when you get reviews like that.

RIBALOW: So you're one of the few writers who believes that the critics can help you.

SCHAEFFER: There are only a few I would like to strangle or throw in the East River. Their reviews may be favorable or "selling reviews," but they're about someone else's book. *That* I resent. I do go to a lot of trouble to write them and I wish they would write a review on the proper book. If a magazine can't find someone who has reading ability, give the book to another reviewer.

RIBALOW: You don't have too many complaints.

SCHAEFFER: Not really, no.

A Conversation with
Robert Kotlowitz

Before the publication of *Somewhere Else* (1972), Robert Kotlowitz was the editor of *Harper's* Magazine and the author of some influential essays on cultural developments in the United States. He wrote his first novel while meeting his professional responsibilities as an executive officer in charge of programming for WNET/13, a television channel in New York City. Four years later, he published his second novel, *The Boardwalk.*

We met in his office on March 11, 1976, and I was surprised to see how well he was able to isolate himself to participate in our conversation. He has a round face, carries a smile easily, and speaks calmly and reflectively. We were interrupted only twice, and each time he spoke in a whisper and with great speed.

Kotlowitz was educated and raised in Baltimore, where his father was the cantor at an Orthodox synagogue. *Somewhere Else,* I discovered, is about his father and his family. He has brought to the novel a deep understanding of Jewish life in Europe and the reader senses a strong affection for the people who inhabit the novel. It is a densely written work of fiction, which covers a long period of time and moves across various cities in Europe, including Warsaw and London, as well as villages and shtetls.

While Kotlowitz is intensely involved in his professional television chores, he is a disciplined man who is able to detach himself totally from his work during weekends and vacations and to concentrate on creative writing. *Somewhere Else* is a polished, well-constructed and finely conceived work of fiction, without the raw edges one finds in the average first novel. When we talked, it was obvious that his mind was focused on *The Boardwalk,* which had moved to the forefront of his artistic consciousness. It had not yet been published when our conversation took place.

Kotlowitz claims that he is most in touch with himself while in the process of writing novels. There are not many writers who can create while working at a tension-ridden, pressure-filled television job. Apparently, he is capable of both.

RIBALOW: How did you turn to fiction comparatively late in your career?

KOTLOWITZ: I had always had ambitions as a young man to be a journalist. I wanted to be a foreign correspondent or a critic. I was infatuated with the notion of international journalism. Then when I got out of the Army, after World War II—or during the war—I really discovered American fiction as a serious expression of American life.

RIBALOW: Where did you serve?

KOTLOWITZ: I served in Europe in the Third Army as an infantryman, so I went through the war in a very real sense. In that interim period I had always read novels and had a long period of Thomas Wolfe when I first went to college.

RIBALOW: We all did.

KOTLOWITZ: When I got out of combat, I was nineteen or twenty years old and it was that interim between the European and Pacific wars, when they didn't know what to do with the infantryman. . . .

RIBALOW: I was in India at the time and they didn't know what to do with me either.

KOTLOWITZ: They didn't know whether they should ship them all to the Pacific to prepare for a Japanese invasion, or what. Anyway, they opened up a whole set of American universities on the Continent and in England, and I went to one for the summer of 1945. I happened to stumble on Kazin's *On Native Grounds* and for the first time recognized American fiction is something I could take as seriously as European novels and European culture in general, which was the center of my home as a child. In any case, I began to write fiction.

RIBALOW: When you came home from the Army?

KOTLOWITZ: Yes. I was twenty or twenty-one. I began to deal with fiction in a serious way, except that I was paralyzed by this old notion: If Leo Tolstoy is a novelist, what is Bob Kotlowitz? I came to New York and tried to make a career for myself in the world—and did, and made very minor attempts at writing fiction. I began to write journalism, criticism, and then a piece, when I was at *Harper's,* called "Baltimore Boy," which dealt nonfictionally with what it was like to grow up in that very well-defined Jewish community.

RIBALOW: Is that the piece that later was reprinted in *Growing Up Jewish*?

KOTLOWITZ: Yes, the same piece, and that stirred up a lot of publisher interest in a book, except that I discovered that I was not interested in doing memoirs, because Norman Podhoretz' were appearing.

RIBALOW: You are too young, anyway.

KOTLOWITZ: I am too young and it was a form I just did not want to fool with. On the other hand, I was very tempted and flattered by publishers' offers. So I thought I had better sit down and start dealing with this as a writer. So I did. I worked for ten solid weekends and then became aware that I was writing a novel. I very often do things behind my own back.

RIBALOW: I was told you are very disciplined, that you don't see anyone on weekends, that you lock yourself up.

KOTLOWITZ: Yes, I am. When I am working on a book we live a very reclusive life. It's not a bad way to live. It does not conflict with the energy I use here because this is so collaborative and disorderly, if not anarchic, and writing of course is exactly the reverse, and—I don't know—it brings me back in touch with myself. That's one of the things that it does for me.

RIBALOW: So you wrote these long weekends on what turned out to be a novel.

KOTLOWITZ: Yes and then I said to myself, "Bob Kotlowitz, you're really writing a novel. You are not writing about Baltimore, you are writing about your father's life." So I called one editor who was most interested and showed him what I wrote. He said, keep going, here's a contract. And so I wrote a novel. That book, which I wrote in my early forties, was the most important thing that had happened to me in terms of my work. Whatever I had been, it confirmed me as a writer to myself.

RIBALOW: Did this happen as you were working on it or after you completed the novel?

KOTLOWITZ: Well, after it was completed. You work on it in some blind sense.

RIBALOW: When did you complete it?

KOTLOWITZ: It was published in 1972, '71. It was completed when *Harper's* blew up in the spring of '71.

RIBALOW: You know your book better than I, of course. But let me read the opening phrases of *Somewhere Else:* "In my family, we tell stories about each other all the time, and what we're not told, I try to pick up by eavesdropping. I like the real stuff, inside information, the sight and bristling sound of other people's dramas, especially when the plots are taken from family life and its fractious heart, the snarled bloodnest of father, sons, and everyone else; there lies the source of every clue about ourselves." Which leads me to ask—and I'm guessing, of course—that this novel tells the life of *your* family.

KOTLOWITZ: My father was a Polish Jew who was the only member of his family to come to the United States.

RIBALOW: Was that Mendel?

KOTLOWITZ: That was Mendel. My father's name literally was Mendel. He had been in World War I in the Jewish Legion in the British Army.

RIBALOW: That is the way *Somewhere Else* ends. I am reminded that Mendel comes from a place called Lomza and goes to Warsaw and London. He is a Jew who travels through space and time. Yet you begin long before Mendel—with your great grandfather Eliezar, right after the Napoleonic era. Then you introduce the grandfather, Mordecai, and the father, Moses, and then the Mendel you are talking about. Charles Angoff has said that his Alte Bobbe, who has become famous in his work, was known to him for only a few months of his life. Obviously you couldn't have known these great grandparents in any way, yet Eliezar is a memorable character.

KOTLOWITZ: I didn't know any of those Poles. What had happened was that all through my childhood, my father had letters from Warsaw or Lomza. They were always coming. They took on a mythic quality for me. I never saw the people and I had a rather intense imagination. With all these cousins and aunts and uncles and grandparents . . . you know, I imagined grand people.

RIBALOW: Are these the actual names of the people or did you change them for the novel?

KOTLOWITZ: I mixed up a lot of it. Then, just before I sat down to work on the book, to do the writing, my father was visiting me in New York and we were talking. I had always been probing and asking questions. Somehow, he said to me, "You know, my grandfather died when he was 104." One hundred and four! I said, and you've never mentioned it to me? How did he die? He told me the story and we started laughing.

RIBALOW: By fire.

KOTLOWITZ: Yes. About that fire: we said if he had not died then, he'd still be living! So that's what I started writing about. That had always taken hold of me, the mythic quality of the family. Then the war and the camps reinforced that. There was a sense of desperation in so many Jews about all of that going, with no record, no memory. I had one cousin who escaped, who had been shipped off to the Riviera in 1939 to get over an unhappy love affair. She passed through France all through the war as a Catholic and escaped. She married an American lieutenant and now lives in New York. Her husband is a very successful sculptor named Bernard Rosenthal. She is the only Kotlowitz, the only one I know, who survived. I didn't say all that to myself before I began to write, but it clearly was there.

RIBALOW: I have a note here on your bridging a hundred-year age gap between the old Eliezar and his own grandson at the time, all of which you handle so well. How did you "absorb" this old man and recreate so many of the others of an obviously earlier era?

KOTLOWITZ: I had no conscious intention of doing any of that. In fact, my plan was to write a book about Palestine in 1917 to 1921, if I had a plan. I thought I would write a novel about my father as a young man in the Jewish Legion in Palestine. I thought I needed an introductory chapter about Poland and a transitional chapter about London. I had never been to Poland, so what did I know? Anyway, I started to write. As you know, half the book takes place in Poland! All of this had been clearly working in me since I was a child. It all began to come out. All my feelings about the people, everything I had imagined about them. I get letters from people who say to me that the Russian church in Lomza was not on the corner where you remember it to be. It was on the other corner!

RIBALOW: I was impressed, in my rereading, by the way you recreated the little village and the streets, the orphanage across the street from somewhere. . . .

KOTLOWITZ: That's all imaginative. I am sure there was an orphanage and there was a Russian church. I spent a day at YIVO looking at whatever atlas material they had about Lomza.

RIBALOW: Just one day?

KOTLOWITZ: One day. I wanted to know the streets and the number of people who lived there and what they did.

RIBALOW: How did you find that information?

KOTLOWITZ: YIVO has records.

RIBALOW: In English?

KOTLOWITZ: In English. I discovered there was a clothing factory on the river so I could use that. That's why you're a novelist.

RIBALOW: Were you familiar then or are you familiar now with Charles Angoff's novels? I ask because he began very much the same way. He started with a couple of short stories. They were published in Jesuit and literary magazines, not Jewish periodicals. Then he began his novels. First he thought he was working on a trilogy. Now eleven have been published. Some of the earlier books deal with very much the same European materials you concern yourself with. I have another note here which you may be unaware of but I'd like a reaction anyway. It came to me when I was first reading *Somewhere Else*. In 1951, a writer named David Miller wrote a novel called *The Chain and the Link*. It was projected as a trilogy, but it never made it, probably because the first volume never really sold. It reminds me of your work in that it begins with Jews in a shtetl, his in Lithuania and yours in Poland, also in the Napoleonic era. I later learned from Gorham Munson, the well-known critic and teacher, who promoted the book, that Miller had written a huge manuscript that was cut into thirds. The first third was issued and the publisher—World—wanted to see the public reaction to it. It must have been indifferent because nothing else of Miller's was published. He was from Cleveland and years later he died. So you see the fate of some books. What, then, was the reception to your novel, apart from the Edward Lewis Wallant Award it won? Let me add another note. Your novel came to me out of nowhere. I knew your name, of course, but not that you wrote fiction and I was glad to be a judge partially responsible for your obtaining the Wallant Award.

KOTLOWITZ: I don't know about David Miller and I'm not aware of how Angoff's work first evolved. Interesting. But in reply to your final question, *Somewhere Else* had a very serious reception in the press. Part of that, I'm sure, is because I had some kind of reputation already. The press reception was wonderful and on the most serious level. It sold its first printing of 6,500 copies. It was published in England. It really says to you that you are confirmed as a writer.

RIBALOW: I keep repeating that Eliezar is very vividly drawn, even though he is a minor character in the book. He has had two wives. The second one is especially interesting. She is bright, opinionated, and aggressive. Is she an idealized woman of her time or do you have actual knowledge of women like her?

KOTLOWITZ: Sure; I have practical knowledge of women like that. I grew up in a society in which powerful women like that really founded Israel. The Baltimore Hadassah community, of which my mother was a hard-working member, had immensely powerful, hypnotic women. Very compelling personalities. That woman just happened to pass through the book. There was no reason why there should be a second wife. That is one of the great joys of writing fiction. People come into the book and take over.

RIBALOW: What struck me later on in relation to this is that your Jewish women in London, later on in the novel, are unappetizing compared to the little Irish girl who works for a jeweler.

KOTLOWITZ: That's interesting, because I *like* the Jewish girls.

RIBALOW: You like them? Yet you drew them in a way that reminded me of how Thomas Wolfe described his lusty, fleshy women. At the same time—not that the two Christian women are necessarily the most attractive—but by comparison it struck me that the Jewish women were not as delicate.

KOTLOWITZ: The Jewish women were really more worldly versions of the Polish bride. The night that I was at the Waltmans, the sponsors of the Wallant Awards, for the award ceremonies, some guest they had came over to me and said, "I want to tell you something. I used to date Ray Pilchick." That was one of the most wonderful things anybody ever said to me!

RIBALOW: Everybody who writes fiction is thrilled when someone recognizes a fictional character as prototypical of a real, live person.

KOTLOWITZ: Right. I, in a way, love those women. They were variations on women I knew as a young man.

RIBALOW: On another theme for a moment. I get an enormous sense of place in your novel. You seem to have been to the towns and the cities of long ago. For example, the novel is first set in Poland, near Lomza. Then, quoting from your book, "Lomza is not far from Warsaw, maybe sixty miles to the northeast, near Zambrau and Ostrolleka on the Narev River. . . ." Then you refer to "a cluster of lakes forty miles north of Lomza . . ." and you name a few of them. Is this all from your imagination, or is it factual?

KOTLOWITZ: No, those towns really existed; so do the lakes. I just sat down with a map. I remember once my father had said to me that one of those towns used to love to call itself "the Jerusalem of Poland."

RIBALOW: Vilna.

KOTLOWITZ: Every town. Baltimore used to call itself "the Jerusalem of America." That had always amused me, this claim of cities to be the intellectual and spiritual centers.

RIBALOW: Still, you describe Lomza in some detail: the cemetery, the orphanage nearby, the bonfires lit by the boys, the cholera epidemic that takes the life of Leah, Eliezar's first wife. Again, was that imagination or research?

KOTLOWITZ: All imagination. There's a cemetery everywhere. We have all heard of cholera epidemics. The bonfire comes out of the novelist's mind.

RIBALOW: Earlier on, you begin with Eliezar who grew up in the Napoleonic age. He was 104 in 1899. He remembers the French occupation in Lomza and the French retreat from Russia.

KOTLOWITZ: Again, all imagined.

RIBALOW: You may not be aware of the point that was striking me.

KOTLOWITZ: It's fascinating to hear your responses.

RIBALOW: I have the strong impression of the difficulty these people have in surviving. Mordecai is the only surviving son of Eliezar. One son, Joseph, dies very young. Another son, Alexander, drowns. There is, therefore, only one survivor. Survival must have been extremely difficult and while it is said quickly and casually, it comes across. Another thing that struck me as remarkable in its way is that you recreate in careful detail four meetings of the Jewish Council of Lomza. At these meetings, Moses becomes very angry because the members don't want him to abide by his sense of justice. You describe how funerals are arranged and the tax problems of the poor. You also draw clearly the kinds of Jews who are the officials in the community. Does this material come from the letters your father received?

KOTLOWITZ: I knew that his father had died of apoplexy and had trouble in the community.

RIBALOW: In the book he dies of pneumonia, I think.

KOTLOWITZ: Pneumonia, right. The fight was over an issue involving yeast. That had been a family story. I knew the council from the board of directors of my father's synagogue in Baltimore.

RIBALOW: Sometimes it pays to be a hazzan's son.

KOTLOWITZ: Right. You know, our treasures lie at our feet. I knew there could not be that great a change from 1890 to 1935. I knew this board. They were Americanized, but powerful men, and so I just sort of tried to put all that together. Then I placed my father in the middle of it as a witness, because that episode proved to be a turning point in the book in a way that I did not intend consciously at all. It was one of the things that ruled this young man's life and, I think in fact, it did rule my father's life.

RIBALOW: He felt a sense of injustice.

KOTLOWITZ: It affected his relationship with the synagogue. I know that. It was very crucial to him.

RIBALOW: On another matter. You have a gift—a valuable touch, in any case—of dealing with the private affairs of your people as you describe parallel events on the larger scene. When Mendel returns from a resort and learns that his mother has remarried, you inform us that there was a pogrom in Bialystok, with seventy dead. You merge the personal with the political. This carries throughout the novel.

KOTLOWITZ: That's very important to me. I do this in the new book, too. I believe very strongly in what external circumstances do to lives. I was highly sensitized to that as a child.

RIBALOW: There are dozens of people in your novel. You really could have expanded the material into two books.

KOTLOWITZ: That's right. There's too much in it.

RIBALOW: In the rereading, I became aware of a great deal of material that was not important to me on first reading and then I realized how tight you had made it, although it is quite a long book. Do you work from an outline or does it "flow"?

KOTLOWITZ: I just do it. My experience as a writer—and this holds for non-fiction, too—is that the arch of the book really is what it is from the beginning. I *never* restructure it. I don't know where all this is maintained; I don't question it, either, because I'm not sure that it bears questioning. What I really rework is the prose. That gets denser and thicker with each rewriting. I *never* cut. The first draft is always very swift and mainly for the structure.

RIBALOW: Do you polish the prose? Add and subtract?

KOTLOWITZ: Add, mainly. That is how it goes with me, which is not a common process, I would think. Usually, it's cutting and cutting.

RIBALOW: Your central character, Mendel, studied the cantorial art yet at no time does he become a full-fledged cantor. He gave it up because he said he didn't believe in God. Later, in a London synagogue, he led the chanting. I assume that is based on your father's experiences.

KOTLOWITZ: Well, my father kept returning to it because it was what he knew how to do. He didn't know English well enough to be able to take the time to deal with a different way of life. I am not sure that he would have. It *is* his story.

RIBALOW: In the early sections of the novel, you describe vocal techniques, on how to narrate music, to create suspense, inflate emotion. Are you yourself a specialist in music?

KOTLOWITZ: I studied music at the Peabody Conservatory. I studied, and still play, the piano. Music is very close to me. That is natural. Music is very important in my new book, too.

RIBALOW: You make references to Mendel knowing Mozart and Beethoven, but not Mahler. Is it realistic? I read this with a sense of semidisbelief that Jews from that area of Poland would be exposed to Mozart and Beethoven.

KOTLOWITZ: He didn't know Mahler. Mozart and Beethoven were played everywhere in a conventional concert program. That's why I separated Mahler from the others.

RIBALOW: And the cantorial institute you introduce—Reb Lilienblum's—did you make that up or were there cantorial schools?

KOTLOWITZ: That was created. My father said that he went off to Warsaw to study. There was no status involved with it and so I created the school and remembered all the teachers who were my enemies.

RIBALOW: The relationship between Mendel and Zygmunt is an interesting one to me. They were cousins. Zygmunt worked in Uncle David's jewelry shop in London.

KOTLOWITZ: My father actually had a first cousin named Zygmunt, who lived in London and had lived there since World War I. I met him for the first time ten years ago. In fact their relationship was not that close and the relationship in the book is almost all created.

RIBALOW: Every once in a while you get, I would not say sermonic, but reflective. Sonya, Mendel's sister, talks of conversion, and you have a fine passage in which you write, "Being a Jew for her was like living at the bottom of a well, a dank, enclosed well, when an open lake, broad and constantly changing, lay nearby." Then, somewhat surprisingly, Mendel is shocked by her thinking and warns her that she will destroy herself.

KOTLOWITZ: In fact, it's my secret belief that my father actually went through that himself.

RIBALOW: Was there a sister?

KOTLOWITZ: Yes, there was a sister named Bronya and a sister named Shifra and I think the book is probably very true to them. I don't know why I say that, but I feel it.

RIBALOW: There is a lot of talk on Zionism, on Socialism, which involved many Jews in that era.

KOTLOWITZ: It was also true of that household; it was not a strange story.

RIBALOW: Back to your father for a moment. He was a member of the Jewish Legion, wasn't he? And what happened to him later must be in your second novel, as *Somewhere Else* ends when he joins the Legion.

KOTLOWITZ: No, it's not in the second book. I thought it was going to be in the second novel, which was, in fact, the first book I was going to write. The first book ends where I thought I was going to begin.

RIBALOW: You have references to Purim celebrations as key events in your novel. There are not many Jewish novelists using Jewish holidays for their material.

KOTLOWITZ: Well, after all it was a big synagogue.

RIBALOW: I know that *you* know, but I'm telling you there are many Jewish novelists who don't know. ... I was also interested in the growing relationship between Dorothy Sullivan, who worked in Uncle David's jewelry shop, and Mendel.

KOTLOWITZ: I found that I liked Dorothy Sullivan. Let me tell you a story about that. I sent the manuscript to my father after I finished the book, eager for him to read it.

RIBALOW: Is he a reader?

KOTLOWITZ: Yes, he was. He died two years ago. He was an intellectual, a reader. He was what Europeans called a member of the intelligentsia, which is not quite an intellectual—it's something else. Anyway, I called and we had a long conversation. He gave me a critique which was highly intelligent and then there was a silence. Then he said to me, "One thing I have to tell you. I never slept with a *shiksa,* especially in the woods." My God, I thought, I really touched something. Anyway, that blew up into a three-month battle with my father. He wanted me to rewrite those chapters, change the names.

RIBALOW: He probably was worried about what other people might say.

KOTLOWITZ: He was worried about that and then I thought I really had touched on something that had actually happened. Because those events were all imagined. That was the one thing he made a major issue of and we were really on bad terms. It was a real problem. Then the book was published. He saw how seriously the book was taken and that washed everything away.

RIBALOW: The business with British vaudeville—how did you get into that?

KOTLOWITZ: He was out with a Gilbert and Sullivan troupe when he first came to America. He told me that he toured with the troupe. And that is how the whole section came out. I set it in London.

RIBALOW: I'm a great lover of London and I enjoyed your setting. How did you get to know London as well as you do?

KOTLOWITZ: I also love it and I have been there many times. But I have not been to the East End, which is where the story is set.

RIBALOW: You write knowledgeably about Oxford Street, Bond Street, and other well-known areas.

KOTLOWITZ: I spent a day at the New York Public Library with a transportation map of London from 1910, because I wanted to make sure there were buses that really ran, that the subway was where it was, and that they went to the correct neighborhood and that there was a brewery there. I also got hold of a book called *The Very Best English Goods,* which is a very thick catalog. It is an anthology of all kinds of material objects available to people in 1910. I used that as a source. There are photographs in the book and I checked and studied them.

RIBALOW: I recognized how well you knew London, so then I began to wonder about Poland. I asked myself, If he knew London, does he also know Poland?

KOTLOWITZ: As I said, the East End is imagined, but the rest of London is not. Once you start writing that way imaginatively, you can't go to a place and have the reality of it intervene. I lost my desire to go to Poland after I finished the book.

RIBALOW: Were you thinking of it?

KOTLOWITZ: I wanted to go to Lomza; that I would like to do. But not the way I used to want to go.

RIBALOW: You have a quotation that puzzles me, not in what it says but in terms of the point of view the novelist is taking. You write, "There is a photograph of the family taken that year," and then you describe each of the individuals in the photograph. From what point in time is that written? I ask because every once in a while, the interior evidence of the book was clear to me the first time around that this is the first of a number of novels. Somewhere—I don't remember where—you make reference to somebody who is going to go to America and the impression is that that person did go to America. Here, looking back, there is a photograph of these people and it's as though when these books are ultimately published, one will be able to see, from the first book, that other things had occurred. Again, in the beginning, the novel starts with "I." Later, you forget that "I" and you write from the viewpoint of Mendel.

KOTLOWITZ: Yes, yes. The same happens in the second book.

RIBALOW: It is clear that *Somewhere Else* is intended as the first of a series of novels. What, then, is the status of the second volume?

KOTLOWITZ: I do have a second book I want to do about Palestine 1917–1921, I think, in which I take Mendel through the experience.

RIBALOW: Beyond *Somewhere Else,* have you completed a second manuscript?

KOTLOWITZ: Yes, but it is not related to the first novel. It's about different people entirely.

RIBALOW: Entirely?

KOTLOWITZ: Yes, but it is about Jews.

RIBALOW: So it is no sequel?

KOTLOWITZ: As I said, it's totally unrelated, although the people are actually the same, the way novelists' people are.

RIBALOW: Where is this novel set?

KOTLOWITZ: In Atlantic City the week before World War II breaks out, late August 1939. It is set in a small Atlantic City hotel. Atlantic City was a big Baltimore resort, so it includes Jews in Atlantic City and German refugees. That's what it is. It's about their lives going on in the context of the war breaking out. It is very focused in terms of timing. It covers a ten-day span and that's it.

RIBALOW: This surprises me because when I had heard you were working on a new novel, I assumed it was a continuation of *Somewhere Else.*

KOTLOWITZ: No, but I am mulling the book on Palestine from 1917–1921.

RIBALOW: Have you been to Israel?

KOTLOWITZ: Oh, yes. I was on a Masada dig. We are going back to Jerusalem and I'll see how it goes.

RIBALOW: Do you think that *Somewhere Else* is a "Jewish" novel? If so, why? —or why not?

KOTLOWITZ: My book is a Jewish novel and it was written by a writer who is a Jew and it's about Jews but it's also about gentiles. Yet, it's about Jewish matters. My very strong belief, which I think is evidenced in everything I write, is that I really believe that the more specificity you can create in a work of fiction, the more universal your work becomes. So I zero in as tightly as I can on the people as Jews, their spiritual lives, their mental growth, the objects that surround them in life. I believe that to be important—the kinds of beds they sleep in, the way they take their meals, the music they listen to. I believe that from those specific things you can create something universal. To be arrogant in the ultimate Jewish way, I believe that if you are authentically Jewish then you are truly universal.

RIBALOW: You know that in all that he wrote in his lifetime for publication, Franz Kafka never used the word "Jew." For that matter, as you probably know, Saul Bellow, in a speech delivered at Brandeis University, and Bernard Malamud, in the *Paris Review*, and Philip Roth almost all the time, reject the label of "Jewish writer."

KOTLOWITZ: The problem with being called a Jewish writer is that it is never really used in the sense that you want it to be used. It is used to delimit you rather than to give you the scope that you feel your writing has. That is really the problem with it. It's like being called a Jewish singer. You know what I mean?

RIBALOW: A Jewish singer is somewhat different from being a Jewish writer. A singer is not using Jewish materials.

KOTLOWITZ: I think that in the public sensibility to be called a Jewish writer is to delimit the writer. Jewish artists paint pictures with specifically Jewish themes. I am writing about the twentieth century, really, that is as authentic as any other aspect.

RIBALOW: Do you read Jewish fiction? Singer? Potok?

KOTLOWITZ: Singer, yes. I read Bellow; I've not read Potok. I read Mailer, Updike, Nabokov. In fact, I only read novelists whom I think are better than I am. But I never read novels when I am working on my own. I will occasionally read nineteenth century fiction because I'm very impressionable and I can't control what I pick up. While writing, I only read nonfiction. But when I finish a book, I read everything I can.

RIBALOW: I'll ask you a question I have been raising with other writers. Cynthia Ozick, in her introduction to her latest book, *Bloodshed*, says that the only reason she has written the introduction is to answer one particular critic who didn't understand one of her stories and she argues with him. She has this observation, "English is a Christian language. When I write English, I live in Christendom."

KOTLOWITZ: It's true. She would love to see Yiddish revived. I have a passage in "Baltimore Boy," in which I talk about how the concept of Jehovah was changed in the Baltimore temples and synagogues as the Hebrew began to disappear from the service and was replaced by English and how Jehovah becomes WASP-like by the mere use of the language. But it's like that. She is right.

RIBALOW: She makes the point also that had her story appeared in Yiddish or in Hebrew nobody could have questioned its meaning.

KOTLOWITZ: I think she is really a great writer.

RIBALOW: Do you write short stories, too?

KOTLOWITZ: No, all I want to do is write books.

RIBALOW: Do you find you can write while holding down this administrative job running programming at a television station?

KOTLOWITZ: It's very hard. I make light of it, but when you go on that three-year routine, and you take all your vacation time and all your weekends, there is a price for the family to pay, although during the writing of these books my wife was getting her Master's degree. But my kids were getting to the tenth grade and eleventh grade and didn't need me all the time. That is when I started to write books. That's all I really want to do now. I believe in the novel as a form and I love the nineteenth century novel very much and also much of twentieth century fiction, but I am an old-fashioned writer in the real sense.

A Conversation with

Chaim Potok

Chaim Potok's novels are concerned with Hasidic Jews steeped in their pious traditions, with yeshiva students mulling the complicated passages of the Talmud, with young Jews distressed and unbalanced by overt anti-Semitism. These books have won for Potok an enormous and faithful following in the United States and foreign lands. It is surprising and unexpected.

No one is more surprised than Potok himself. A chunky, bearded man of fifty, Potok is a yeshiva product with rabbinical ordination from the Jewish Theological Seminary of America, a Conservative Jewish institution. Potok also has earned a Ph.D. in philosophy from the University of Pennsylvania.

He has taught Hebrew school, has been editor of the Jewish Publication Society of America and is mainly a novelist. After a run of successful works of fiction, he published *Wanderings* (1979), a popular Jewish history, profusely illustrated, a narrative written with many personal asides. It, too, was a best seller.

When his first novel, *The Chosen*, was published in 1967, it received the Edward Lewis Wallant Book Award (other winners include Hugh Nissenson, Susan Fromberg Schaeffer, and Robert Kotlowitz). More significantly, it became a national best-seller and Potok soon developed into a highly popular novelist. Each of his novels that followed, *The Promise, My Name is Asher Lev,* and *In the Beginning,* adhered to the same pattern: wide acceptance, paperback reprints, and international acclaim.

We had met socially and casually in Jerusalem some years before we talked about his work and career in New York City on April 8, 1976. Potok has a home in Jerusalem and another in Philadelphia. When he came to the United States on a brief lecture tour, we met at a business office. He had to fit in our conversation between a number of other commitments. Nevertheless, he spoke unhurriedly, in the measured cadence of a man accustomed to lecturing. He is familiar with the professional language of psychoanalysis (as his novels and his personal conversation attest), and, of course, is extremely well versed in Jewish religious, cultural, and social issues.

Potok has a cohesive view of himself as a Jew and he seems completely aware of what he is trying to achieve in the writing of fiction. In the course of our talk, he said—more than once—that he felt himself to be a "freak" in that Orthodox Jews generally do not write fiction or deal with serious Jewish issues through imaginative works. He is, however, quite prepared to continue writing novels and, reflecting on his success and vast readership, it is no wonder.

RIBALOW: Are you surprised that your books have become best sellers?

POTOK: Amazed. I really thought I was writing about a tight little world. I wondered how many Jews would be interested in that tight little world, let alone those who are not Jews, people who haven't the remotest notion of what that world is all about. It's been as much a mystery to me as it has been to a lot of people. In some circles it has been rather an embarrassment, particularly in some intellectual circles, that is to say, the popularity of these books. I'm not altogether certain I understand *why* they are popular. The fact that they are popular is a never-ending source of surprise to me.

RIBALOW: You once publicly observed that you questioned the importance of imaginative writing in the Jewish tradition. What do you think now?

POTOK: Well, I think the imagination as such, the faculty of the imagination and its lonely outpourings, have always been suspect to the intellectual. Maimonides, for example, wrote with great suspicion about the workings of the imagination. One of the reasons for this is that the intellect has boundaries and functions in disciplined form. Without discipline, and without boundaries, the intellect cannot maneuver. Even when it maneuvers right up against its boundaries, and makes attempts to push the boundaries away, there is always a sense of set configuration, established norms, insofar as intellectual maneuvering is concerned. One works with ideas that have form. The imagination takes inordinate leaps. One of the characteristics of the imagination is precisely the fact that it will fight boundaries; it will jump beyond boundaries. Also, it nourishes from an element of the human being which those who are very much taken with matters intellectual are very often frightened of. And that is: the imagination nourishes from the more volcanic aspects of man; that is to say, his unconscious or his subconscious. That gives rise to very mercurial material and the intellect is almost by very definition very leery of that kind of jumping. As a matter of fact, one of the basic problems in modern philosophy, the one posed by Hume, and possibly by some preceding Hume, has to do with one element of the imagination that must be utilized if science is to make any progress. And that is the jump that is made in the process called induction. It is a jump or a leap of the imagination and a scientific mind does not quite know how to cope with that inductive leap. It has remained to this day one of the basic problems in epistomology. Now, if that key element of scientific model-making is a puzzle to the intellectual mind, the whole faculty of the imagination is clearly going to be bewildered to the intellectual mind. Since the Jewish tradition very strongly emphasizes the workings of the intellect, the mind, particularly scholarship, more specifically scholarship in Jewish sources, in the Talmud, the workings of the imagination on that produce creativity bounded by aesthetic norms—that kind of working has always been suspect in traditional Jewish sources. It remains so to this day.

RIBALOW: In line with this, I was reading the English novelist Alan Sillitoe, who wrote *The Loneliness of the Long Distance Runner* and *Saturday Night and Sunday Morning*. He is, by the way, deeply involved in Jewish subjects and is a supporter of Israel. I was reading in an autobiographical work called *Raw Material,* and I came across a line I thought I would ask you about, "Everything written is fiction, even nonfiction." Then he adds, "Anything which is not scientific or mathematical fact is colored by the human imagination and feeble opinion."

POTOK: The fact of the matter is that even hard scientific data and "mathematical fact" are colored. But the point that he is making is a very important one and that is that we are essentially model-making beings. We don't know what reality is. We take the raw data that impinge upon our consciousness, our perceptions, and when we think that data, we are already giving it structure and configuration. So that even when a mathematician thinks a model, that thinking is a construct. I used to think, when I was doing my doctorate at the University of Pennsylvania, in secular philosophy, that at least logic was the bedrock of human thought. Until I read Quine's *Mathematical Logic.* He makes the point very clearly that it is even possible for models of logic ultimately to be impinged upon to such a degree where we will have to alter even that bedrock itself. There really is nothing that is fixed and permanent in principle insofar as human thought is concerned. By the way, Edward Albee made an interesting remark some years ago when someone asked him what fiction was. He said, fiction is fact distorted into truth.

RIBALOW: In how many languages do your novels appear?

POTOK: In French, German, Hebrew, Japanese, Portuguese, Danish, Dutch, Swedish. . . . I must have left a few out.

RIBALOW: Many in paperbacks, I'm sure.

POTOK: As a matter of fact, they are in hardback in virtually all the editions. There is one country that publishes initially in paperback—France—but, if I remember correctly, *Asher Lev* appeared there in hardback. The first two appeared simply in soft covers.

RIBALOW: Is anything of yours being filmed or staged?

POTOK: Nothing staged, but there is a production company that has been formed to do *The Chosen* as a movie, and there is an option on *Asher Lev.* [In 1980, *The Chosen* was filmed.]

RIBALOW: What kind of mail do you get?

POTOK: I get a lot of mail from the hardback readers, and a lot of it runs now all the way back to *The Chosen,* where people pick up the book for the first time. I would say it is easily fifty to sixty percent non-Jewish. Usually, people tell me how warmly they reacted to the book. I suspect that the people who don't like the book don't write.

RIBALOW: Why do you think non-Jews read your books?

POTOK: I think I have inadvertently stumbled across a cultural dynamic that I didn't quite see clearly myself until sometime toward the end of the writing of *The Chosen.* I think what I am really writing about is culture war. The over-arching culture in which we all live is the culture we call Western secular humanism, the culture that Peter Gay of Columbia University calls modern paganism. Within this culture there is a whole spectrum of subcultures. The basic characteristic of the over-arching culture is what I call the open-ended hypothesis; that is to say, nothing is absolute in any kind of permanent way. A model is a shifting or temporary absolute on the assumption that additional data will be discovered that will impinge upon a given model. That model must be altered. So there is a constant search for new knowledge that is built into the civilization that we live in, this over-arching civilization. But imbedded inside this civilization we have a whole series of cultures which come into this world with *givens,* with models that are fixed absolutes. If they are alterable, they are alterable only under inordinate pressure. What happens is that these subcultures clash in a variety of ways with the over-arching culture, as somebody from this subculture grows up and encounters elements from the outside model.

RIBALOW: How does your work fit into this?

POTOK: Now, *The Chosen* was about someone from the center of the Jewish tradition clashing with one element from the model of Western secular humanism; that is Freudian psychoanalytic theory. *The Promise* is about a boy from the center of the Jewish tradition clashing with one element from the center of Western secular humanism; and that is text criticism. *Asher Lev* is about a boy from the center of the Jewish tradition clashing with one of the fundamental elements of Western secular civilization; and that is its *art*. And the last book is about a family clashing with the underbelly of Western civilization; that is its anti-Semitism. So what I am trying to present here is a clash of cores of culture, centers of culture. Bellow has his Jews along the periphery of the Jewish tradition, connected emotively to their pasts, but they are in the center of Western secular humanism. Now Western secular humanism has many problems of its own: alienation, dread, the fragmentation of the human being, a hunger for a scaffolding for a particular life. When a person in the center of Western secular humanism encounters the problems of Western secular humanism or modern paganism—if he is still connected emotively to his past—he will see those pagan or secular problems through the tonalities of his particular past. So the Bellow heroes are Western secular humanists but they see the problems of that humanist through Jewish eyes. The Updike people are Protestants so they see the problems of Western secular humanism through Protestant eyes. That is another kind of culture clash. You get the culture clash where people are along the periphery of two cultures. Philip Roth's people are all the periphery of things Jewish. They think Judaism means *kneidlach* and gefilte fish.

RIBALOW: *Bauch Judentum.*

POTOK: That's right. At the same time, they really don't know the essential nature of the richness and wealth that is at the heart of modern paganism.

RIBALOW: Modern paganism?

POTOK: Western secular humanism. I use the terms interchangeably. I don't use them in a pejorative sense at all. I'm simply using the term that Peter Gay is using. I think he is using it correctly. He thinks that Western secular humanism is Venetian blinds, wall-to-wall carpeting. When you get a rub up of periphery of cultures, you get cultural monstrocities that are created. That's the world that Roth explored in his Jewish books, *Goodbye, Columbus* and so on. So you get various models, you see, of cultural conflict. *The Portrait of the Artist As a Young Man* by James Joyce was another such model. What I seem to have stumbled across is a kind of core-to-core cultural confrontation. What non-Jews are doing—if I can get it from the letters they are sending me—is that they are simply translating themselves into the particular context of the boys and the fathers and the mothers and the situation that I'm writing about. So instead of being a Jew, you are a Baptist; instead of being an Orthodox Jew, you are a Catholic; and the dynamic is the *same*. The culture war is the *same*. The particular words or expressions that might be used might be Jewish or what have you, but they are simply putting themselves into the place of the subculture which is clashing core-to-core with the umbrella culture in which we all live.

RIBALOW: You were a teacher and a rabbi. How did you happen to turn to the writing of fiction.

POTOK: No, I started to write when I was fourteen years old. I've been writing since I really was a kid. I wanted to write the day I finished reading a novel that really changed my life. It was a novel about upper-class British Catholics.

RIBALOW: Really?

POTOK: You won't believe this story. Evelyn Waugh's *Brideshead Revisited*. It absolutely changed my life. It was an extraordinary encounter with that novel. It was the first serious adult fiction I had ever read. I lived inside that book with more intensity than I lived inside my own world. It was the exact reverse of anything you would think would affect a nice Jewish boy in New York going to a Jewish parochial school. When I closed the book, I was *overwhelmed* by my relationship to that book. I remember asking myself, "What did he do to me? How do you do this kind of thing with words?" That's where my commitment to write began. It was really born —very concretely—out of that encounter, with that *one* book. And it lasted.

RIBALOW: Have you read his other work and did any of it have the same effect on you?

POTOK: Yes, I've read others, but no, it was that *one* book. It may have been because it was a religious book that it had this effect on me.

RIBALOW: I have been working on a literary study of American Jewish writers and I thought I would begin with a definition of a "Jewish" writer. I have read what writers consider a Jewish writer; I have read through symposia on the subject and it really became terribly confusing. The truth is, after you get through reading forty people, all of whom have thought about it, there is no definition. I'll ask you, then, have you a definition of a "Jewish" writer?

POTOK: No, but I'll say this. I'm an American Jewish writer, and I'll accept that definition if you say to me that Updike is an American Protestant writer and O'Conner was an American Catholic writer and Hemingway was an American Midwestern writer. It's much better, I think, just to say whether you are a good writer or a bad writer and leave it at that. The most banal kind of definition would be, "An American Jewish writer is an American Jew who writes about Jewish subjects." You know, that solves all your problems right away. Therefore, John Hersey, who wrote *The Wall,* cannot be an American Jewish writer. Norman Mailer, who is Jewish, isn't an American Jewish writer because he writes nothing Jewish. But then you have a double problem when you have an American Jewish writer who sometimes writes about Jewish subjects and sometimes doesn't, or when you have a situation like an American Orthodox Jew who doesn't write about Jewish subjects at all, like Herman Wouk. I think that the struggle for the definition is not a profitable one. No matter what definition it yields, it doesn't really clear up anything. I suspect that we are much better off if we just move away from that kind of category.

RIBALOW: Graham Greene wrote two kinds of books, one of which he called "entertainments" and the others were, obviously to him, "serious" novels. Are you writing "entertainments" or are you trying to be educational, or are you "giving a message"?

POTOK: If you want to give a message, you better write public relations. I'm really trying to track this core-to-core cultural confrontation in as honest a way as I can. I'm not interested in writing public relations nor am I particularly interested in writing "entertainments," nor do I regard these novels as entertainments, to tell you the honest truth. I can't imagine how anyone could regard them as entertainments.

RIBALOW: I read your novels in a special way. I got through reading *In the Beginning* not long ago, and I see that you and I attended the same yeshiva. Our backgrounds are somewhat similar. So as I read the novel, I find it a remarkable achievement that you make dramatic things that one imagines cannot be made dramatic. A *shiyur,* an intellectual argument between a rebbe and his student. Theoretically, anything can be made dramatic, but I sometimes think I'm especially intrigued because I've experienced some of it. But most readers haven't.

POTOK: Non-Jews seem to be interested in that, too. I think that is one of the essential tasks of a novelist, and that is what Henry James and others used to say, "Dramatize! Dramatize! Dramatize!" Tell the story in a way that dramatizes what it is you have to say.

RIBALOW: Will you write fiction about non-Jews, too?

POTOK: The first novel that I wrote, which was almost published and which turned out to be the source for a fight inside a publishing house, had no Jews in it at all. It was all about Americans and Koreans. That novel was ultimately not published. The editor-in-chief of the house accepted it. The publisher did not want it. He didn't feel that it was going to sell. I withdrew it and the editor-in-chief resigned subsequently. I'm glad, in retrospect, that I withdrew it because I know now how to handle the material. I wasn't quite sure how to handle it then.

RIBALOW: To jump to another subject. May I ask why you have elected to live in Israel?

POTOK: We don't live in Israel, we sort of reside there for part of the year and then come back here. We used to be in the States ten months and in Israel for two months.

RIBALOW: Jerusalem.

POTOK: Yes, Jerusalem. Then we decided, in '73, to take a crack at Israel for a year. Then the war broke out so we decided maybe we'd better extend it another year so that the children don't get a feeling that Israel is such a depressing place in which to live. We'll probably be back here in a year or so.

RIBALOW: Do you plan to write about Israel?

POTOK: I think not so much about Israel but about Jerusalem. I want to explain the dimensions of that city in fiction.

RIBALOW: Are there any of the modern Hebrew writers who impress you?

POTOK: Yes, I'm particularly impressed by two or three. Amos Oz, Aleph Bet Yehoshua, and by Aharon Megged.

RIBALOW: Do Israelis know American Jewish novels, stories, writers? I hear complaints by many American Jewish writers who visit Israel that Israelis seem to be oblivious to American Jewish writing.

POTOK: That's a fair generalization. They do not particularly care about it; they think it is another world.

RIBALOW: What you are writing about, then, is a world twice removed.

POTOK: Well, no. As a matter of fact, it's interesting that it is otherwise. A Yemenite came over to me once and said he felt the same experience in terms of culture clash in Israel as one of the characters in the book. This was after I gave a talk about the novels at the University of the Negev in Beersheba. The dynamic is identical. It's going on in Israel just as well as it's going on here, in the same way. You have subcultures inside the over-arching culture. Israel is essentially a secular culture. The culture war goes on. The problem in Israel is that it is all subdued beneath the over-whelming effort of the country to stay alive and secure inside that on-going battle, the war it is having with the Arab nations. But this cultural tension continues.

RIBALOW: Do you read contemporary Jewish fiction?

POTOK: Yes, I try to keep up. I feel myself very much a part of the stream of novel writing and I try to keep up with it as best I can.

RIBALOW: As a Jewish editor—which you have been—what do you think of modern Jewish fiction?

POTOK: I think it is one of the most exciting things that has happened in Jewish history in a very long time. We are a people with a long history of culture warfare . . . four thousand years of culture wars. The first was with the culture of the river civilizations in the Near East, particularly its Caanan-ite expression. Out of that culture war came a literature called the Bible. We were then involved in a culture war with Greek and Roman paganism. Out of that culture war came a literature called the Talmud, Midrashic works that were not accepted by the Jewish tradition, and so on. We were then involved with a culture war with Christianity and, for a period of time, with Islam. Out of that came another literature, some of it polemical in nature. The war with Islam was a core-to-core confrontation in Spain and produced an *exquisite* literature. We call that "The Golden Age of Spain." We are now involved in a fourth culture war and that is with secular humanism. I don't know what kind of literature is going to be produced by that culture war. But one aspect of that literature is already becoming discernible, and that is the novel. Some Jewish novelists are tracking aspects of this culture war, whether they know it or not. Bellow is doing the periphery confrontation. I'm trying to track the core-to-core confrontation as best I know how. Others are doing other variations of it. Some may end up doing secular core to secular religion confrontation because the battle goes both ways. It isn't unusual for me to go to a campus today and find a Lubavitcher Hasid who was once brought up in an absolutely secular home but somehow the Hasidim got to him and all of a sudden he's a *baal t'shuvenik*; he's being transformed. So the dynamic functions in many models and in all directions. I think that what is exciting about this American literature is that it is tracking, whether it is aware of it or not, various kinds of cultural confrontation. I have no way of knowing now, no way of guessing, what kind of final shape this literature will take. It's *very* exciting.

RIBALOW: As I listen to you, a question comes to mind. You have been editor of the Jewish Publication Society of America, so I would like to address this question to you. Why has the JPS always been backward in publishing creative writing?

POTOK: Precisely because the Jewish Publication Society represented a bastion of the Jewish intellectual, the scholarly intellectual. It's exactly in line with what I said before: the novel is a flippancy, a frivolity, and how could you conceivably offer a novel to a serious scholarly audience? If it is good, it is dangerous. If it is poor, it is banal. So why bother with it? That's been changed since I came to the Society. The whole configuration of the Society is quite different today from what it was when I inherited it. It was a publishing house whose basic intent it was to produce scholarly works. The emphasis was, just as it always has been in the Jewish tradition since the close of the Biblical period, on matters of the intellect. So since Sol Grayzel—God bless him, he has just turned eighty—was interested in history, there was a heavy emphasis on historical works. Had a Talmudist been the editor, there probably would have been an emphasis on that aspect. I came in; I was interested in belles lettres and, very slowly, the balance shifted.
[Dr. Grayzel died in 1980.]

RIBALOW: On Hasidim . . . does your knowledge come from your personal background or from your research?

POTOK: It comes from two aspects. First of all, it comes from personal knowledge.

RIBALOW: It's in all the novels.

POTOK: Except the last one. It's not there because the Hasidim don't teach the Bible. It was impossible to set the last novel in any kind of Hasidic framework. It had to be set in a Galician-Lithuanian framework, as it were.

RIBALOW: But your people are still religiously observant.

POTOK: Very observant, because I'm talking about the core of a culture in confrontation.

RIBALOW: At the very end of *In the Beginning,* the father is just as upset with the son's going into Wellhausen Biblical criticism.

POTOK: The novels were arranged, when I planned them. . . .

RIBALOW: You planned them?

POTOK: Yes.

RIBALOW: When you began with *The Chosen,* had you planned the others?

POTOK: No, no. But toward the end of *The Chosen,* it became very apparent to me that the novel I was writing was running away with itself.

RIBALOW: Was *The Chosen,* when it was published, the complete book? I had heard that you had written a book and that it was submitted, that it was edited and that *half* of the novel was published.

POTOK: What happened was . . . this is what I'm trying to say to you . . . toward the end of *The Chosen,* it became apparent to me that it would be impossible for me to include within the boundaries of that one book all the problems I wanted to handle. The novel was suffering from a surfeit of plenitude. It was just an impossible aesthetic situation. Bob Gottlieb, who read it, sensed that also. I took it home and cut it. I threw out the whole section I couldn't use anyway. It involved hundreds of pages. What was left of it involved some rewriting. *That* was the novel ultimately published as *The Chosen.* Already in the writing of the last part of *The Chosen,* it became apparent to me that I could not handle it. Problems that I wanted to handle began to divide themselves into four basic elements. I set them up in a sort of nebulous way at first. Then it began to take clearer and clearer shape in a hierarchy, a kind of rising crescendo of core-to-core cultural confrontations. Danny Saunders in *The Chosen* is able to make some kind of accommodation between his Orthodoxy and Freudian psychoanalytic theory. Reuven Malter in *The Promise* is able to make some kind of accommodation between his Orthodoxy and text criticism on the Talmud. Asher Lev sometimes can make an accommodation between his Orthodoxy and Western art and sometimes cannot. The point to Asher Lev, of course, is that since the Jew has not contributed any aesthetic vessels, as it were, to Western art, his range and maneuverability in the area of aesthetics is very limited. If ever there is an experience that will require him to utilize a certain motif that is a horror aesthetically to the Jew, he will utilize it as an artist because an artist chooses for his art. Now *Asher Lev* is written purely in the realm of aesthetics. It is not an halachic problem. Halachically, you can paint all the crucifixions you want.

RIBALOW: Really?

POTOK: Yes, you are not violating Jewish law so long as you don't paint them for purposes of worship. It is *not* an halachic problem that Asher Lev violates.

RIBALOW: What is it, then?

POTOK: It is an aesthetic line that he crosses. In the eyes of the Jew, the Orthodox Jew, the Crucifixion immediately triggers images of rivers of Jewish blood, because of the deicide charge. For Asher Lev it was a mold. Into that mold he pours Asher Lev just as Picasso also drew a Crucifixion at a critical moment in his life; Chagall puts Russian Jews on crosses and paints Crucifixions. This is, basically, the way the novels were arranged. I began to see that I had a set, as it were, of problems. The final one absolutely cannot be handled within the boundaries of Orthodoxy and that is the problem of text criticism applied to the Bible. And that is bound up with anti-Semitism, certainly in the last century. The last problem is the whole spectrum of traditional Jewish responses to one core element of Western secular humanism—its anti-Semitism.

RIBALOW: You mentioned this earlier.

POTOK: It is important. Bound up with that anti-Semitism is the way so-called objective scholars handled the Hebrew Bible in the last century. The problem with that is if you just push the anti-Semitism aside and if you come from the core of the Jewish tradition, you discover that despite the anti-Semitism, there are truths to the problems that they posit. You then have to ask yourself, "Do I run away from those truths? Am I in a kind of Jewish tradition that says to me I can't look at the truth? That I can't confront the truth in the marketplace of ideas?" The dilemma here is that it is precisely your love of the Bible that brings you to this kind of scholarship. If you are an honest enough individual, and really hunger for the truth, you are going to have to contend with this scholarship. The irony is that you cannot contend with it within the framework of Jewish Orthodoxy. You've got to leave that boundary.

RIBALOW: Your *rebbes* always seem to understand this.

POTOK: I am convinced that within Orthodoxy there are minds who fully understand the dilemma of the extraordinary student.

RIBALOW: You make that clear.

POTOK: They are there. They are willing to take the risks or have their best students take the risks rather than have them stagnate or rather than have them break entirely with Judaism.

RIBALOW: You have touched on some of the incidents and themes I have been wanting to ask you about. Nonetheless, let me formulate a few of the ideas that struck me in reading *The Chosen*. Your major young men are Danny Saunders and Reuven Malter. The first is the son of a Hebrew teacher and Reuven is a member of a distinguished Hasidic rabbinical family. Yet Reuven moves from his rabbinical background to clinic psychology and Danny moves to the rabbinate. Isn't that paradoxical?

POTOK: There is an underlying symbolic structure to *The Chosen*, which somebody discerned in a piece that he wrote on the novel in a scholarly journal. He sensed it and explored it. I'm talking about the core of the Jewish tradition. I'm talking about it all the time. I decided right off the bat when I was writing *The Chosen* that I had better define what I meant by the core of the Jewish tradition. And that's the reason for the baseball game in the opening scene. In that baseball game you have two aspects of Jewish Orthodoxy in contention. You have the Eastern European aspect, which prefers to turn inward and not confront the outside world. You have the Western European more objective scientific aspect within the core, within Orthodoxy, that is not afraid to look at the outside world that produces scientists. These are in interaction with one another inside the core. That's the baseball game. The way the kids play ball, their styles, the way they think of one another. Then the way David Malter teaches his son Hasidism is an example. I didn't just stick that in there just so that people should learn about Hasidism! There's a point to that! The point was to show you how a Western-oriented, more scientific Orthodox Jew handles historical data. He's very sedate; he's very calm; he'll question this or that aspect of the life of the Baal Shem Tov; he'll talk about the development of Hasidism; he'll talk about the various Hasidic sects. This is his style of teaching as over against the synagogue exhortations of Reb Saunders, which is a more traditional way of teaching, the Eastern European way of teaching. Those two speeches, those set pieces, were my way of defining for myself, and for the reader, what I meant by the *core* of the Jewish tradition. Then, once I had that definition, I take it and confront it with one of the elements from a core of Western secular humanism, that is to say, Freudian psychoanalytic theory, and the book goes on from there.

RIBALOW: I've made this point before. In *The Chosen* and, of course, *The Promise,* you use the Talmud as dramatic material. It works very well. How did you conceive using the Talmud this way? When I first read *The Chosen,* I was excited by the very concept of the center of the drama being an intellectual debate on the road to earning a *smicha.*

POTOK: First of all, it *is* exciting. If you have experienced it, it really is exciting. My problem was how to make it exciting inside the pages of a book.

RIBALOW: I think you succeeded even more with your Reb Kalman.

POTOK: Yes, yes.

RIBALOW: Because the reader starts to hate him, changes, feels sorry for him. . . .

POTOK: Doesn't know how to react to him and finally is ambivalent.

RIBALOW: He is sort of. . . .

POTOK: Sympathetic, yes.

RIBALOW: He ends up a real, living person.

POTOK: Yes, I felt that way myself about him as I wrote him.

RIBALOW: You did have many problems in writing these novels, didn't you?

POTOK: I was confronted with an aesthetic problem that I had to solve in dealing with the Talmudic passages. If I were to do the content of a Talmudic dispute, the whole thing would get bogged down. So I did away with the content and I abstracted the form. So what you are really reading is the interpersonal dynamics of Talmudic disputation—*contentless.* You will note that I almost never insert an actual piece of content inside one of these dramatic Talmudic confrontations. I tried to do that with the last book, *In the Beginning,* with the Bible, but it was impossible. There I had to give very concrete examples of what it was that I meant.

RIBALOW: In *The Promise* you have this fourteen-year-old boy, Michael, with his breakdown, and a clinical psychologist trying to bring him out of a catatonic situation. Then you have Reb Kalman, who is rigidly Orthodox, threatened by modern scholarship. He is somehow uncertain about his own situation, not unlike Michael. With Kalman, is this part due to his experiences in the concentration camp?

POTOK: Yes, that uncertainty comes from the suffering that he has experienced and leads, in turn, to his certainty. He says to himself, I cannot have gone through what I went through and have lost what I lost if it's all meaningless. Therefore, the very experience serves to reinforce his commitment to the past. The alternative is to say that Hitler succeeded, that everybody really died for nothing. That reinforces his certainty. At the same time, he has lost his whole world. He is in a strange, bewildering world here. He is listening to the music of that past world. And somehow he manages to find it in the way Reuven Malter studies Talmud. Yet Reuven studies Talmud in a way that is threatening—to Talmud, and threatening to the way that his world studied Talmud, because Reuven Malter takes a Talmudic text and makes it something fluid. That is terrifying to any fundamentalist mind, because the very basic notion of a fundamentalist mind is that the text is a given, it is fixed and our task is to understand it. To reconstruct the text first! That's a terrifying notion to any fundamentalist mind. So here is Reb Kalman in his incredible dilemma finding a boy who has the same love passion for the Talmud and studies it with the same music that Reb Kalman heard his best student studying it back in Europe, but at the same time this boy poses the biggest threat to his, Reb Kalman's, love for the Talmud. That is another piece of the underlying structure of the novel.

RIBALOW: What makes it so original is that who else is writing about such things in America today? I don't know if you can undertake to write on such a subject unless you have the discipline and the training for it.

POTOK: The experience. . . . Do you know what the ultimate irony in all this is? I heard Maurice Samuel once complain about what it was people like Philip Roth and others were doing with Jewish tradition. And I said to him, "How do you know about the Jewish tradition? The only place you can ever really learn it is if you go to a yeshiva and study it from the inside, from the core." The irony is the longer you go to a yeshiva, the less regard you have for the whole enterprise of writing novels. They look upon it as an utter waste of time, as *bitt'l Torah*. Why are we surprised that yeshivas don't produce novelists? They don't want to produce novelists!

RIBALOW: Who is surprised?

POTOK: He was. I said, You're not going to get people who understand the core from the core because the core doesn't write about itself because the core denigrates writing. It is only concerned with Talmudic scholarship. I'm a freak! I really am a freak! I had to fight my way up through the yeshiva all the years that I spent there after the time I made my commitment to writing.

RIBALOW: It seems clear this is so from the way you create your people. Obviously it is personal. Your Mr. Malter and Mr. Gordon are based on actual people.

POTOK: Yes, yes. Michael Gordon's dilemma. . . .

RIBALOW: The love-hate conflict.

POTOK: Yes, the love-hate is one of the prices you have to pay for a core-to-core cultural confrontation. I don't mean at all to make it sound Pollyanish. There's a terrible price that is paid sometimes for this kind of situation where it can't be handled and the result is a complete paralysis of creativity. You love and hate the same person at the same time—you are absolutely paralyzed. I might add that the isolation experiment that is run in *The Promise* was actually run by a clinical psychologist six or seven times. In two of those instances, the child became catatonic and the therapy was stopped. The catatonic state terminated. The therapy was resumed and in all the instances, the children became amenable to normal therapy and ultimately were returned to normal life.

RIBALOW: That's what happens in your novel.

POTOK: Yes. That's based on clinical data.

RIBALOW: Some critics have complained that you don't deal with love, romance, sex. What do you say to them?

POTOK: It all depends on how you deal with it and what you mean by "dealing." If I had to deal with romance in my novels as part of the aesthetics of the novel, that is, if it were really necessary, I would deal with it. If I had to deal with sex—with the sex act—as part of the need, the structural need, for a novel, I would deal with it. I'm not averse to dealing with that kind of material. But I'll be damned if I'm going to put that stuff in just to spice up a book.

RIBALOW: In rereading *The Promise,* I found exciting material. The *smicha* exam, for rabbinical ordination, with the questions on the emendations of the texts and the different and varying editions of the Talmud. Is that fiction or reality? The Napoli edition, the Yerushalmi. . . .

POTOK: Reality. That all exists. There are editions like that. You can check them.

RIBALOW: Are you saying, then, that many of the yeshiva rabbis and scholars are ignorant of them?

POTOK: Yes, oh, sure. They may not be ignorant of them but they certainly don't deal with them in the sense of parallel texts the way somebody, let's say in the Jewish Theological Seminary, would deal with them. As far as they are concerned, the text that they have, the Shulsinger Talmud, is *the* text.

RIBALOW: Which yeshiva did you attend?

POTOK: Yeshiva University, Rabbi Yitzhak Elchanan. And Salanter, the Talmudical Academy, which is the high school of Yitzhak Elchanan.

RIBALOW: I also attended the Talmudical Academy, but then I also was a student at the Beth Medrash Lamorim, the nonrabbinical school.

POTOK: I went to the yeshiva, not the Beth Medrash Lamorim.

RIBALOW: I recognize, of course, the difference. . . . My first question on *My Name Is Asher Lev* is different from what I thought it would be. As I read it, it hit me that you are the only American novelist who has written about Russian Jewry. That is, aside from Arthur Cohen in *A Hero of His Time,* which came out somewhat later. In *Asher Lev,* as well as *In the Beginning,* you do this well: you depict and describe what is happening in the "outside" world as it impinges on your people. In *In the Beginning,* you take the time to deal with Father Coughlan and the emergence of Hitler. Where Asher's father is a *shaliach* of a sort, you introduce the subject of the Russian Jews. No one writes about this in fiction. To a degree, I wonder why. Do you ever reflect on this?

POTOK: They don't know that world. A novelist writes about the world that he knows best.

RIBALOW: Malamud, in "Man in the Drawer," wrote a short story about a Russian Jew and, of course, there is Cohen's novel. Have you read it?

POTOK: No, I haven't seen it yet, but, yes, I know of it. It's about the Russian poet who comes to the United States, yes.

RIBALOW: There's very little being done on the subject. Let me get on with Asher Lev. He is from the Crown Heights section of Brooklyn and I assume you are, too.

POTOK: My wife is from Crown Heights.

RIBALOW: And the Ladover yeshiva in your fiction I assume is the Salanter yeshiva.

POTOK: No, the Ladover yeshiva is a Lubavitcher yeshiva.

RIBALOW: I see. In line with something I said earlier, the passage of the holidays, the way in which you see everything through Jewish eyes—a woman wears a dress and you call it a *shabbos* dress—these observations, I would think, come instinctively. And, of course, it all gives richness to your stories.

POTOK: Right.

RIBALOW: You also have the father speak of illegal yeshivas in Russia and throughout Europe and as Asher Lev travels about. . . .

POTOK: He sees them. As I said before, the novel is on the level of aesthetics, entirely. The father also has his aesthetic world. The father's aesthetics is *Tsimmes* on *Shabbos*. The father's aesthetic material consists of the Jewish people, which he is trying to remold and rebuild and save. The father's aesthetic world consists of the yeshivas that he is creating; that's also a kind of creativity. Asher Lev is engaged in one sort of artistic creativity. One might say of the Jewish tradition that its real artists were the rabbis, that the raw material of the rabbis were the people and that the goal of creativity was the sanctification of the total people in all its areas of life. That's the last thing in the world you would say about a Western artist. The Western artist's material is his paint, his canvas, his colors, his hues—right? And his goal is to express his own particular vision of the world.

RIBALOW: Yes, you make this point throughout the novel.

POTOK: There's a whole library of aesthetics in the Western world; there's no library of aesthetics in Jewish writing.

RIBALOW: How did you think of writing of a painter?

POTOK: I have painted before I was writing.

RIBALOW: Have you ever sailed, as one of your heroes does?

POTOK: Oh, yes. I love that.

RIBALOW: I ask because these are seeming contradictions. I was just wondering whether you simply chose those subjects from out of the blue or drew from your own experiences.

POTOK: No, I took them from myself. Also to show that in certain areas one can be inside the secular world or "the world" without necessarily having to be any sort of threat whatsoever to the core of the Jewish religion.

RIBALOW: What of the gambling scene in *The Promise*?

POTOK: That's something else. You see, the point I'm trying to make is that you can be inside the core of Judaism and at the same time enjoy the world. But, at certain points, particularly the ideational elements of the world, you are going to come into serious conflict. But sailing, playing ball—you can enjoy that. Gambling in *The Promise* is fundamental to the whole structure of the novel. I have in my house in Philadelphia 1,100 pages of typescript that I threw out, that ended up being the first fifty-eight pages of *The Promise*.

RIBALOW: You have just answered one of my questions. I was curious to know if you do much rewriting.

POTOK: Uh. Over again and over again, to get that very simple style that so many people go crazy about and can't stand. I will strip something down to its barest bones. First of all, I have this feeling that florid prose often covers up obtuseness of ideas. Secondly, I was very much taken, when I was young, with the sonnets of Milton. I remember studying them. My major in college was English Lit. I was tremendously influenced by one particular teacher at Yeshiva University.

RIBALOW: What was his name?

POTOK: David Fleischer. I'll never forget studying the sonnets of Milton and being awed by the utter simplicity of the language of those sonnets. The language is *so* simple and yet he takes those simple words and he puts them together and makes out of them configurations of exquisite beauty. I never forgot that. I was writing prose at the same time. From that point on, I felt myself beginning to cut down and pare away the prose that I was writing. My notion is that a sentence has to be transparent. You've got to be able to look right through it. If it's somehow thick and unwieldy, it's bad writing and you're hiding something. There's something somehow that you haven't expressed correctly. Some people go crazy over this, because they cannot stand this kind of prose. Now I have a great regard for Updike's prose, for example, and I love reading the good stuff of Nabokov, but I can't write that way. It's a very personal preference on my own part.

RIBALOW: I have a reference here to the constant confrontations between Asher Lev and his father on art and Judaism. Asher's mother observes, "Your father sees the Jewish people as one body and one soul. When a head hurts in the Ukraine, your father suffers in Brooklyn."

POTOK: Yes, that's the Jewish concept of "all Jews are responsible to one another."

RIBALOW: You include a passage in *The Promise,* of which I'm not sure of the source, whether it's from the Midrash or whether it's your own. You say there are three kinds of Jews in the world. . . .

POTOK: That's from the *Taanya.*

RIBALOW: The *Rosho,* the one who sins and has evil thoughts. The *Benoni,* the one whose acts are without fault but cannot control his thinking. . . .

POTOK: And the *Tzaddik,* the righteous man.

RIBALOW: And the *Tzaddik;* only *Tzaddikim* have control over their hearts.

POTOK: Their hearts and their actions. That comes from the *Taanya,* which is, I would say, the central book in Lubovitch Hasidism.

RIBALOW: Jacob Kahn, the old master artist and teacher of Asher Lev, is also a very interesting character. There is a tendency to try to guess who these people are, but we have to assume they are imagined characters. Kahn says, "Art is not for people who want to make the world holy."

POTOK: *Absolutely not.* Correct.

RIBALOW: It is a sentence that struck me when I read it. Again, Kahn says, "Art is a religion" and calls it a tradition of goyim and pagans, and its values as goyish and pagan.

POTOK: By goyish, of course, he means Christian and pagan.

RIBALOW: Your Asher Lev is in a dilemma. Right in the middle. But he does feel responsible for his people.

POTOK: He has a tremendous sense of responsibility and that's the anguish.

RIBALOW: And Kahn says that the responsibility of the artist is to his art.

POTOK: Right, to his art.

RIBALOW: Yet Asher Lev's mother seems to understand this to a greater degree than Asher's father. I'm not sure whether it is understanding or whether she wants to encourage her son.

POTOK: Part of the reason that the mother understands it is that she is able to stand away from both of them simultaneously. The father is involved in his work; he is always running around. She is alone standing by the window. Asher Lev is suddenly involved with his work and he is gone. She stands at the window and can think. Can you imagine what the mother is thinking of as she stands all those hours and all those days by the window? She is able to achieve a distance, some kind of perspective on both of these people. She is also doing her own work, you see. It is not that she is a vacuous individual. She is a significant person and is able to think. It is because of that that she is able to sympathize both with the husband and with the son. At the same time, she is torn by the two of them.

RIBALOW: You seem to know a good deal about the techniques of art. You have painted, as you said a while back.

POTOK: Yes.

RIBALOW: There is the slow realization that the attraction of Michaelangelo's Pieta motivates Asher Lev to begin to think in terms of the Crucifixion. No doubt you have been to Italy.

POTOK: I saw the Pieta and I had the same reaction to it.

RIBALOW: How did you arrive at the concept of the observant Jew identifying with the Christ image?

POTOK: That was one of the longest, most agonizing processes I've ever lived through in my life. The reason for it is that I kept fighting it.

RIBALOW: Just like Asher Lev.

POTOK: I absolutely kept fighting it. In the back of my mind, I knew it was something that was going to happen.

RIBALOW: I've made a note here, saying, "agonizes over Crucifixion." So it was not only Asher Lev. It also was you.

POTOK: I wrote the book and kept living it as I was writing it. It was the strangest kind of experience because I kept saying to myself, "There's going to be another way out of it." And I kept checking it with people—what would you do? What would you do? What would you do?

RIBALOW: I remember that a few years ago, when I was in Jerusalem and we met in Professor Moshe Davis' home, you were in the midst of the novel and you did raise this question.

POTOK: Yes, I was always asking. I kept checking with people. It seemed inconceivable to me that I had stumbled across an idea that led to such an absolute blank wall. There is no other form in Western art other than the Crucifixion that a Jew can use to depict ultimate, solitary suffering? There has to be! Well, there isn't. Now, on the assumption that this Jew is committed to his people—he comes from the core of the Jewish tradition and is at the same time committed to Western art, which is what Asher Lev is—when he is confronted with the particular dilemma that *he* is confronted with, he will choose for his art. And the only vessel available to him at that point in his life by means of which he can express his feelings of his mother's protracted solitary torment, the only aesthetic mold available to him, is the Crucifixion. Jews haven't participated in Western art. Religious Jews haven't participated in Western art. There are no Jewish molds in Western art. So he turns to the Crucifixion. Again, he is not violating Jewish law. What he is violating is an aesthetic line he is crossing.

RIBALOW: It is the same thing when he draws the nudes.

POTOK: Exactly. But the nudes are containable, you see. But the Crucifixion evokes images of rivers of Jewish blood. Jews were slaughtered for that. So the *rebbe* cannot excuse that kind of thing. He has a revolution on his hands in the terms of the community. The *rebbe* cannot answer his people any more, and so he sends Asher Lev away.

RIBALOW: What has been the "Jewish" reaction?

POTOK: I get it in the head—constantly. Every time I speak, somebody says, "Why did you *do* that?"

RIBALOW: They do?

POTOK: Yes. They ask, "Why that?" or "Pick the Holocaust." I said that, first of all, the Holocaust is not a theme in Western art yet. It's not a mold. Nobody knows what to do with the Holocaust. On the assumption that it will become a mold in a hundred years, the last thing in the world it is going to be is an aesthetic mold for ultimate faith. There is no other mold in Western art than the Crucifixion to depict that particular feeling.

RIBALOW: When I started reading *In the Beginning,* I recalled a few lines by A. E. Housman, who was a favorite of my youth: "I am a stranger and afraid, in a world I never made." James T. Farrell used these lines for the titles of two of his novels. I thought of these lines in connection with your work because your novel, in a way, deals with Jews in "a world full of goyim." This did not hit me when I read your earlier novels. But here there is a special quality in your descriptions of anti-Semitism, the street hoods, of whom one is Polish and one is Jewish.

POTOK: That's right.

RIBALOW: How did you come up with the image of a Jewish hood, one who attends the same Hebrew school that David Lurie goes to?

POTOK: There are bullies all over. I picked a Jewish bully, first, to show that bullying is something endemic to growing up; secondly, to show the difference in quality between a goyish bully, whose bullying is based on anti-Semitism, which is something inexplicable. The Jewish bully's actions are based on envy. He doesn't evoke the kind of terror that the Polish boy evokes. His reasons are comprehensible. The other one— bewildering! Also he has a thousand years of hate behind him. He represents something.

RIBALOW: You have David Lurie growing up in the Bronx. Your earlier books are set in Brooklyn. Where are you from?

POTOK: I was raised in the Bronx, right where I wrote that book.

RIBALOW: Again, you bring many current events into your work: The Hebron pogroms in 1929 and the Depression and the Wellhausen Bible criticism.

POTOK: They called it higher anti-Semitism.

RIBALOW: These Bible critics weren't Jews, were they?

POTOK: No, they were Protestants.

RIBALOW: One reviewer of *In the Beginning* comments on the constant ailments afflicting David. He gets colds frequently. He has a leg infection. He undergoes surgery. Why do you make him sickly?

POTOK: First of all, he was. Second, one of the things I wanted to do with this boy is put him into a world filled with bewildering accidents. One of the most bewildering of accidents is anti-Semitism to the Jew. That is to say, one never knows where and how it is going to strike. The accident, plus the photograph, form the basic controlling metaphors of *In the Beginning*. The concept of accident, and how the Jew handles it—what do you do after an "accident"?—by accident I can mean anything from killing an animal to a major catastrophe. What do you do the Monday after the Sunday of the accident? How do you lead your life? That, plus the controlling metaphor of David Lurie's relationship to the photograph, to what went on before the photograph, what's in the photograph and what came out of the photograph—those two poles comprise the controlling metaphors of that book. And I'll let others figure out how those two poles work.

RIBALOW: There are constant references to contemporary history: to Father Coughlin and his anti-Semitism, to Vladimir Jabotinsky, the father. . . .

POTOK: Of Revisionism.

RIBALOW: And the concentration camps. The camps enter your story with great impact. It wasn't what I expected to find as the novel was going along.

POTOK: That's the greatest accident of all.

RIBALOW: The half-dozen pages on the impact of looking at the photograph. . . .

POTOK: You see how the two metaphors finally are joined at the end?

RIBALOW: The pictures?

POTOK: It is the pictures of the concentration camps. It is the photographs of the greatest accident of all. You see how the book is structured. It is the photographs of the greatest accident of them all that the Jewish people has experienced. Fused together, they take David Lurie out of his Orthodoxy and tell him, "I've got to dedicate my life to fighting what it is that these accident-makers are doing with something that I take to be the most beautiful photograph of all; that is to say, the picture of my people as given in the Bible."

RIBALOW: There is a hint of that in the earlier photograph taken of a group of Jews, posing with knives and guns in Poland, ready to fight for their own survival and identity.

POTOK: Exactly. That's one of the basic elements of the way the book is structured.

RIBALOW: You also list a lot of the books one should be familiar with.

POTOK: You can do your own course of Bible criticism by just reading this material.

RIBALOW: Let's return for a moment to the two photographs. The first shows a group of European Jews—armed. And David Lurie is admonished to forget it because it was illegal at the time for Jews to carry weapons. The second depicts death camp agonies, with bodies piled on bodies. That's what motivates David to move to the side of the secularists.

POTOK: Right. Very good. It's the union of the two metaphors that run all the way through the book that finally turns him away in an attempt to really understand, by entering the world that caused the accident to his people, that is to say, the secular world. As a result of the fusion of these two metaphors, he leaves his Orthodoxy, enters one of the metaphors: the secular world, in order to understand better the other metaphor: the photograph, the Bible, which is the picture of his people at a certain period of time. He has got to use secular instrumentalities on a sacred book, secularize that book in order to get out of the book what it is that is truly unique about his people. In other words, what were their beginnings really like?

RIBALOW: Yet the father cannot forgive him for what he calls "going to the goyim." This father is not a *rebbe*. He is removed from the Jews you wrote about in your previous novels. Yet he is just as rigid and adamant as they are.

POTOK: He suffered at the hands of the goyim, remember. How can any father let his son go to the goyim and let him use their instrumentalities on the *Chumash*? It's incredible.

RIBALOW: That's an echo of what happened earlier, when Rav Kalman went to the Talmud to examine different texts.

POTOK: The difference there is the rabbi's son can make his accommodation with Freudian psychoanalytic theory. He drops the Freudian anthropology, he drops the sociology and he uses the therapeutic process to heal human beings. That's an accommodation. You can quarrel with that accommodation, but it is valid and he says to you, I'm helping people. Reuven Malter takes scientific text criticism and uses it on the Talmud. He won't use it on the Bible, because for him the Bible is a divine work, whereas the Talmud, we can see, is the creation of man, we know when it was edited and so on, and people debate it. So he will not take it into the boundaries of the Bible. Once you do so, the Biblical text becomes fluid and the Orthodox Jewish tradition cannot contain the notion of the fluidity of the Biblical text because all of Orthodox Jewish law is based upon the fixity of the Biblical texts, particularly the first five books of Moses. So you cannot apply this methodology to the fundamentalist text.

RIBALOW: What of the Higher Biblical criticism?

POTOK: The Higher Biblical criticism is even worse than text criticism. It talks about sources and editors, so you end up not knowing what comes from where. It's a very powerful and dangerous instrumentality as far as the Orthodox Jew is concerned. In order to do it, you have got to leave Orthodoxy.

RIBALOW: I have a question I have been wanting to pose to you. Cynthia Ozick has a new book called *Bloodshed and Three Novellas.* She has an introduction to the book in which she goes to some lengths to explain one of the stories, because she struggled to make the story particularly clear and one non-Jewish critic didn't understand what she was writing about. In this introduction, she writes, "English is a Christian language. When I write English, I live in Christendom." She makes the point that had that particular tale been written in Hebrew or in Yiddish, no Yiddish or Hebrew reader would have had trouble with it; it would have been crystal clear to that reader. Because the critic was a goy, *naturally* he didn't understand it. So let me ask you: Is English a Christian language?

POTOK: English is not a Christian language, although there are Christian elements in the English language. English is an amalgam of I don't know how many languages. There are whole elements of English borrowed from pagan culture as well and borrowed from Mediterranean paganism and borrowed from Teutonic paganism. . . .

RIBALOW: Do you think she means that if you are writing like Yehezkel Kaufmann for Jews in a Jewish language, only the Jews know what he is saying when he is being critical? This way, if she is writing in English, somehow or other, things she is trying to say Jewishly get blocked?

POTOK: Well, then, the problem in a situation of that kind is for the writer somehow to abstract from his material the particularist elements in such a way that the dynamic of what it is that he is trying to express is capable of being communicated. It isn't only language that has this problem. Art has it as well. There are artists who are transcultural; there are artists who can only talk to their particular region. This is not a problem unique to language. It is a problem that any artist has: How to jump from *your* particular to all the particulars of all the readers who might one day encounter you? How did Evelyn Waugh jump across his world to me? He did it somehow. Evelyn Waugh was not writing *Jewish*. He was writing *English*. I'm a Jew. I read him as a Jew. How did he jump across to me? My problem as a Jew, when I write English, is not as a Jew. I don't have a Jewish problem. I have a problem as an artist. My problem is how to create a particular world in such a way that, first of all, it is crystal clear to me and to my eyes, what it is that I am saying. The boundaries have got to be sharp.

RIBALOW: Isn't it the failure of some of the Jewish writers that they are un-certain as to what they want to say?

POTOK: They are murky. They don't really understand what it is they are writing about. And if you are murky and don't understand what you are writing about, a Christian won't understand what you are writing about. It has absolutely nothing to do with the fact that the English language is Christian. It is not Christian. There are Christian elements in it, there are Greek elements, there are German elements, there are Jewish elements, Middle English. ... How can anyone say the English language is Christian? It is not! Its beauty lies precisely in the fact that it has absorbed the language systems of so many cultures. That is its richness. And I rather suspect that somebody who says that the English language is Christian is really saying that what he is writing is murky and cannot be understood.

RIBALOW: I'm bothered when I see certain writers become successful and I think little of them. It happens very infrequently that I read someone like you and enjoy both the work and your success.

POTOK: Thank you.

RIBALOW: And yet I'm not alone. Having been raised to some extent in your world, I think I'm closer to your books than other readers are. I can't help wondering—when I see your novels become best sellers—"Who are all these readers; where do they come from?" But it is happening and it is a very fine thing.

POTOK: Yes, and I also try not to think about it too much. Because when you begin to write for people, you are through. I'm grateful for it. I accept it for what it is. I'm constantly mystified by it. And when I'm in my room, doing my work, I'm writing for myself.

A Conversation with

Hugh Nissenson

Hugh Nissenson, at forty-six, has a large reputation for a man who has published comparatively little. His two volumes of short stories contain a total of fifteen tales. He is the author of a slim Israel journal and a short novel, *My Own Ground* (1976). His short story collections are *A Pile of Stones* (1965) and *In the Reign of Peace* (1972). *Notes from the Frontier* appeared in 1968.

I visited Nissenson on April 21, 1976. He lives, with his wife Marilyn and two children, on the Upper West Side of Manhattan on the twentieth floor of an imposing building. His spacious apartment commands handsome views of New York City's East River. His workroom is large and his desk faces a wall. When I asked him why he preferred to look at blank space instead of the river, he said he did not wish to be distracted by the view.

Nissenson looks younger than his years and far slimmer than his photographs indicate. He has books spread all over the apartment, but in the living room in which we sat, there was a select handful of volumes, mostly written by personal friends. There were inscribed books by Cynthia Ozick, Chaim Potok, Alfred Kazin, and less well-known writers with whom he had studied at Stanford University.

He is an articulate man and responds with clear answers to questions. Although he was unprepared for my particular questions, it was obvious that he had addressed himself to them before. He also tells a story with dramatic flair and in detail. He reads other writers—which is not true of all novelists and short story writers. He has a healthy confidence in his own work although, as he explained to me after our talk, he was having trouble with his current assignment. He was writing on Israel, following a recent quick trip, and was secretive about the assignment and where his work would be published ultimately. He was working from copious notes. He rewrites heavily and works with great concentration.

Nissenson is a stylist and has been called "the most theologically oriented of the contemporary group of American Jewish creative writers" by Robert Alter.

RIBALOW: How do you earn your living as a full-time writer? There are many writers I know who teach, who write while holding down public relations jobs, and so on.

NISSENSON: I am fortunate in that I have a little money, my wife works and I teach as much as I can and lecture as much as I can.

RIBALOW: Where do you teach?

NISSENSON: I taught at Manhattanville College and lectured extensively. I delivered, for example, a series of lectures this past fall for five synagogues in Westchester.

RIBALOW: What do you lecture on?

NISSENSON: On the Bible as literature. I discussed five stories in the Bible as literature, comparative religion, myth. One of the fun things about preparing these lectures was that I had to read about thirty books. That was terrific! I had to find out what was going on in scholarship in terms of Biblical exegesis.

RIBALOW: You are the author of four books: *A Pile of Stones, Notes from the Frontier, In the Reign of Peace,* and now *My Own Ground.* What are you working on now?

NISSENSON: I have over the years kept and published parts of an Israeli journal.

RIBALOW: I assume that appeared in *Notes from the Frontier,* where you went twice to the same kibbutz in Israel. By the way, what is the name of the kibbutz?

NISSENSON: Mayan Baruch. It is actually six kilometers north of Kiryat Shmoneh. It is now on Fatah-land. They are at war. It is an armed camp. Everybody carries around an automatic weapon. They take care. I stood *shmirah,* as I always do, and there was a buddy of mine behind a machine gun in a steel tower facing Fatah-land and it is no joke. You don't play around. But I love these people and I am part of them when I am there.

RIBALOW: You went there, I understand, when you were twenty-five.

NISSENSON: I got there quite accidentally. I got my first professional job in the arts, so to speak, through a fellow named Larry Frisch. I attended Swarthmore and when I graduated I went for a year up to Columbia University, in the School of Dramatic Arts. I was not sure why, but I was sort of interested in playwriting. Obviously, I was doing a bit of floundering. I quit that and took a job at the *New York Times*.

RIBALOW: Were you a reporter?

NISSENSON: No, I started out as a copyboy. Then they offered me another job and I had a decision to make. Was I going to be a journalist or was I going to turn into an artist? I had to give it a try. Otherwise I would not be able to live with myself. So I politely turned down the *Times* offer for advancement. My parents were very sweet and supported me. For three years I lived at home and wrote endless reams of crap. I was writing and writing, trying to learn my craft. I had to start out writing sentences and then paragraphs, you know, what everybody has to do. I was twenty-five, I guess it was two years later because I got out of college at twenty-three. Then I wrote a story for Larry Frisch.

RIBALOW: He was not an editor, was he? What was he doing that you wrote a story for him?

NISSENSON: He was producing films and I already had an incipient, a well-developed interest in Israel. I wanted to get over there.

RIBALOW: Did you have a Jewish background of any kind?

NISSENSON: In a complex way, yes.

RIBALOW: You ultimately learned Hebrew?

NISSENSON: The Hebrew I know is bad vernacular Hebrew I picked up.

RIBALOW: In Israel?

NISSENSON: Yes. I was Bar Mitzvah'd, but I cannot read Hebrew. I totally blocked out that experience. In a sense, my brain refuses to become absorbed in the structure of another language. My interest is in the American language. I hear music in our language and that's it. America is my country, to paraphrase Camus. The American language is my country. That is what obsesses me, interests me, and that is what I work at and try to perfect and hone and use to the best advantage. That is my lifelong ambition.

RIBALOW: So you were twenty-five when you went to Israel.

NISSENSON: Yes. Larry and I got connected—I think it was through someone at the William Morris Agency—and he said he wanted to do a film in Israel. He seemed to be twenty-eight or twenty-nine and appeared to have a lot of money. He had done one film and now wanted to do another. He came to me and said, "Write me a story about the war in 1948." I sat down and wrote for him the first film treatment I had ever done, which was a curious combination of half-baked and intensely dramatic material. There was already in it what was latent in my later work. A lot of the themes were there in a way that I did not understand. On the basis of this treatment, Frisch sold a studio in Israel. They put up money to match his money and asked me to come over. I told myself, "Here's a chance! Go! Take it!" With my parents' blessing, I took off and arrived in the country.

RIBALOW: When was this?

NISSENSON: Let me think. It was after Suez—'58 or '59. On the second day, Larry said to me, "You've got to get to know something about this country." I said, "You're right." Then he said, "There has just been a shelling up at Kibbutz Dan, up in the north. You had better go up there and find out what life is like on the frontier." So I said, "Sure." I borrowed his army coat and I put a pack on my back. I took a bus and *shlepped* up to the Galilee. It was getting dark and they would not let us into Kibbutz Dan because the kibbutz had sustained some casualties, so I was left in the bus, which terminated at Mayan Baruch. The bus driver, who was not a *chaver* of Mayan Baruch and eventually turned out to be one of the great heroes of the War of Independence, said to me, "What are you doing? You can't stay out here after dark." I said, "I don't know." He insisted, "You can't, you'll get murdered out here. You don't wander around here after dark." I told him, "I have no place to go." He then said, "Come with me, I'll take you to Mayan Baruch."

RIBALOW: And that is how you got to that kibbutz.

NISSENSON: I walked across the lawn to Mayan Baruch and a guy, who is now dead, came up to me and said, in English, "What are you doing here, kid?" And I explained to him. He said, "Okay, don't worry about it." He introduced me to a couple by the name of Gila and Eitan Roz, with whom I have been in love ever since.

RIBALOW: Did you use them in your stories?

NISSENSON: Oh yes. I am writing about them now. That book, *Notes from the Frontier,* was in a sense unsuccessful. I was not prepared at that point to be as honest as I wanted.

RIBALOW: You were guarded?

NISSENSON: Well, I was guarded. Also aesthetically I was not on mature ground. I was young and it did not have the power that it should have had. But that is the way you learn—by doing. They took me in. He is a sabra who was a member of the Palmach. He stands five feet tall and is made out of steel, a super guy. They have how many kids now? Mira, who is married and living in Jerusalem; they have Shai, who is in the commandos, the frogmen; and they have Pal, who is sixteen; they have a little one, Ronen, who is six—four kids. I have watched them all grow up and I know all about them. Eitan is one of the founders of the kibbutz, one of the *vatikim*. He was in the Palmach. He started out to be an architect. He dreaded joining the Palmach because a friend of his was butchered and cut up on the road to Haifa in 1947. But he fought and fought and survived. Then he joined the *garin*, with Jews from South Africa and the Americas as well as sabras to form Mayan Baruch. They settled there in '49.

RIBALOW: So when you arrived in Israel for the first time you were comparatively young.

NISSENSON: I certainly was. The first night I was there—they kind of laughed about it many times since. I sort of naively said that I wanted to find out what life is like on the frontier. Eitan turned to me and said, "Okay. Get up five o'clock tomorrow morning." You see, this was an immediate put-to-the-test. You get up in the morning and go out with the cows, but they used to pasture them on the then Syrian frontier. I get up and show up at the *refet*. I remember I had these rubber boots and thin socks and I was chilled and got terrible blisters. And I walked and walked with this damned herd of cows.

RIBALOW: You had no agricultural background, did you?

NISSENSON: This was my first time on a farm, much less a kibbutz, much less a frontier! There were three guys with us, one of whom has since died a horrible death. In '67, he called down an air strike on himself outside Jenin. He was a scout and he and his jeep ran into a bunch of Jordanian Pattons. He called down an air strike and his fellow Israelis said, "Get out of there!" He said he had no time, his armor was behind him. He was hit and they napalmed him. I was up on the Golan when an officer right after the war discovered an Israeli soldier. The officer said they found his body, which was shrivelled up to the size of a doll. So one of the boys was that sweet boy, with a sensitive face and a moustache. And another boy, who has since become a father many times over and is a dear friend, by the name of Peretz, and a particularly tough guy, who was in the Palmach. He is called Tojo because he looked like a Japanese. He has kind of round glasses and he is so tough he is scary. The guys had between them—as I remember—two 303 Enfields.

RIBALOW: These are the people you went out with?

NISSENSON: Yes, with them and the damned cows. I did not know where I was, but we finally arrived at a spot. I had never been in the army. I was 4-F because I was asthmatic when I was a kid. I had never handled a rifle or a weapon, much less seen one. We arrived at this spot and I was exhausted. Peretz or one of the others asked me the time. I looked at my watch and said, "Nine o'clock." He said, "Aha," and they talked together and then one of them returned, again I think it was Peretz. He said, "You know how to work this?" and he handed me a Karl Gustav submachine gun. I said, "No." He said, "It's very simple. All you do is release the safety and fire it." I said, "Oh." There was an abandoned Arab village right near us and a dry wadi. It was a sort of artificial canal. Peretz said, "Lie in the canal with the machine gun." I asked, "Why?" He replied, "Because if at this time their shepherds have not generally shown up, it means they have been called back and their troops will open up on us." So I said to myself, "Oi Vey!" I just saw it happening—my mother getting the letter. But I was determined to hold. I'm not going to break and run. I said, tentatively, "Can we leave the cattle?" They said, "No. Our job is to get the cattle." So I said, "Okay." If these were the rules, I would play by the rules. I lay there and the cows were mooing all around me, chewing their cuds.

RIBALOW: You were lying in a ditch?

NISSENSON: In a kind of a ditch. The other guys with binoculars had gone out behind a rise to take a look. To see. They had rifles. Peretz said to me, "Don't open fire until they reach this bush." Three feet away! I said, fine and set myself, determined to play it out. I lay there in a sweat. You get so frightened that you are no longer frightened. I looked at myself objectively and laughed. "It's like a B movie," I thought. "What are you doing here?" My God, I looked up and on the opposite hill I see a figure that I cannot distinguish. God, I said, that's it. They're bringing up their troops! Now I am going to have to kill or be killed. For about three minutes I waited as they came closer and I remember lifting the gun up and I carefully calculated that when they come to this bush I am going to open fire, I guess. I was going to shoot. I wasn't going to run. Finally, Peretz came back to me and said, "It's okay. We checked them out. They are shepherds. They're late." So that was when they saw that I. . . .

RIBALOW: Prepared to do what you had to.

NISSENSON: Prepared to stand my ground; I was with them. From that point I have been subjected to a series—for fun obviously—of tests. They would take me off to all sorts of preposterous places.

RIBALOW: So you were in this kibbutz for four weeks in 1965. Then you returned during and after the Six-Day War in 1967.

NISSENSON: I had been in Germany. Marilyn was working for CBS. I did not know whether I could work in Germany or not, but it turned out that it was okay. I worked on *Notes from the Frontier* and all of a sudden the war started up. I figured I had better get out there to see what was going on, to say nothing of my worries about my friends. I got out by pulling strings at the airport. It happened that the guy who was running El Al knew a friend of mine at Mayan Baruch. It was one of those funny things. So I got on the first plane and arrived in the country. I grabbed the first car at the airport—it was a red Volkswagen, I remember—and I am a terrible driver, especially with shift cars. It was night, but I went to the Hilton in Tel Aviv. That is where CBS was and the headquarters for all the correspondents. CBS had a tie-in line with Germany and I knew I could call Marilyn to assure her I was safe. When I reached her, she asked about our friends and about Mayan Baruch. I started to talk but the censor cut the conversation.

RIBALOW: Then what?

NISSENSON: The next morning I got up early and ran over to the Government Press Office to find out what was going on up north because there had been, up to then, no news from the north. I had a buddy at the office, Lionel Paton, a wonderful fellow, from South Africa, who apparently is no longer there. He had taken a liking to me over the years. He sort of looked at me and I asked him what was going on in the north. "Well," he said, "tomorrow or the next day we're running some correspondents up there." Again I asked what was happening. He replied, "Can you get a car?" I said, yes. He said, "If I were you, I'd throw my stuff in a car and I'd go." I thanked him and followed the military convoys north, the tanks, the Centurions being driven up, and the truckloads of troops who had been fighting on the West Bank. I passed at one point a group of them singing "Yerushalayim Shel Zahav," and I started crying. Guys with bandages and singing. They were going up to the Golan to fight. I arrived at Safed and ran in to give blood at a hospital, where they were bringing the wounded with helicopters. But I was turned away because they had enough blood. As I came out of the hospital, I looked up and who did I see but Mandy, a buddy of mine at Mayan Baruch—in uniform and with a Uzi and a jeep. He is in his fifties, originally from the Bronx, a wonderful guy. I ran to him, embraced him, and asked him, "How is everything?" He said, "Well, we are being shelled, being mortared, but everyone is okay." I asked, "How can I get out of here? The MP won't let me through." He said, "It's closed off," but then added, "If I were you, I'd take a chance, go along the northern frontier road, the Lebanese road, things are very quiet up there. Try it. The worse that can happen is that the Lebanese will intern you. You're not going to get shot."

RIBALOW: I guess that is what you did.

NISSENSON: Yes, I took the Volkswagen and I picked up two kids, I remember, who lived in Kiryat Shmoneh. One was a Cochin Indian, the other a Moroccan. I drove like a madman and I had never seen the road before. Finally, I arrived and there ahead of me is the battle for the Golan, spread out like a film. I see the planes, their wings catching the sun dropping, napalm, the tanks moving up—some on fire—guys getting shot. When I get to Kiryat Shmoneh, I go directly to the police station because I cannot get through the road that goes to Mayan Baruch because they are bringing up troops. The MP says, no, they are shelling up there, they are mortaring. Absolutely no. You have to remain in Kiryat Shmoneh tonight. So I run back to the police and say, Look, do me a favor. Get me a line to the bunkers at Mayan Baruch. There was a very sweet policeman there who put me through. Unfortunately, I got through to Ralphie, not Eitan. Eitan would have come and got me. But Ralphie said, and probably quite wisely, Look, we're being mortared here. You'd be smart to lay over tonight.

RIBALOW: In Kiryat Shmoneh?

NISSENSON: Yes. Stay there tonight and come tomorrow. As it worked out, I watched the battle at night from Kuinetra. The whole sky was sort of glowing. The next day I arrived on the *meshek* when everybody was coming out of the shelters and I stayed there for about ten days.

RIBALOW: It was on the basis of these additional ten days that you wrote the addenda to the book.

NISSENSON: Right. Right.

RIBALOW: Getting away from Israel for a bit, let us get back to your background in America. According to the jacket blurbs on your books, you attended Fieldston, Swarthmore, and Stanford. And from the interior evidence of your stories, as well as *Notes from the Frontier,* you do speak Hebrew.

NISSENSON: As I said before, my Hebrew is a bad vernacular Hebrew. But I find that all the friends I have overseas are bilingual and when we start really talking seriously, we start talking English.

RIBALOW: What about your Jewish and Zionist background? Did you know much before you went to Israel?

NISSENSON: Not really. I had a sentimental attachment to Zionism, but I began to read and also my conscience began to tell me that something was happening here. . . . I grew up with the Holocaust, which scarred me immensely. I am writing about that now. My sense of shame at being a Jew as a child was terrible.

RIBALOW: Where were you raised?

NISSENSON: In Brooklyn, at first, then in Manhattan. I knew very early on, I knew the details when I was eleven or twelve, that kids my age, and people like my parents, were being killed and that Jews were victims.

RIBALOW: What was the shame?

NISSENSON: The shame was . . . no child wants to be a victim. A child always blames himself for what is done to him. It is the psychology of a kid. My humiliation and rage at my father's hopelessness . . . not understanding his weeping and praying. . . .

RIBALOW: What do you mean—praying?

NISSENSON: He is very religious. At the same time, I adored God and tried to submit to His will and tried to find some answer to this horror.

RIBALOW: You say you were ten or eleven at this time?

NISSENSON: Yes, ten, eleven, or twelve. It left me with a deep sense of humiliation and shame that my people were in terror, that my people were victims. Not only that, but I said to myself, Roosevelt and Churchill, whom I adored, were not doing anything about it and it could happen here.

RIBALOW: When you were in Israel in 1967, during the fighting, did this feeling of helplessness still assail you?

NISSENSON: No, no. I resolved this the first time I went to Israel. These people have restored my honor as a Jew.

RIBALOW: That is what I was asking.

NISSENSON: Yes. I knew that immediately. The *first* thing that I knew about these people, and what they were doing, was that they had restored my

honor as a Jew. And since then I have been a *passionate* Zionist. One of
the things which has struck me very deeply, beyond this, overcoming
this primordial shame, which, you know, is natural to a child, not to a
man, because you don't blame the victim for being victimized—you
blame the people who do it. And I learned about that. One thing that has
struck me deeper and deeper is the fact that three years after the
destruction of European Jewry, which is from whence I come. . . .

RIBALOW: From where?

NISSENSON: My father comes from Warsaw and my mother was born here but
her parents come from Lemberg, Lvov. I am very conscious of the
immigrant thing. One of the things that struck me forcibly was that here
the Jewish people, having just been murdered, literally—Hitler won his
war against the Jews, no question about it, he did!—we willed our own
rebirth. What we did was we reentered history as an ordinary nation,
which means that we have the courage again, or at last, to take our fate
into our own hands, which is what a grownup does, and to accept the
responsibility for our own existence and, more than that, I believe that
deep down in a lot of Israelis and, I think, certainly myself and a lot of
Americans, there is a deep realization, at last, that the Jews are indeed like
everybody else, alone in a meaningless universe. That there is no God.
There is no Redemption. That the only chance we have. . . .

RIBALOW: There is no God and there is no Redemption, yet Robert Alter
somewhere says that you are the only religious writer we have.

NISSENSON: It is true, because I am obsessed by religious themes. I am obsessed in a sense that the dialogue goes on within me. Part of this last
book of mine, for example, is precisely that. Jacob our father in the book,
Jake, the kid, has a dream not as Jacob the Patriarch, of heaven, but of
earth. It is a nightmare in which he sees the holy moist mother earth who
gives birth to us, who nurtures us and then devours us alive. And that's it!
More than that, there is to me, and in Jake's unconscious in the dream, a
sense of numenusnis about it. I can't help it.

RIBALOW: A sense of what?

NISSENSON: N–u–m–e–n–u–s–n–i–s. It is to me holy. This mystery of this awesome process evokes in me a sense of holiness and it has nothing to do any
longer with a sense of a personal God. It is numenous. I cannot help it. I
am filled with a numenous awe at the mystery of. . . .

RIBALOW: What does the word mean?

NISSENSON: It is Rudolph Otto's word on the idea of holy. It is a wonderful word because it defines something which is awesome, which is religiously inspired, inspires in you a sense of the awe of things. That is the final statement in this book: that the boy, the old man tells him, "Take off your shoes from your feet. This is holy ground. Everything on it is holy and even though there is broken glass scattered all over the floor, which comes from Schlifka's bottle tossed in the whorehouse—and your feet are going to get cut—you have to stand on the earth."

RIBALOW: Let us get to *My Own Ground* a little later and deal with your work chronologically. I have some notes here about the attitudes of some of your characters to Arabs and I wonder whether they are your own. In *Notes from the Frontier,* a Shlomo Wolfe says, "The Arabs hate us so much, it's hard to believe." And Aliza, Shlomo's wife says, "You have to live in a country of your own, among your own kind. And it's not possessions that matter, but people." Yet Aliza was an atheist following the death of her parents in Auschwitz, apparently giving up the concept of God. You worked physically in the kibbutz, not only when you first went there, but later as well.

NISSENSON: Actually, I worked mostly when I first went there.

RIBALOW: Afterwards, you came as a guest?

NISSENSON: Yes. What I do is walk around and talk to people and they know I am taking notes.

RIBALOW: One of your characters says in the journal, "On a kibbutz exploitation is impossible" and that "alienation is inconceivable" and "labor has become an end in itself, as it should be." Later on you make the point that something like three percent of all the people live on kibbutzim and yet the kibbutz ideal of social justice is bound to have some influence in a country as small as Israel.

NISSENSON: It requires, I think, an extraordinary personality to live on a kibbutz. I know that I could not because I am an artist for one thing.

RIBALOW: Doesn't Amos Oz live on a kibbutz?

NISSENSON: Amos does, but they give him six months a year off and he has a special deal going for him. I, for example, had a conversation with a very gifted graphic artist by the name of Guzman. He is thirty-seven and was wounded by shrapnel in '67 in the back of the neck. I visited him in Hadassah Hospital. He was totally paralyzed, except that he had some ability to use his left hand. He squeezed my hand and said shalom. Now he has recovered, although he is sick periodically. One evening, Guzman showed me his work. And he is, it seems to me, a remarkably gifted artist. I said to him, "You're thirty-seven and you are going in one point and you ought to develop."

RIBALOW: You mean, to get off the kibbutz?

NISSENSON: "You have to go and see what is going on in the United States," I told him.

RIBALOW: That conflict is an old one.

NISSENSON: It certainly is. I said to him, "Don't you want recognition?" He said, "No." Well, I do not know honestly whether it is denial and a means of not putting yourself on the line, because, as I said to him, "Sooner or later, as an artist, you have to face the critics. That is part of the game."

RIBALOW: Moshe Sharett's brother Yehuda, was a composer, who wrote "Kinneret." He lived on a kibbutz and the problem was, does he go off and compose? Meyer Levin wrote the first novel in English. . . .

NISSENSON: Yes, *Yehuda.*

RIBALOW: . . . on the kibbutz covering that particular crises.

NISSENSON: About a violinist.

RIBALOW: Yet you make a point somewhere where one of your characters says that apart from defending the frontier, the kibbutz is of little practical value.

NISSENSON: I think that *this* kibbutz has become increasingly viable economically because they now have an automated factory and they are producing cotton in the Huleh and they are growing apples. Everyone said apples could not grow; they have a fantastic cash crop.

RIBALOW: Are there many kibbutzniks who feel that the lives they lead are provincial lives? A sabra is quoted in your journal, saying, "As a sabra, he has no feeling of Jewish inferiority, but is plagued, instead, by a sense of inadequacy as an Israeli."

NISSENSON: In some instances this is true but there has been a substantial change in the Israeli psyche since '73.

RIBALOW: Are they no longer on tranquilizers, as you indicate in your book?

NISSENSON: That is Kiryat Shmoneh. That is a different problem, in towns.

RIBALOW: You also have a description of children having Bar Mitzvahs in the kibbutz, which once upon a time was detached from religion.

NISSENSON: They have never really quite resolved the problem of what to do with festivals and celebrations.

RIBALOW: They make them national celebrations rather than religious ones.

NISSENSON: Well, yes. But it seems to me to be an unsatisfactory solution because it has no mythic base. It does not move you in an unconscious way.

RIBALOW: Well, yes. But it seems to me to be an unsatisfactory solution because it has no mythic base. It does not move you in an unconscious way.

RIBALOW: Well, there is a sentence of your own, in which you observe, "How can they possibly learn to appreciate the moral values of a civilization while rejecting the faith from which they're derived?"

NISSENSON: I think that is a dilemma I would ascribe to all human beings now, not only in the kibbutz but modern civilization in general. It was pointed out very early on by Dostoevsky that Ivan says that if there is no God, everything is possible. And we are all faced with this problem of how do you evolve a humanistic ethic which is based simply on a relative relativism? There is no fiat from above. This is a basic problem that we are going to have to solve.

RIBALOW: Let me get to a couple of your story collections in which some of the stories derive from what we have been talking about. *A Pile of Stones* contains seven stories. They were first published in magazines. Your stories made your artistic reputation. Yet I am sure you earned more money from the sale of the individual stories than you did from the royalties from the books.

NISSENSON: Exactly.

RIBALOW: The first two stories in *A Pile of Stones* were set in Poland. One is "The Groom in Zlota Street," which originally appeared in *Commentary*. It deals with anti-Semites in Poland and is about a Jew who subjects himself to having his beard pulled by an anti-Semite. Was this conceived by you or is it something you had heard about?

NISSENSON: It was a fantasy that came to me.

RIBALOW: Of course, the point is that the Jew has the option of refusing to have his beard pulled.

NISSENSON: Right. By the way, I recently learned that a group of my stories are being translated into Italian.

RIBALOW: On this subject: Have you been translated into other languages?

NISSENSON: Yes, I don't remember how many. French, for one. Norwegian, English editions, and now Italy. I am being taught at the University of Verona. I find, I must say that my work, even though I have transcended it and moved on, has a life of its own.

RIBALOW: You never know what happens to the printed word, the effect it has.

NISSENSON: I am always hearing about something I did ten years ago. I am told "I was very much moved," or "I started crying on a subway when I read 'The Crazy Old Man.'" It is all a dream to me now.

RIBALOW: "The Blessing" is the story—published in *Harper's*—about the Jew who refuses to attend the funeral of his eight-year-old son, an innocent boy subjected to cancer. The father resists the idea of going to the funeral. Is that based on something that happened in Israel?

NISSENSON: No, it is set in Israel and I wrote it when I was twenty-two. It was the first mature story I did. With it, I suddenly found my theme and my metaphor and my voice.

RIBALOW: At that time of life or through this story?

NISSENSON: At that time of life. I suddenly realized that this problem, this religious obsession and this conflict, and one's relationship to a universe which is either meaningless or, you know, is going to be a central theme in my work.

RIBALOW: That is what happened?

NISSENSON: That is exactly what happened.

RIBALOW: In "The Well," which is, again, a story set in Israel, the young Jew is a friend of Ali, an Arab and the son of a sheik. The Jew, Grossman, has a sense of justice and fights to make water available to the Arabs who haven't any. Grossman believes that the sheik will give the water freely to his people, but instead, the sheik taxes them for it. Finally, Ali curses Grossman for being a Jew. This all reminds me a bit of Moshe Smilansky, who used to write stories in Hebrew about Arabs. His stories, written some forty or fifty years ago, were romantic stories. He was an early settler in Palestine and found his material in Arab life. He was romantic very much like the British Arabists. But in "The Well," the Jew and the Arab are enemies.

NISSENSON: I think I was more of a prophet than I knew.

RIBALOW: The story of yours that is reprinted in my anthology of Jewish short stories, *My Name Aloud,* was "The Law." It is a Bar Mitzvah story. Almost everybody who is Jewish who writes Jewish fiction at some point writes about a Bar Mitzvah.

NISSENSON: Because I think it is unconsciously the rite of manhood, that rite of passage crucial to our own existence.

RIBALOW: Yes, but many writers use it as a social comment on the hundreds of guests, the rabbi's speech, the food. . . .

NISSENSON: No, I am not interested in the social comment.

RIBALOW: Right; here in your story, the plot is based on the boy being a stammerer. With all the torture that he goes through, nevertheless, he wants to experience the Bar Mitzvah service and ceremony. The outsider who is telling the story thinks this poor kid is being whipped, flayed, and agonized. In the end, the boy stumbles through the service. He takes on the responsibility of manhood.

NISSENSON: How does it go? He begins to "assume the burden of what the reiteration of the Law of his Fathers had demanded from the first."

RIBALOW: I find it interesting that the title story was really a non-Jewish story to a greater extent than all the others. "A Pile of Stones" is about the fellow who was the Presbyterian and the Yale lawyer who becomes obsessed with religion, God, the Jews, and Buber and then dies meaninglessly.

NISSENSON: But his prayer is fulfilled. The irony is that God answers his prayers and takes him at the moment of his greatest happiness.

RIBALOW: In the next book, which is *In the Reign of Peace,* again I made a list of where all the stories appeared. I assume that "The Throne of God" makes its first appearance in this collection.

NISSENSON: Right. I wrote that very late and did not have time to publish it elsewhere. Of all the stories in it, I never make this kind of mistake; I am too good a technician. That story was written from the wrong point of view.

RIBALOW: It is about a sixteen-year-old Jewish assassin. . . .

NISSENSON: It is written unfortunately in the first person and months after the book was published, I realized it should have been in the third person. I almost never make that kind of fundamental error. I pride myself on my technical facility. I was shocked to discover this, because I knew the story did not quite make it. I was shocked to discover the reason was that I had simply made a wrong-o, aesthetically chosen to tell the story from the point of view of the doctor, who was the nationalist. What I should have done, to get more power out of it, was to tell it from the third person.

RIBALOW: It is about the boy who comes down with pneumonia and, in the end, he is still running loose and you don't know what has happened to him.

NISSENSON: Because in the end the murderous principle has been released.

RIBALOW: In the story that follows it, "The Crazy Old Man," the one you made reference to a few moments ago, your viewpoint is quite original. The old man shoots an Arab in order to take the onus of murder away from the Jew who had had the privilege to have been born in Israel. Therefore, the old man takes the crime upon himself. You said that people were affected by that story?

NISSENSON: A couple of months ago, in a charming incident, a kid who was an admirer of mine, said to me that "When I read that story on a subway, I suddenly burst out crying." And I said, "Well then I did my job."

RIBALOW: Here is a very interesting passage from the story, "All of you who were born here have had enough and will have your State. For you, the exile is over. Not that it wasn't deserved. . . . We sinned and were punished for it. It was just. But He has relented and in His mercy has given you one more chance. So you must be careful." Of course, the old man recalls the pogroms of his own country and therefore appreciates doubly what is being achieved in Israel by these people.

NISSENSON: Right. However, they had to go into murder in order to achieve it. That is the basic irony of the story. They have to torture and kill in order to accomplish their mission, which is indeed to fight.

RIBALOW: You have a couple of stories set on the East Side in these books. I would not be making this point, except that later, of course, I read your recent novel, which deals with the East Side. In the story called "Charity," where the father makes welcome every *shlepper* who may come to his home, he also gives refuge to a con artist named Reb Rifkin. The mother has pneumonia. She finally recovers and the father believes that she had overcome the disease because he had fulfilled a *mitzvah* by allowing all people to enter his home.

NISSENSON: No, the boy thinks so. It is all told from the point of view of the boy and the father corrects him at the end and, in a very ambivalent statement—I intend both—, he says to the boy, it was not done for Momma but it was done for him. But who was that? Is it this *shlepper* or God?

RIBALOW: I reread the title story in *In the Reign of Peace* shortly after I had your journal in hand and I find that you are drawing for your fiction from your raw material.

NISSENSON: Oh, sure. It takes place in Mayan Baruch.

RIBALOW: The Orthodox Moroccan was at Mayan Baruch?

NISSENSON: Yes—Chaim, whom I loved. He worked in the apple orchard but the rest of the story is fantasy.

RIBALOW: Chaim was a special sort of man, "The Sabbath had preserved him." And he does not understand the kibbutzniks who are nonreligious. He does not quite understand what is Jewish about them. When you tell him that nobody follows kashruth and that the kibbutzniks don't believe in God and don't believe in the Messiah and yet, at the same time, when a field mouse is being eaten by ants, then, somehow or other, there is a religious conclusion drawn.

NISSENSON: It is not that, except that he points out that, with the wisdom of the ages, that *they* think they had achieved Redemption—a just society— but Redemption will not be achieved until the universe itself is just.

RIBALOW: Until this no longer happens.

NISSENSON: Right. Until a mouse is not eaten alive by ants. But unfortunately cosmologically, and talking in terms of evolution, that is the way it is. We eat or are eaten.

RIBALOW: In "Going Up," where the narrator's Uncle Mendel comes to their kibbutz, even though he does not approve of it and, as you already have said, it was during the fighting in the Golan when he realizes the ferocity and the cruelty of what goes on.

NISSENSON: He sees the corpse of a sixteen-year-old boy, as I did. It was the first corpse I saw in that war. . . .

RIBALOW: And obviously it was the first corpse the old man had seen.

NISSENSON: Yes, and I realized suddenly he was an innocent, a shepherd boy who had been killed by some damn shell.

RIBALOW: For no reason at all. A concussion, as I remember, so he doesn't look really damaged.

NISSENSON: Yes, there was no mark on his body. His face was rotting. There was literally no blood.

RIBALOW: Then, of course, the religious or theological motif comes in again, when the old man reflects that "God never sleeps. It wouldn't be so bad if I believed He was asleep." So he cannot justify, or accommodate to, what is happening. Your story "Lamentations" is, I don't want to use the word "peculiar," but. . . .

NISSENSON: It is the best story in that book.

RIBALOW: Yes, in its way. What Bashevis Singer does is this: he takes something totally incredible and you believe it as you read it. This story has such a peculiar, incredible thesis or premise that you somehow believe it. I have a curious question about it: Is it within Jewish law, to marry someone who is dead? To make it clear to someone who does not know the story, Elani and Uri, who are referred to somewhere in *Notes from the Frontier,* are a young couple who fall in love, or she does with him. It looks for a moment that they may become a couple but you drop it. Anyway Elani becomes pregnant, although they have not been married. Now that he has been killed, she wants a wedding ceremony at the graveside!

NISSENSON: I based this story on the fact that several Israelis had told me this actually had taken place.

RIBALOW: It is a very moving story.

NISSENSON: They *told* me. I said, well, if it has or hasn't, regardless, its mythic, too good to leave, not to use. The lamentation of the story is, of course, the lamentation, ultimately, Zion spreadeth forth her hands and there is no one to comfort her. There is a realization on the part of the sabra, Yigal, at the end, that there is no God, there is nothing. We are alone— and he weeps.

RIBALOW: Yet the girl has enormous strength of character.

NISSENSON: She is bearing life. She is mad, but she is bearing life. It seems to me, in ten pages, to sum up an awful lot of what the universe as I see it is about.

RIBALOW: Your novel *My Own Ground* stunned me, in the sense that it was to me totally different in many ways from everything of yours I had read.

NISSENSON: I think it is.

RIBALOW: I remember talking to you before we have gotten together. You said then that Wilfred Sheed had liked it but that it was "too slender" in commercial terms to become a Book-of-the-Month Club selection.

NISSENSON: Yes, yes, that was too bad.

RIBALOW: You wrote this novel in such a way that one does not really know that the story is being told in the present about the past. It isn't until the last page, where you see the name of the author, written in 1965 in Elmira. Then suddenly the reader sees that the story is a total flashback. Why didn't you do it as a straight narrative?

NISSENSON: Because technically I wanted the immediacy of the scene. From the first sentence. Cynthia Ozick recently told me on the phone that she went out to Pittsburgh to teach a course in creative writing and what she said is that I'm putting that first sentence up on the blackboard and I'm discussing that and the title and they'll learn something about writing. I mean to say you are *there* in that first sentence.*

RIBALOW: The story, of course, without having to repeat it too much, is about a rabbi's daughter who is seduced both physically and emotionally by a pimp.

NISSENSON: And spiritually.

RIBALOW: On the subject of language. It is quite raw. Do you think such language was used then, in 1912?

NISSENSON: I think it was used then. I took this cue from my father. He grew up in a Yiddish-speaking environment, speaks English absolutely perfectly, without *any* accent, but who all his life told me stories about his past in the American vernacular. When I was searching for the voice of this book, I said, "That's it! My father is giving it to me!" All my life he has told me stories in a profoundly American tone and melody about what happened in the past. The wonderful juxtaposition of using it is too incredible to be missed. It's a wonderful aesthetic playoff.

RIBALOW: The research of the East Side, which a number of critics have praised so highly—where does that come from? Not from Irving Howe's *World of Our Fathers,* which was published at about the same time as yours.

NISSENSON: No, no. Mr. Howe sent me one chapter on crime on the lower East Side, which was not helpful at all.

RIBALOW: He sent it to you while you were working on the novel?

NISSENSON: Yes, I knew he was writing his book and he was very kind and sent it to me, but I had to fabricate.

RIBALOW: When I talked to Robert Kotlowitz on where he got the geographical locations in his shtetl in Poland, he said that, among other things, he went to YIVO and looked at maps and said, well, the river is here and he knew there was a factory there. . . .

NISSENSON: That's right.

RIBALOW: What did you do about it? I know you went to YIVO, as the librarian, Dina Abramowicz, when she saw me holding your novel, told me you had been there.

---

*This is the opening sentence in *My Own Ground:* In the Summer of 1912, when I was fifteen years old, Schlifka the pimp offered me ten bucks to tell him when Hannah Isaacs showed up on Orchard Street in the building where I lived.

NISSENSON: I started in without yet knowing the theme of this book. I was convinced that I was destined to be a short story writer. That was it. I was convinced of it in my late thirties that . . . so what? After all, Isaac Babel had written short stories.

RIBALOW: Very good short stories. There are those who believe that Isaac Bashevis Singer is better as a short story writer than as a novelist.

NISSENSON: The short story is a great form. But I also was determined not to write a novel until I had a theme commensurate with the form as I understood it. Publishers had "hocked" me for years and I said, "No, this is *my* life and I'm pursuing *my* obsessions." They are not suffering with me in the art of creation. *I* am. I was determined that no matter what they said I was not going to produce a work of juvenilia or litter the landscape with half-baked autobiographical early novels. I have too much respect, in a sense, for the form of any literary structure and a great passionate love for what can be done if one knows what one is doing with the novel. I started in about November '69, I don't know why, it was brewing, I guess, writing notes.

RIBALOW: On the East Side.

NISSENSON: Yes, and images, writing images.

RIBALOW: That seems clear. The book is full not only of the East Side but a lot of stories out of Europe.

NISSENSON: Right. One of the technical devices of the book are arias which the major characters deliver about life. Each one has an aria specifically pertinent to the thematic development about what is happening.

RIBALOW: By the same token, why is the enslavement, sexual and otherwise, of Hannele, more or less offstage? It is as though it were told. It may be, I guess, because it is the narrator doing the telling and he is not always present.

NISSENSON: Exactly. The point is that it is all filtered through the consciousness of a fifteen-year-old boy. In the climactic struggle between Jacob and the Angel, Jacob and Esau in the whorehouse, the boy sees her in her full degradation. She is revealed with her nipples rouged. The rest, as with all adolescents, is filled with looking and hearing and smelling and spying.

RIBALOW: He only partly understands it.

NISSENSON: Because adolescents do that. They spend their lives sort of sniffing around.

RIBALOW: Are you familiar with the review of your book and Jerome Charyn's that was published in the *New Republic* by Peter Shaw?

NISSENSON: Oh, yes. I must say I know Peter. I just wrote him a letter. He ascribed Schlifka's past to Jake.

RIBALOW: Let me read from the review: "Nissenson and Charyn are not simply concerned to recapture unsavory types, who in any case can be found in Yiddish literature itself. There is a long tradition of conflict between *proste* (vulgar) and *edel* (refined) types in both Jewish life and literature. For the first time, though, I believe, we are being shown Jews who are utterly debased spiritually. In *My Own Ground* Jake Brody's uncle kills an anti-Semitic peasant without a qualm."

NISSENSON: But it isn't Jake Brody's uncle. It's Schlifka's uncle, which is the whole point of Esau. Schlifka is the red, the hairy red one. His dark revelation on that road when his nostrils are stuffed with dirt and he hears an owl and a weasel hunting and an owl with a mouse in its claws, he has a mystical revelation of darkness at the end of days which is the result of murder. And that is what forms him. His uncle takes the same flat rock, white rock, that appeared earlier in Mrs. Tauber's revelation about the Garden of Eden, about eating the apples, which no one has come upon— and which is the center of the book! The vision of this woman, who is transfigured into Mother Earth herself. This is made possible by her sexual and religious emancipation very early on when she talks about . . . it's a play about Eve and the Garden of Eden. It is in an apple orchard and when she is given the rotten apples by the peasants from our moist Mother Earth and she eats.She has a revelation realizing that the apples fall—very beautiful it is, if I say so myself—they fall so that others may indeed grow in their place and that death is not a punishment—as she has been taught—but death is what has to be.

RIBALOW: Why does Hannele kill herself?

NISSENSON: For two reasons. One is she realizes that she has totally succumbed to the lust of Schlifka. "Kill him," she cries, kill him with that stick. Secondly, the personality which is so fascinated obviously with self-degradation, self-annihilation, ultimately must destroy itself. A classic example of a perverse masochist who, because she was unloved by her father who was in love with God and won't touch her—he doesn't touch her hand; he drops the keys into her hand because she is menstruating— so all of her passion is focused upon what she sees to be a living God and she becomes, in a sense, the *Dopelganger* of Mrs. Tauber. It is the great mother and the holy prostitute. These are archetypes I am dealing with.

RIBALOW: You therefore are more or less agreeing with something that struck me as being slightly odd when I was reading the reviews. Christopher Lehmann-Haupt, in *The New York Times,* read all sorts of symbolism into *My Own Ground.*

NISSENSON: I think Chris is right.

RIBALOW: My question is: Is it his imagination or yours?

NISSENSON: No, no. One of the interesting things about this book, which is comprehended thus far, I must confess, by really a few, is that people have not grappled with it as yet.

RIBALOW: It is a difficult book.

NISSENSON: It sure is.

RIBALOW: Any reader familiar with your work and your writing finds at the outset that *My Own Ground* is so different in *milieu* and in language from your other work. In the back of the mind, there is always the realization that this man is trying to do something.

NISSENSON: Not *trying* to do something; *doing* something.

RIBALOW: I don't know who the reader is who picks up any fiction. Some do so when the reviews are good, or if they know the name of the author. But here is a novel by somebody who has not been a novelist before. I don't know what will happen with the paperback, but I am sure that it could lend itself to a garish cover and the quotations can deal with everything that will sell the book to the Harold Robbins reader.

NISSENSON: I couldn't care less. The book exists on its own; the statement is there in *all* of its complexity and *all* of its metaphysical implication and all of its power, and all of its horror and all of its beauty.

RIBALOW: You still have stories within stories. I have Stanley Kauffmann's review here in the Sunday *Times*.

NISSENSON: He didn't get a word of what I wrote. I might as well have written in Chinese.

RIBALOW: As you know, he says you are a short story writer.

NISSENSON: The idea of a movie critic trying to deal with the book is. . . .

RIBALOW: He is, or has been, a novelist, the author of *The Philanderer*.

NISSENSON: Mazel Tov! I know he has not got a literary sensibility.

RIBALOW: I read a piece in the *Saturday Review,* in the April 17, 1976, issue by Anthony Burgess on the work of Flann O'Brien. This sort of promiscuous reading brings up questions worth raising. And he says this, "Action is a great bore to most serious novelists since it tends to breed cliché. But how, without action, do you maintain narrative interest? Well, you can push it onto the margins, where it is merely heard about, or into chunks of parody, extracts from ancient heroic annals, newspaper reports, dreams. . . ."

NISSENSON: I don't believe it.

RIBALOW: He continues, "Your average best seller gives you violent action and simple language. Joyce and Flann O'Brien assault your brain with words, style, magic, madness, huge vocabularies, and unlimited invention, in other words, they are literary writers, which loads the dice against their popular acceptance."

NISSENSON: I don't know whether this has any meaning, because the carefully plotted works of, for example, Thomas Mann, in which the action is so compelling and so magnificent, it seems to me that Joyce, for all the verbal play, has a hell of a lot going on. It moves, God damn it, that book moves! To say nothing of Proust, or to say nothing of Andre Biely, who was one of the great novelists of the century, in which a bomb is ticking throughout the whole thing. Is the son going to murder his father, with the bomb in a sardine can? It seems to me that all of these fiction devices are used because there is, it seems to me, a primordial sense in all of us. It is like my child. She wants to know what happens next as we all want to know what happens next. The narrative, no matter what you do with it— you may chop up times or manipulate as Faulkner does in *The Sound and the Fury,* but you cannot produce a distinguished work—nor can I think of a truly distinguished work of fiction—that does not have a narrative drive.

RIBALOW: Let me quote Robert Alter to you. He calls you "the only genuinely religious writer in the whole American Jewish group." He explains this by saying, "Where other Jewish writers haul in forefathers by their pious beards to provide scenic effect of symbolic suggestiveness, the introduction of such figures in Nissenson's work is an act of serious self-examination." How would you respond to this observation?

NISSENSON: He's quite right. I am obsessed with the religious sensibility and with the atheistic sensibility. The metaphysical *Weltanschauung* is of primal interest to me. I *must* deal with this, again and again, because I can't help it. This is what obsesses me. I must look and try and find and work out as best I can some basis upon which I can face the universe in which I live. I am obsessed by myth. I always have been and all my work is saturated with myth. I am obsessed by the religious *Weltanschauung* because it is a fundamental and ancient human expression of one explanation of what this universe is about. It is the one, indeed, that I was given as a child by my father, which obviously is the reason that it obsesses me.

RIBALOW: What does your father do?

NISSENSON: He is now retired. He was in the dress business. A very intelligent man, deeply religious, whose obsession with religion obviously influenced me. At one time I went through a deeply mystical period, at the beginning of college continuing into my twenties, which I now understand to be a resolution of severe psychic conflicts. But I continued to be obsessed by this, because I think there is great ineffable beauty in these religious myths. Whether it is indeed the myth of Adonis, or the myth of Divine Christ, or the myth of the Jewish Creation, the myth of Jacob and Esau, who is connected in this book with Gilgamesh. Also, one of the reasons that this book is about the underworld is because it is literally a journey *into* the underworld. It is an archetypical journey, both figuratively and literally, into the underside of human experience. Therefore, it all takes place under the El. There is a scene literally in hell, in the whorehouse, when the pimp dumps shit all over the girl and all the anal and sadistic. . . .

RIBALOW: Toward the end of the book?

NISSENSON: No, about the fifth chapter.

RIBALOW: I am thinking about the climax, towards the end.

NISSENSON: Ah! Towards the end! It is an archetypical journey in the underworld, as Gilgamesh intimates. That is what interests me. These great journeys into the underworld from which we hope, by suffering them, to come up with some treasure, which is to say, some understanding.

RIBALOW: Alter predicted, back in the '60s, that "the vogue of Jewish writing, quickly exhausting its artistic possibilities, offers many indications that it may be falling into a declining phase of unwitting self-parody." Do you find any sense in that?

NISSENSON: No, I don't understand what that means. You never know what is going on in the minds of artists. There are a lot of distinguished writers around today, really first-rate writers.

RIBALOW: Whom do you have in mind?

NISSENSON: Well, Cynthia Ozick. Philip Roth, obsessed with the Jewish métier and civilization. Johanna Kaplan. There are an awful lot of people out there who are busy trying to understand this mystery of what Jewishness is all about. It happens my next book is not going to be about Jews.

RIBALOW: You are not the first Jewish writer to tell me that. You may know that Chaim Potok's first novel was not about Jews. Another writer I recently was talking to told me his next novel was not going to be about Jews, either. So that was my next question to you: Are you working on new fiction, or a novel?

NISSENSON: Yes, I have a new book in mind which is tentatively called *The Tree of Life,* in which I am going to try and deal with the metaphor of Protestant sectarianism.

RIBALOW: You are beginning to think about it?

NISSENSON: I have structured it out.

RIBALOW: I have been wanting to ask you about our Jewish writers. Leon Uris, in an interview in *Publisher's Weekly*, talking about *Trinity*, a novel he wrote about the Irish problem, said he was inordinately pleased to be classified as a Jewish writer. On the other hand, Saul Bellow, in a speech at Brandeis University, said that he, Bernard Malamud, and Philip Roth are the Hart, Schaffner, and Marx of American literature. He keeps repeating it.

NISSENSON: He's very pleased with that.

RIBALOW: When Bellow speaks in public or submits to interviews, he says, I'm not a Jewish writer, I'm not a Jewish writer, I'm not a Jewish writer." Although I understand he is now completing a nonfiction work on Jerusalem. [Published under the title of *To Jerusalem and Back.*]

NISSENSON: Yes, I do know. He is extremely fortunate insofar as the academics have, for some reason, found him and praised him to the skies. He is interesting. He knows, technically, what should be done. He does not have, so far—and it seems to me by now he should have—the wherewithal to dramatize his stuff. Our job is to dramatize. As Conrad says, to make you see.

RIBALOW: Bashevis Singer says that all he tries to do is to tell a story. He may be oversimplifying.

NISSENSON: Singer's genius is that every sentence he writes is tactile. You feel it, you see it, you smell it. It vibrates on the page. And that is what writing is all about. That's your *sole* job. If you have a vision, all to the good, wonderful! That makes you a better writer. If you have an obsession, that makes you an even better writer. As Graham Greene once said, All writers worth our attention are, in the eighteenth century use of the word, poets, which is to say they are the victims of an obsession. I think this is true. Those writers who really matter and who seem to matter, are those who are working out some private, obsessive problem that they have about their relationship between themselves and the universe. That is why it is so fascinating to study the career of any first-rate artist, because you watch the way this is dealt with over the years, the way the metaphor changes, but the same things keep reappearing. If indeed these conflicts did not exist, then I don't think you would bother writing. Art is one way in which you can work out. You can't do it in life.

A Conversation with
Isaac Bashevis Singer

This interview took place some three years before Isaac Bashevis Singer was awarded the Nobel Prize for Literature, but he already was one of the best-known writers in the world. While I comment on him and his work in the introduction to this book, I should point out that when we met formally to talk on the last day of Passover in 1976 (April 22), it was not the first time we had discussed his career, his novels and his stories. Thirteen years earlier, he allowed my daughter Reena to interview him for a high school assignment and both he and his wife Alma were invited to my daughter's wedding reception in 1970.

He was much the same man in 1976 that he was in 1964, and remains unchanged to this day.

We talked in his home on the Upper West Side in New York City, in a sunny, spacious apartment. In the living room there are bookshelves which include, of course, all the Singer titles, in various languages. I saw his books in Japanese, German, French, and the Scandinavian languages. Many are in paperbacks, especially Penguins. Since winning the Nobel Prize, his American paperbacks have proliferated and on a recent trip to England I noticed that Penguin has reissued his books in new, attractive, artistic covers.

Singer's attractive wife and her sister, Mrs. Bruno Foa, were at home when we talked and, from time to time, Mrs. Singer offered an opinion of a Singer novel or short story.

Singer, at seventy-two (his age at the time we conversed for this book), is small-boned and seems to be frail. Actually, he is sturdy. I always find him pleasant, humorous and wise, thoughtful, friendly and outgoing. I have heard that he can be caustic and is quick to disapprove of people. Once, I attended a lecture of his and he was not polite to those who asked him unintelligent questions. Clearly, he does not suffer fools gladly.

Singer speaks with wit and care. He is a good listener and he remembers each of his stories quite precisely, their phrasing and the effect that he wants them to have. He recalls last lines, reviews, and what critics say of his work. I mentioned that he appears more frequently than any other short story writer in the *New Yorker*. Gently, he corrected me. "No," he said, "Donald Barthelme is there more." He also is a scorekeeper.

On a previous visit to him—to another West Side flat—I saw that he had a few birds flying about. Alma explained that because of their schedule they no longer kept birds. It is impossible to keep birds if you are not always at home. In asking him what differences success has brought to his life—and this before the Nobel Prize—he said that now he is free to travel.

A great deal has been written about Singer. At this writing he has become almost an academic cottage industry, but he did say a number of things in the interview that follows which are worth remembering and pondering. I found it difficult to ask questions about stories that were familiar to the writer and the interviewer but perhaps not to the reader. This is why, from time to time, I found it necessary to offer a few lines of exposition about a story known to the two of us. I often assume that the reader is acquainted with the stories and novels we discuss.

RIBALOW: There are many books on you and your work. Do you know how many?

SINGER: There must be about four.

RIBALOW: Four. Irving Buchen's, the brochure by Ben Siegel, the collection by Marcia Allentuck, and Irving Malin's work, with its bibliography and chronology. Then you have your many interviews. . . .

SINGER: I've given so many interviews that I have to repeat myself.

RIBALOW: Why do you make yourself available so much?

SINGER: I will tell you why. I just haven't learned to say no. When a person asks to interview me, to say I don't want to give you an interview, I cannot say no. And then I think, "Why shouldn't I say what I think?" I make a big mistake in this.

RIBALOW: There is the interview in *Commentary* by Joel Blocker and Richard Elman.

SINGER: Yes, this is an old interview.

RIBALOW: Then there is one with Marshall Breger and Bob Barnhart in 1965 in a University of Pennsylvania magazine, which appears in Malin's collection. Do you remember it?

SINGER: No. I will tell you: A little girl came to me, an eight-year-old girl, and she said, "I want to interview you." So I sat down and spoke to her an hour and a half. Then I asked her, "What are you going to do with this?" She said, "I'm going to show it to my teacher."

RIBALOW: Harold Flender did a few interviews with you. He had a *Paris Review* interview and one in the *Intellectual Digest.*

SINGER: Yes. He was a very fine man. He's dead, you know.

RIBALOW: Yes. Then, a woman named Cyrena Pondrom published a long interview in *The Contemporary Writer* in 1968. And Elaine Gottlieb in the *Reconstructionist.* Also my daughter, Reena Sara Ribalow, as she was then, also published a *Reconstructionist* interview with you.

SINGER: If you are going to count all the interviews, there will be no time left for us.

RIBALOW: Then, of course, so many critics have written about you. There's a tremendous literature on you now.

SINGER: Act as if we were just born.

RIBALOW: I have figured out that you have one hundred and twenty stories published in your collections of short stories.

SINGER: I don't believe that. In these six volumes I have not more than six times fifteen.

RIBALOW: Let me tell you. In *A Friend of Kafka,* there are twenty-one. In *Gimpel,* twelve. . . .

SINGER: You are right. You are right.

RIBALOW: No doubt, you have a number of uncollected stories.

SINGER: No. Very few. Those that are not collected I sort of threw away.

RIBALOW: And, of course, you have all your children's books.

SINGER: I recommend that you read *A Little Boy in Search of God.* It's new and it's autobiographical.

RIBALOW: Is that a book for children?

SINGER: No. It's for grownups.

RIBALOW: From what I gather, you have a couple of unpublished novels, *Shadows By the Hudson* and *A Ship to America.*

SINGER: These novels are both unfinished and unpublished and untranslated. In other words, these are only half things.

RIBALOW: Were they published in Yiddish?

SINGER: Yes. Not in a book. Serially in the *Forward*. But I have other books, more ripe. They already have been translated but are not yet edited. Anyhow, I wait. I hope to God—if God gives me health—I will see to it that all of these little things should be edited, polished and ready for printing.

RIBALOW: What about the time that is taken from you for the dramas, like *Yentl*?

SINGER: I don't take myself seriously as a dramatist.

RIBALOW: Still, doesn't it take up your time and energy?

SINGER: Everything takes up energy.

RIBALOW: I remember that *My Father's Court* was staged.

SINGER: That was done by David Licht; he did a dramatization.

RIBALOW: And *The Mirror?*

SINGER: *The Mirror?* I rewrote it. It was played in New Haven and produced by Robert Brustein. Also, *Schlemiel the First* was played in New Haven, but I never saw it because I was then in Israel.

RIBALOW: With *Yentl*, you now have had four plays staged.

SINGER: Three-four. I don't know myself. I will tell you; I don't count my energy. I think my energy has to be used.

RIBALOW: Are all your novels and short story collections in paperback editions?

SINGER: Except for *Passions,* which is new.

RIBALOW: Into how many languages have you been translated?

SINGER: Mr. Flender, peace be with him, wrote I was translated into fifty-four languages. Actually, it is about fifteen. Those who always translate me immediately are the Japanese. They translate everything I write. Adult books, children's books. They also publish me in English, with Japanese notes. In other words, they teach the children English. . . .

RIBALOW: Through your stories.

SINGER: I once said they'll end up learning Yiddish this way. . . . Yesterday I got a letter from a Japanese writer who just translated a story of mine called "A Friend of Kafka." My impression is that the Japanese translate everything. They are *so* productive.

RIBALOW: There are a lot of writers they don't translate, I assure you.

SINGER: I don't know.

RIBALOW: Let me get to Yiddish for a moment. You are constantly asked, I know, about Yiddish, its future and your feeling about writing in a "minor" language with a small and limited readership. I won't burden you with that aspect. . . .

SINGER: No, no. Burden me, burden me. Whatever you feel like asking you can ask me.

RIBALOW: I did have in mind to ask you. . . .

SINGER: I will tell you. I once said that if I would be the only person who would speak Yiddish, I would still write in it. I'm not writing in Yiddish because I want to do Yiddish a favor. I'm writing Yiddish because I want to do myself a favor. I know that in Yiddish I will write better than in English or in Polish or in Hebrew. So because of this, I don't worry about the situation of Yiddish. If they all stopped speaking Yiddish and I still speak it, I write in it and I'm happy. But since I'm not an idealist, I do it just for my own sake.

RIBALOW: You once told an interviewer, "Though I love Yiddish, I'm not a Yiddishist."

SINGER: Exactly. What I mean by that is I don't make propaganda for Yiddish, although sometimes I do. I say to the young people, "If you would know Yiddish, you would know yourself better, you'd know your parents and grandparents better." But I'm really not the kind of a man who makes propaganda for a language. For me, Yiddish is my language. There are people in Albania and they speak Albanian. Do they care that only a million people speak Albanian? They don't mind. They are among their own people; it's their language—and it's the same with me and Yiddish.

RIBALOW: When the Albanians, or the Finns, or the Swedes write in their native language, they visualize at least a homogeneous readership, an audience. Do you have a readership in mind, too?

SINGER: Almost everything I write, I publish in the *Forward*. The *Forward* still has about 40,000 readers. The *Forward* reader may be an elderly man, but he was brought up in Poland, he knows the language, and since it is a very small newspaper, a few pages, they read all of it—including the advertisements. So I'm sure that I have at least 20,000 readers immediately. I know it, because if I make a mistake, I get 20,000 letters. I once wrote that they said *Yizkor* in the synagogue on the second day of Rosh Hashanah, which was false; they don't. So I got bags of letters every day, correcting me. They are waiting for a chance to correct me, and I know they are waiting, and I'm careful. I wouldn't say, then, that in Yiddish I have no readers. They are my *first* readers and few writers nowadays have 20,000 readers when they write. I still use the methods used in Russia or in the time of Dickens. I publish in a newspaper in a serial, so that people read it.

RIBALOW: On the subject of your popularity or lack of it in the Yiddish world, among Yiddish writers—I don't have to name some of these people. . . . I have an uncomplicated mind. I attribute the whole thing to jealousy.

SINGER: Believe me, it's a good reason. All the woes in the world and all the troubles come from jealousy. Man is the only animal who is jealous. An animal is not jealous. If a dog has eaten and he sees another dog eat, he is not jealous. If he hasn't eaten, he takes away, but he is not jealous. Men are jealous.

RIBALOW: Did you ever expect world recognition, writing in Yiddish about a vanished world?

SINGER: No, I neither expected world recognition nor Jewish recognition, or Yiddish recognition. I didn't work for recognition. When I began to write I said this was a hopeless business, I'm a hopeless man. I didn't worry too much about it. I said there were many writers like myself who wrote for minorities and I thought if I managed to make a living and I have earned enough for paper and ink, I would be satisfied. To get more than that is pure profit.

RIBALOW: Many of your Yiddish readers, like the critics, are bothered by your use of the devil, demons, and imps.

SINGER: Let them be bothered. I don't give a hoot.

RIBALOW: Are they literary symbols to you?

SINGER: They are literary symbols and I believe in them, too. I believe that there are demons. I don't know exactly the difference between a spirit and a demon, or a demon and a nymph, but I know there are powers. I will give you an example. When my wife goes away—to see her sister in Washington or wherever she goes—I leave the light burning in my bedroom because I am afraid of the demons.

RIBALOW: Of the dark?

SINGER: Of the demons! I really believe in them. Since I'm afraid of them, this means that I believe in them. They exist for me.

RIBALOW: Years ago, when I edited an anthology of American Jewish stories, you reviewed it under your pen name Warshavsky. One of the things you said about it was that a book can't be Jewish if it is written in a non-Jewish language, meaning it has to be written in Yiddish or Hebrew.

SINGER: Well, I don't feel that way any more. More Jews speak English than Yiddish, ten times as many. As far as Hebrew is concerned, since it has so many new words, it has become a secular language and it is not any longer a *Loshen Kodesh,* a holy language.

RIBALOW: I found out when I was in Israel and I listen to the radio, I have my problems with Hebrew. When I hear a lecture on Bialik, I understand it all. But when the news broadcast comes on, I'm lost. I can't understand the Hebrew.

SINGER: Neither can I. I would say they want to be like all the other nations and they have reached their goal completely. They are like other nations, except that they don't have the good luck of other nations. They have the troubles of Jews. But as far as culture is concerned, they try to be like other nations. I wish them a lot of happiness. Since the *Galut,* so to say, is bankrupt, let them have at least some joy out of life. I myself am still connected with Yiddish and with *Loshen Kodesh.* I cannot say *parnasa,* I can only say *parnuseh.* Not *tachlit,* but *vos vet zein der tachlis.* I cannot say *Shabbat,* I can only say *Shabbes....* In other words, I love them and I go to Israel, my books are translated there, my son speaks Hebrew, his children were born there and speak Hebrew. I am a Zionist. But my real love is Yiddish. Yiddish and old-fashioned *Loshen Kodesh,* which is also Yiddish.

RIBALOW: I have a number of quotations in which you refer to Yiddish. You have said, "I like to write ghost stories and nothing fits a ghost better than a dying language."

SINGER: Absolutely.

RIBALOW: You added that, "I believe not only in ghosts but in resurrection. I am sure that millions of Yiddish-speaking corpses will rise from their graves one day and their first question will be: Is there any new book in Yiddish to read? For them Yiddish will not be dead."

SINGER: True, true, I said it.

RIBALOW: Then you made the point about Hebrew, that Hebrew was considered dead for a couple of thousand years and it came alive. The same thing may happen to Yiddish.

SINGER: It may happen to Yiddish but I hope they are not going to change the Yiddish accent. In other words, they shouldn't begin to say *Shabbat.* I hope they will still say *Shabbes.* If it is going to be *Shabbat,* it will not be Yiddish any more.

RIBALOW: A critic, Eugene Goodheart, wrote in 1960 the following, "The placing of Singer with the great Yiddish masters is unfortunate. That Singer is a genuinely gifted writer is beyond dispute, but his real affinities, it seems to me, are with writers outside the Yiddish tradition. Indeed, Singer is an alien figure in his own literature." Do you agree with that?

SINGER: I am an alien figure in Yiddish literature. I am an alien figure among Jews; I am an alien figure among goyim; I am an alien figure altogether. And I made peace with it a long time ago.

RIBALOW: I'm impressed—on the basis of the reading I've been doing recently on your work—with all the references you make to your brother, Israel Joshua Singer. Of course, he was a famous writer, the author of *The Brothers Ashkenazi* and *Yoshe Kalb.* You write so differently from one another and yet you insist he was an enormous influence on you.

SINGER: I consider him my teacher and master. He taught me many things. The most important thing he taught me is to tell as many stories as possible and to give as little commentary as possible. For this rule itself, I am grateful to him to the last day of my life.

RIBALOW: Is there any truth in the feeling I get, from reading biographical and other material, that you are under the influence and—without using the word adversely—the shadow of your brother, in a way? After he died, you seemed to write so much more, and differently.

SINGER: I was never under his shadow. While he was alive, I wrote *Satan in Goray* and a number of stories. In this country I stopped writing for a number of years, six or seven years, so that takes care of that. But actually, my brother encouraged me as much as a brother can. He rejoiced when I wrote something and when I stopped writing, he was sad about it.

RIBALOW: When *Yoshe Kalb* was performed by Maurice Schwartz—it must have been the opening night—my father took me to the show. Your brother sat two rows behind us. My father introduced me to him and a little while later, my father said to me that Singer has a younger brother— meaning you—*"er vet zein besser fun em,* he'll be a better writer than I. J. Singer."

SINGER: Is that what he said?

RIBALOW: Yes.

SINGER: Only a great man can say a thing like this. Small people are always jealous.

RIBALOW: You know who is not jealous? Those who are not in competition with the writers.

SINGER: I understand it very well. I will tell you what the situation is: God has given us not too many qualities. He was stingy in every respect. He didn't give us enough eyesight, enough of the power of smell. But when it comes to egoism, He was very lavish. He gave to everybody a million times as much as he needs. So every human being, no matter how little he is, must love himself and admire himself. He cannot help it. These little writers— they have to find faults in me to strengthen their egotism.

RIBALOW: Your father, we know, was a rabbi, and you have written a great deal about him, especially in *In My Father's Court*. I assume you attended a yeshiva.

SINGER: Not really a yeshiva. It wasn't called a yeshiva. A yeshiva was in another town, where the student ate at other people's tables. This I didn't do.

RIBALOW: And you don't have a *smicha*?

SINGER: I don't have a *smicha*, but I studied in a rabbinical seminary.

RIBALOW: Are you familiar with Chaim Potok's novels, which are about Hasidim in America?

SINGER: No, really not. I looked into them, but I have no time, really, to read them. Maybe I will some day.

RIBALOW: I read somewhere that, in your restricted life, you discovered Sherlock Holmes and the stories set your imagination going. Is this true?

SINGER: Yes. Sherlock Holmes looked to me so great, so wonderful. . . .

RIBALOW: You read him in Polish?

SINGER: In Yiddish. I'm afraid to read Sherlock Holmes again, knowing I am going to be disappointed, no matter how good it is. It can't be that good. It sounded to me like heavenly music.

RIBALOW: I understand you don't read much current fiction and I read that you believe no one around compares with the classic Russians.

SINGER: Yes, the French also.

RIBALOW: What kind of mail do you get?

SINGER: People who say to me, I've never written a letter to a writer. This is the first so-called fan letter which I am writing.

RIBALOW: Where do the letters come from?

SINGER: From England, from Israel, from the United States—all sorts of places.

RIBALOW: I am reminded of Somerset Maugham in a quote of yours. You know, he constantly wrote that his function was to entertain. Here is something you told one of your interviewers, Cyrena Pondrom, "The basic function of literature, as far as I can say, is to entertain the spirit in a very big way—it's basically an entertainment and it has only qualities of entertainment—which means, if you are not entertained while you read a book, there is no other reward for you."

SINGER: Absolutely.

RIBALOW: But the reader gets more than just entertainment from you.

SINGER: He certainly gets more than entertainment. But entertainment is the minimum. *This* it certainly has to be. If it has all the other qualities, but no entertainment, it's worthless. Let's say, if you go to a French theater, you are learning French at the same time, and you are entertained, and at the same time you meet a nice girl there and you make acquaintance and you go to a restaurant—all these things are good. But if you are not entertained, all the other qualities don't count. In other words, whatever we do in life. . . . This time I will speak a little longer. We have something to get out of it. You know this Yiddish joke: When you ask a Galitzianer what time it is, he says, I know, but what will I get out of it if I tell you? When you read a book you have to have some pleasure and if you don't get any pleasure, there is no reason to read fiction, unless you are a critic and you make a living out of it. Then you can read anything, but you are not considered a reader. It's not enough for a novel to tell the truth. If you tell the truth in such a way that the reader has no enjoyment, it doesn't lift up the spirit, nobody is looking. In science, if a scientist will come along and say that "next month a comet will fall down and destroy the earth," you have to accept it, whether you like it or not. It's science; it's the truth. In fiction, you don't have to accept anything. If you don't enjoy it, you can put away the book and say, "I don't give a hoot about it." And this is something which in a great amnesia the writers have forgotten. They are so eager to tell what they call the truth, they are so eager to express themselves, to find their identity, that they forget that there is such a thing as a reader. He also has to get something out of it. But thank God, I never forget the reader. I will not write ten pages when I know the reader will be bored after the second page. I will finish a chapter knowing I can give him so much in this chapter. This is what the masters of the nineteenth century never forgot. When you read *Anna Karenina,* you will see that Tolstoy has little chapters, four-page chapters, three-and-a-half-page chapters, never a chapter of fifty pages, because he knew that the reader doesn't want such big chapters. They adjusted themselves to the readers. They were kind people. And just as when you meet a man and if you are a person of ethics, you will not try to bore him to death, but will try to be nice to him and to entertain him and to make him feel good. This is the way the writers of the nineteenth century felt. They felt that the reader is a human being, while the modern writer sits down to find his identity and writes about it for fifty pages, boring the reader to death, doesn't give a hoot about another human being. He is not ethical and this is the reason he is not aesthetical.

RIBALOW: But also, of course, there is entertainment and entertainment.

SINGER: I would say so. A great writer entertains great readers. A small writer entertains small readers. A cheap writer entertains cheap readers. As long as he entertains someone, he is a writer. If he entertains no one, he is nothing.

RIBALOW: You have certain stories, without being overly complimentary, that remain in the mind for years.

SINGER: Thank God.

RIBALOW: Yet you say you are "entertaining" your readers. It has to be more than that.

SINGER: I say that entertainment is the minimum.

RIBALOW: All right. A great deal has been written and said about your belief in the supernatural, except that you say it is all part of nature and we call "supernatural" that which we don't know or understand.

SINGER: Of course, of course. If they exist, they are a part of creation not just something "supercreation." As a matter of fact, before people knew about electricity, if a man took off his garment at night and he saw sparks, he was convinced those sparks were something supernatural. He didn't know what they were, but when he learned, he got a name for it called "static electricity" or whatever it is called, and he knows it is a part of nature. If the demons do exist, they are a part of nature. Also, there are millions of other parts of nature of which we have no inkling and we may never have an inkling. No matter how much we study nature, nature has such a way of concealing itself, that we only see a small part of it.

RIBALOW: You seem to object to being called a prolific writer. You know, of course, the young American writer Joyce Carol Oates.

SINGER: Yes, she is very prolific. I will tell you the difference. I have lived over seventy years and I have published thirteen books.

RIBALOW: You have published more than thirteen books.

SINGER: No, except for children's books, the little stories, which really don't count. So for seventy years, thirteen books is not prolific. It is true that these thirteen books were published in a short period of time. The reason for this is that they began to translate my books when I was already in my late forties. Oates has already written twenty books and she is only thirty-two or thirty-three. You cannot compare us. When she will be my age, if she continues like this, she will probably have written a hundred books. Even this is not an accusation. If these books are good, it's not anybody's business. I don't accuse her or defend her. Whether I would accuse her or defend her would depend on the book itself and not on how many she has written. If you want to have twenty children, but if these twenty children are good children, I have no right to accuse you of anything. Twenty good children are better than one bad child.

RIBALOW: In a very interesting short piece I read about you by your nephew Maurice Carr, he makes the point that you have told him that you get up, put on your robe—and you write. Do you have any set working hours? Do you isolate writing hours each day?

SINGER: The best time is after breakfast, between breakfast and lunch.

RIBALOW: Carr also reports, or quotes you, to the effect that you have advised him, "Treat yourself as you would a musical instrument and learn to play yourself."

SINGER: I never said this. It's not in my character. I'll tell you, I never speak about using a musical instrument. I am so far from music, I know so little about it, that I would never use this kind of phrase.

RIBALOW: Do you write from outlines?

SINGER: I work always from a plan. I must have a plot, a story, or I'm not going to write. I *must* have a story.

RIBALOW: You don't have journals from which you draw, do you?

SINGER: Yes, I have notebooks. Sometimes I forget to look into them. I lose them. I forget them on trains. But I keep on scribbling ideas all the time.

RIBALOW: I notice that in book after book, you seem to have different translators. How do you work with translators?

SINGER: Actually, lately I do the translation myself, because most of my translators don't know Yiddish, except for my nephew Joseph Singer. I do the rough translation and—I will tell you the truth—I have learned so much that they are no longer rough. After they translate, I do the polishing myself.

RIBALOW: How do you account, not only for your own acceptance, but that of so many Jewish writers in recent times? Ludwig Lewisohn and Maurice Samuel—they were labeled as Jewish writers, placed into an ethnic group. They were accepted by the Jews, but when general literary histories were written, they were omitted.

SINGER: I will tell you. Ludwig Lewisohn was not omitted. He was accepted.

RIBALOW: In part. He was accepted before he wrote fiction. When he started to write "Jewish" fiction, and autobiographical works about himself as a Jew, he was called an eccentric and was put aside.

SINGER: Well, Lewisohn was a writer. The others are the so-called "Jewish writers."

RIBALOW: Are you saying now that there is an acceptance of Jewish writers because today they are better writers?

SINGER: I would say the public accepts the so-called better writers now. Most of them are not really so good, but they are not worse than the others.

RIBALOW: In your *Paris Review* interview with Flender, you have a line that surprised me, "I don't think that a fiction writer who sits down to write a novel to make a better world can achieve anything."

SINGER: Absolutely not. If you sit down with this idea that you are sort of entertaining the reader, or lifting up his spirit, and are going to accomplish something by it, you have already missed your goal. If at the same time an entertainer wants to create a revolution, or whatever he wants to create, he creates nothing. If you sit down and want to write a good novel and this novel happens to disturb the minds of people, the writer may at least create the desire for a better world. In Soviet Russia, where the writer sits down to write to serve the revolution, or if you want to serve the counter-revolution, or if you want to serve Zionism, or Socialism or any other "ism," you have already failed.

RIBALOW: Yet of Harriet Beecher Stowe, who wrote *Uncle Tom's Cabin*, Lincoln once said, when he met her, "So you're the little lady who made the Civil War."

SINGER: It's not true at all. It's not such a good book, either.

RIBALOW: That's the point. *Exodus* wasn't a good novel, but it moved and stirred people.

SINGER: Listen! A few brochures created Communism. The *Judenstaat,* helped create modern Zionism. In other words, doing things is one thing and writing well is another.

RIBALOW: I discovered, to my surprise, that you once had a writing block. Is it because you were a foreigner in this country and adjusting to it?

SINGER: Because I was a foreigner in this country, yes. Also, I couldn't make a living and I felt that Yiddish is already going down. I became pessimistic. Also, I did something that I should not have done, which was silly. I tried to write an American novel. I thought, I am already a year or two in America, let me write it from the point of view of a foreigner. It took me years and nothing was accomplished. I learned then that you have to be in a country at least thirty years to write about this country. Even so, now I only write about Yiddish-speaking people who come from Poland to America. I don't write about people born in this country.

RIBALOW: You have written under more than one name, including Warshavsky. Why do you do this?

SINGER: I also wrote under the name of Segal, but this was only journalism. Warshavsky also wrote mostly journalism, but a number of novels about which I was not sure at the beginning were written under the Warshavsky name. *Enemies, A Love Story* I wrote under Warshavsky. *In My Father's Court* I also wrote under the name of Warshavsky.

RIBALOW: You told Elaine Gottlieb in 1959 that you were going to write a book on *The Cabala and Modern Man.* Did you ever get around to it?

SINGER: Not a book, but I wrote a speech on "The Cabala and Modern Man," which I made in many cities.

RIBALOW: You left Poland and came to the United States in 1935, before the Nazi Holocaust. What prompted you to leave at that early point? Was it because your brother was here?

SINGER: First of all, my brother was here and then the fear of the Nazis.

RIBALOW: That's why I asked the question, because a lot of Jews were not that prescient.

SINGER: I knew one man, a publisher, who came to this country in 1939, in the summer, and in July he said he was going back to Poland. I asked, "Why are you going back to Poland?" He said, "I have to publish a book of poetry, Yiddish poetry. I promised the author it will come out in September." So he went to his death.

RIBALOW: To publish a book of poetry.

SINGER: Some people are so optimistic and I was so pessimistic, that when I was supposed to go to America in April 1935, my travel agent called me and said, "The *Normandie* is going to have its maiden voyage and if you wait two weeks you can go on the *Normandie* and you will see all the important people. I was afraid to wait two weeks because I thought Hitler might march in during that period.

RIBALOW: This was 1935?

SINGER: Yes, 1935. I have enough imagination to see what terrible things might have happened. This man, the publisher, came in 1939 and went back in August!

RIBALOW: I understand you began your journalistic career in Poland by interviewing Yiddish writers.

SINGER: Yes, I was an interviewer. I interviewed many writers—Hillel Zeitlin and a lot of American writers like Moshe Nadir, Menachem Boraisha.

RIBALOW: Philip Toynbee wrote in 1967, when he reviewed *The Manor,* "Until I read this book, Isaac Bashevis Singer was no more than a name to me. . . . He had seemed—vaguely—the absolute, nonnational, nontemporal Jewish writer—the *supremely* Jewish writer." The reason I quote this is that there are so many people saying that you are a Jewish writer and others saying you are not a Jewish writer. You have written on what it takes to be a Jewish writer and your conditions were so severe that on that basis there are very few who are Jewish writers.

SINGER: There are very few writers.

RIBALOW: You have to start with that. You have to start with talent.

SINGER: And if he has talent, he is already more than a Jewish writer.

RIBALOW: You said to Rochelle Girson of the *Saturday Review* in 1962. . . .

SINGER: Yes, yes. I remember her.

RIBALOW: She made the point that you switched from Hebrew to Yiddish because, you said, Yiddish is one of the world's richest languages because the idioms of many other languages have accreted to it.

SINGER: Exactly. It's rich. When I began to write, I began in Hebrew, which was not yet a living language. I had to look up the dictionary to see how to say "saltshaker" in Hebrew. Since my heroes spoke Yiddish, there was no sense in making them speak Hebrew. It would have been translation, not writing.

RIBALOW: In 1965, in *Jewish Heritage,* you are quoted as having said, "If sex and murder were to be removed from literature, there would be little literature left."

SINGER: Absolutely. Especially sex.

RIBALOW: Then you added that Sholom Aleichem was "a good middle-class man" and knew little of the darker aspects of life and sex and the same was true of Bialik. But Sholem Asch, Zalman Schneour were different and then you were explaining this seeming shock of realizing that sex exists didn't begin in Yiddish literature with you.

SINGER: Yes, it did not. Take away love and sex and there is no literature. Actually, every novel—a novel in a European language is called a *roman,* which means a love story—without a love story there is no story. In a short story you can, once in a while, write a story without love. But a novel without love is impossible. And I want you to know that people tried. They tried novels about factories, about Socialism, about Communism. All this came to naught. There must be a love story. There is no way out; we have to do it.

RIBALOW: At the same time, you don't use four-letter words.

SINGER: Never. They are not necessary at all. There is also a good reason not to use them. These words are created for the power of shock. If you use them once, let's say, if a gentleman and a lady had made acquaintance and had gone through the process of love diplomacy and they finally go to bed and if a man uses this word, it has a shock power that it can do a lot for him. But if you use it all the time, it becomes nothing. It's like taking drugs. The more you take, the less you feel them.

RIBALOW: Again, in terms of your various successes. Alden Whitman wrote in the *New York Times* in 1970 in an interview with you in which you said, "The only difference that success has made for me is that I work more."

SINGER: How true!

RIBALOW: "and that I don't have this fear, which I had for many years, that I will starve."

SINGER: This is true, although the way inflation works today, I am getting this fear again.

RIBALOW: Let's talk for a bit about *The Magician of Lublin,* which is looked upon by most critics and readers as a major novel.

SINGER: I'm glad.

RIBALOW: Do you have any favorites among your books? I'll start by saying I like *The Slave* best.

SINGER: I would say that *The Slave* and *The Magician of Lublin* are two short novels which I myself like. [At this point, Mrs. Singer, working in the kitchen, said "*The Slave* is a masterpiece."]

RIBALOW: The first half of *The Slave* is remarkably evocative. It shows how a man is isolated and, through the power of his mind, retains everything that is important to him.

SINGER: As I say, I like *The Slave* and *The Magician of Lublin*. I would not have published them if I would not have liked them.

RIBALOW: Yasha Mazur is the magician. He is forty and married to a barren wife. He performs as a magician in many Polish cities and has mistresses in all of them. One, you will recall, is Zeftel, whose husband is a gangster. So Yasha meets gangsters and becomes an unsuccessful thief. Later, he becomes a fugitive and realizes a kind of fulfillment in a synagogue among ancient Jews observing ancient rituals. You have a quotation somewhere in *The Magician of Lublin* that goes like this, "The prayer house was like a barracks. There God's soldiers were mustered."

SINGER: I make Yasha the hero, a saintly person.

RIBALOW: I am reminded that some critics remark they are unhappy with the endings of some of your books. *The Slave*, to me, has a very moving, touching ending.

SINGER: Oh, sure.

RIBALOW: Yet it is so different from the way the book began, that some would call it sentimentalized, or symbolic.

SINGER: No writer really listens to what other people will say. The moment you publish, they can say anything.

RIBALOW: What about "Gimpel the Fool," the short story that seemed to be so important in projecting you into a certain kind of literary world, different from the one you came from?

SINGER: One never knows why one story is more successful than the other. There really is no sense contemplating it. Sometimes a story touches almost everybody, which means that it doesn't have much individuality.

RIBALOW: That's *one* interpretation. The phrase that "the world is entirely an imaginary world, but it is only once removed from the true world," is something that can touch a lot of people.

SINGER: Yes, it can. It can.

RIBALOW: It is a memorable tale of this poor man married to an unfaithful shrew who tells him, on her deathbed, that none of her six children are his. He is shocked and becomes a wanderer over the face of the earth. The end is especially vivid. When Gimpel is ready to die, he says, "When the time comes I will go joyfully. Whatever may be there, it will be real, without complication. . . ."

SINGER: Well, if you defend it, I am not going to quarrel with you.

RIBALOW: ". . . without ridicule, without deception. God be praised; there even Gimpel cannot be deceived."

SINGER: Many feel that since every man is a potential Gimpel, it has touched so many.

RIBALOW: And it is such a *short* story to say so much.

SINGER: I would say this is the explanation, because every man feels in his heart, "Is my wife true to me?" It touches a general feeling. But I have stories that touch not many men, but a few men, and I like them just as much. It is not really my intention to entertain everybody. For me it is enough if I entertain somebody.

RIBALOW: With each given story?

SINGER: Exactly.

RIBALOW: I think of "The Gentleman from Cracow" as a great story.

SINGER: Thank you. You are kind to say so.

RIBALOW: For those who don't know it, let me read my few notes on it. It takes place in Frampol, a poverty-stricken town. A stranger comes with unlimited funds and is eager to pass out his money. Gradually, the stranger persuades the townsfolk to reject their belief in God. He asks for a bride and has his choice of Frompol girls. The people cavort, throw money around, shed their inhibitions and participate in an orgy. The "Gentleman" is the chief of the devils and the bride is also a devil. He burns the town. Frampol is not only poor—now it has been destroyed as well. It could make a fine. . . .

SINGER: A movie.

RIBALOW: Or an opera.

SINGER: Many of my works can be made into movies or operas.

RIBALOW: "The Mirror" was made into a play and that was such a brief, condensed story. An imp persuades a vain, beautiful woman to come to Hell.

SINGER: "The Mirror" I made myself. I dramatized it myself. I added many facts. But as I told you, as a playwright I consider myself a sheer beginner. An old beginner.

RIBALOW: A word or two about your prose. Every once in a while, the prose becomes remarkably vivid. Some of the time it serves the purpose of carrying forward the narrative. In "Shidda and Kuziba," you have uncommon images, which I should like to point up—and to ask if they are yours or the translator's. Shidda's body "was made of cobwebs. . . ."

SINGER: This is mine ... *shpinveh*—I wrote it.

RIBALOW: "Her hair reached to her anklebones; her feet were like those of a chicken. ..."

SINGER: It's all in the Yiddish.

RIBALOW: "And she had the wings of a bat." "Her son resembled his mother," but had "donkey ears and wax horns." These are fascinating images.

SINGER: Yes, they should be. If they are not vivid, they are no good.

RIBALOW: Then you put into the mouth of one of them what seems pessimism or cynicism of a kind, when Kuziba asks his mother, "What are human beings?" She says, "They're the waste of creation, offal; where sin is brewed in a kettle, mankind is the foam. Man is the mistake of God."

SINGER: "Foam" is not good; it should have been "the scum."

RIBALOW: "Man is the mistake of God." It's a dark view of life.

SINGER: I can understand that Shiddah should feel so. That I sometimes also feel so? This is my trouble.

RIBALOW: In "The Black Wedding," I. ...

SINGER: That's a story about insanity.

RIBALOW: About madness. The girl sees everything as though it were reality. Then you realize, at the end, that it is just images of the insane. The girl marries a rabbi and a moment after the ceremony, she sees her brides-maids and husband as devils.

SINGER: She sees what her mind wants to see.

RIBALOW: And "The Destruction of Kreshev." There, too, we have a story of violence.

SINGER: It is also a story of homosexuality, because the husband actually gives his wife to the coachman. Directly.

RIBALOW: And then she hangs herself. First she is emotionally and bodily enraptured by her husband, who talks her into committing adultery.

SINGER: Yes.

RIBALOW: Yet her husband divorces her, because of the adultery. Why?

SINGER: Because he repents. According to the law, he is not allowed to live with her any longer.

RIBALOW: These stories I'm talking about come from different collections, but it really makes no difference. "The Last Demon" is actually a very sympathetic "person."

SINGER: Yes, he sits there in an attic and reads an old Yiddish book.

RIBALOW: He says, "I, a demon, bear witness that there are no more demons left." I don't know if he means there are no more demons or no more *Jewish* demons.

SINGER: There are no more *Jewish* demons left in Poland.

RIBALOW: Then he continues, "Why demons, when man himself is a demon?"

SINGER: Ah, yes.

RIBALOW: Then he reflects, "I am a Jew, what else, a gentile?" I must say, a lot of readers don't pay enough attention to the humor in much of your work. There is a great deal of humor.

SINGER: Let me tell you. What I write is not really for the average reader. The average reader also finds something. It's for a reader who really understands, has an idea about Jewishness and about culture and literature. I say that every writer must entertain someone. It's my ambition to entertain the intellectual, the person who senses and knows. If the simple reader also gets something out of it, I'm happy.

RIBALOW: In a story ostensibly about demons, the demon says, "I've heard that there are gentile demons, but I don't know any nor do I wish to know them." That's funny, and yet it is within the context of a nonhumorous story. Then the same demon says, "I've seen it all, the destruction of Tishevitz, the destruction of Poland." The Holocaust is reflected in so many ways in so many stories. And then, "The Messiah does not come. To whom should he come?. . . . There is no further need for demons. We have been annihilated. I am the last, a refugee." Even the demons themselves, in a sense, are being annihilated.

SINGER: Because the demons are also human beings, of course.

RIBALOW: You don't know this, because we don't see each other that often. I'm busy defending you all the time—not that you need defense—but I do hear criticisms and I'm explaining your work. Take "Blood"—that's the story people don't understand.

SINGER: People criticize it. This is a story of sadism.

RIBALOW: Your people become animals.

SINGER: Sure.

RIBALOW: But I've heard readers remark on the story about Risha, who betrays her scholarly husband and takes a shochet as a lover. They insist there never was a shochet who killed animals in order to obtain sexual satisfaction—as this shochet does to arouse Risha.

SINGER: How does the reader know there never was a shochet like this? Do you know that there is a story in Jewish life where a shochet slaughtered a rabbi? Believe it or not, it happened in Poland.

RIBALOW: *Slaughtered,* not just killed?

SINGER: Slaughtered. He was angry with the rabbi. He killed him, but. . . .

RIBALOW: The ritualistic way, the way a shochet kills a chicken.

SINGER: Yes. People are so sure that it never happened. How do they know that it never happened? There isn't a thing yet which hasn't happened.

RIBALOW: In "Blood" you also write, "The Cabalists know that the passion for blood and the passion for flesh have the same origin. And this is the reason 'Thou Shalt Not Kill' is followed by 'Thou Shalt Not Commit Adultery.'"

SINGER: I *say* something here.

RIBALOW: Do you think this is your most controversial story?

SINGER: I don't really care whether it is controversial or not. It was highly praised. One of the people who praised it highly is an English critic—I have forgotten his name.

RIBALOW: Ted Hughes?

SINGER: No, not Ted Hughes; another one, who writes criticism and is also a short story writer.

RIBALOW: V. S. Pritchett?

SINGER: Pritchett!

RIBALOW: "Yentl the Yeshiva Bochur." . . .

SINGER: It became a play.

RIBALOW: Yes, but when it was first published as a short story, I remember how intrigued I was with it and, as I remember, Stanley Edgar Hyman said some very nice things about it.

SINGER: Yes.

RIBALOW: Irving Malin, who has a book about you, talks about the "open" novel and the "closed" novel. He categorizes them. The "open" novels are the chronicles, *The Family Moskat, The Manor, The Estate.* The "closed" novels include *Satan in Goray, The Slave,* and *The Magician of Lublin.*

SINGER: It's as good a name as any.

RIBALOW: You don't pay any attention to these labels?

SINGER: It never occurred to me that one is "open" and one is "closed."

RIBALOW: Was *The Manor* written as early as the 1930s?

SINGER: No, later. It was written in the 1950s.

RIBALOW: In that novel you deal with the whole gamut of Jewish experience. It is the story of Calman Jacoby and his children, from the 1860s to the 1880s and deals with the conflicts of worlds and generations, assimilation, Socialism, Zionism, the breakdown of Jewish life. Philip Toynbee, a critic and the son of Arnold Toynbee, had written about it and called it a "cool" book. I'm not sure why he said that.

SINGER: I will tell you why he called it "cool." Because Ted Hughes said. . . .

RIBALOW: Oh, yes. He said you were a "blazing" writer.

SINGER: Right, right.

RIBALOW: Toynbee added that there was little attempt to get into the characters. Yet Robert Alter has written that you never sentimentalize and that most marriages end in betrayal, divorce, or lovelessness. Saul Maloff calls you "Balzacian." Every critic has his own comparison to make. *The Estate,* of course, is the same book.

SINGER: The same book.

RIBALOW: It traces the decline of the family and all its misfortunes. Calman moves beyond the ghetto. A daughter marries a wild, Christian count, and another daughter marries a Hasid who turns to science.

SINGER: Yes, it's a continuation, the same book.

RIBALOW: In *The Seance*, I'd like to talk a moment about "The Slaughterer," I guess it is called "The Shochet" in Yiddish. Yoineh Meir hates to kill animals yet is fated to be a shochet. He is divided in his thoughts between the conviction that he has been ordained by God to do this job and his compassion for the creatures he kills. He hates his work, himself and, finally, God.

SINGER: This was the first story of mine that the *New Yorker* ever published.

RIBALOW: Did they have others to choose from?

SINGER: No, no. My agent, Lila Karpf, said to me, "I sent a story to the *New Yorker.*" I said, "What story?" She said, "'The Slaughterer.'" I said, "If there is a story which you shouldn't have sent them, this is it. The *New Yorker* would never publish it."

RIBALOW: You were a poor prophet.

SINGER: I was a poor prophet, yes, which I often am.

RIBALOW: This reminds me of an actual case.

SINGER: This is also an actual case, my dear man.

RIBALOW: I'm talking of another subject. There is a novelist named Henry Roth, who wrote. . . .

SINGER: I know, *Call It Sleep.*

RIBALOW: I had a major role in its revival, in 1960, after it had gone out of print twenty-five years earlier.

SINGER: Really, really?

RIBALOW: Roth wrote the book when he was twenty-seven years old and it was published late in 1934. Roth later went to Maine. When I met him in Maine, he was a quiet little man, a fowl farmer. He earned his living in three ways. He did some tutoring in mathematics and Latin, his wife taught music in a local public school, and he raised ducks.

SINGER: Ducks!

RIBALOW: Yes, but he made fifty cents a pound for plucking duck feathers, because when you kill a duck, there is so much blood from the duck that the local duck farmers didn't have the stomach for the job.

SINGER: So he did it? Oh My God!

RIBALOW: He did it. So he was the little Jewish fellow from the East Side, who became the shochet, which the others didn't have the heart to do.

SINGER: I'm surprised. I wouldn't kill at all. I am a vegetarian already for fourteen years. I wouldn't kill an animal if you would give me all the money in the world.

RIBALOW: Yes, I know. . . . To another subject. Was *Satan in Goray* your first novel. When was it written?

SINGER: Yes, it was my first novel. I wrote it when I was about twenty-eight, in Poland.

RIBALOW: It was published late in the United States. 1958?

SINGER: Yes.

RIBALOW: There are those who believe that it is the best book you have written.

SINGER: It's possible.

RIBALOW: Many of the themes and patterns of your later work are here, too. Orgies, people going mad.

SINGER: Yes, everything is already there. It foretold the character of my writing.

RIBALOW: It foreshadowed so many of the elements of your writing. It's the story of a false messiah and the Chmielnicki massacres in 1648, but you manage to convey the sense of religious frenzy you bring to other books and stories.

SINGER: Yes.

RIBALOW: On children's books. I have a few of them and have read them with pleasure. In my files I have an article of yours from the *New York Times* of 1969 on the subject. I have an interesting quotation from it. Here it is, "I have convinced myself that while adult literature, especially fiction, is deteriorating, the literature for children is gaining in quality and stature." What children's literature have you read apart from what you have written?

SINGER: I can't say because I can't quote any special book, but let me tell you; children are the best readers. An adult will read a book that is written by a great authority, although the book is no good. He comes to it with a prejudice. A child doesn't have this prejudice. If the book doesn't please him, he throws it away. A grownup will read a book because a famous critic praised it. A child doesn't give a hoot about critics. A grownup will read a book because it was advertised in a big way. A child doesn't care about advertisements. A child is an independent reader. This is the reason I love children. I write for children.

RIBALOW: You have written that "No writer can bribe his way to the child's attention with false originality, literary pun, and puzzles. . . .

SINGER: Exactly! Exactly! If the child doesn't like it, he spits on it.

RIBALOW: You added, "I came to the child because I see in him a last refuge from a literature gone berserk and ready for suicide." What do you mean by "a literature gone berserk"?

SINGER: What I mean is that all this modernism, all this so-called false avant-gardism that people write so that you don't know what they are talking about—they talk nonsense or they talk ugly words.

RIBALOW: I am reminded of the complaint one critic had about Somerset Maugham. All he can do, the critic said, was to tell a story.

SINGER: How difficult it is! Ab Cahan said about one writer, "He is a peculiar talent. You cannot read him." There are many such peculiar talents in our day.

RIBALOW: Let's talk about *The Slave,* which is so imaginative a book. The whole concept, how did you get it?

SINGER: Don't ask me how I got it. All I can say is. . . .

RIBALOW: I didn't ask you this question about anything else, but about this I am most curious.

SINGER: For years I wanted to write this story. I found my notebooks and in one of them I found this line, "Jacob is being converted." You know, I played with all kinds of ideas. You don't come straight to the idea. Slowly, slowly there is a way of selection and of evolution in a novel. You make many mistakes, or you intend to make mistakes, but they are eliminated by self-criticism. Before I made these notes, before I wrote it, I was looking to see how the story should develop. So for a moment it occurred to me that maybe Jacob should become so embittered with the Jews and so in love with Wanda that he should convert. After a while, I decided, no, it should be the reverse: Wanda should convert. This shows me that a writer, like everyone else, can make the right decision after you go through scores of possibilities of bad decisions.

RIBALOW: Selectively.

SINGER: Selectively, exactly. Sometimes it comes straight and sometimes it doesn't.

RIBALOW: For those who are unfamiliar with it, *The Slave* is about a Jew named Jacob, whose family is killed by the Cossacks and he is enslaved. Wanda, his master's daughter, falls in love with him while he manages to keep his Jewish faith in a remarkable act of will and strength of memory of the Jewish calendar and Jewish rituals. She converts and becomes Sarah. It is a moving tale.

SINGER: Thank you.

RIBALOW: You have a story called "Three Encounters," in which the first segment is so familiar to me now because you talk of your own life—being a proofreader, working in a literary *milieu* and then it leads into this woman whom, you recall, you say to her, "You are a pretty young woman, why are you stuck here?" She comes to see you a few times and then *she* is converted.

SINGER: In her case, this was right.

RIBALOW: There, too—whether it is imaginary I have no way of telling and it's not important—but *The Slave*, it seems to me, is a phenomenally imaginative achievement.

SINGER: Thank you. But this is an entire novel and "Three Encounters" is a short story.

RIBALOW: Still about *The Slave*. Jean Stafford, a well-known novelist herself, wrote about it in the *New Republic* and said of you, "He is a spellbinder as clever as Sheherazade." To jump a bit: May I ask you how did Ted Hughes come to write about you at such length in the *New York Review of Books?*

SINGER: I don't know. He read my work and liked it. I never met him. There are people who, when they read something and like it, praise the author all the way. Others are jealous and stingy.

RIBALOW: Hughes, in writing about *The Slave* in 1965 says, "In this book one of Singer's deep themes comes right to the surface. Singer implies . . . that there is an occult equivalence between a man's relationship to the women in his life and his relationship to his own soul—and so to God."

SINGER: He's right.

RIBALOW: It was also Hughes who called it "a burningly radiant, intensely beautiful book. But when people make complaints about sexuality, he is going that step further from the woman, to the soul, to God."

SINGER: He is a man who understands things. More than this, he is a man with great intuition.

RIBALOW: Irving Howe, in writing about *The Magician of Lublin,* says of you, "He writes in Yiddish but is often quite apart from the Yiddish tradition."

SINGER: I am. I am.

RIBALOW: The reason I mention it is that others strongly disagree. Ben Siegel is a literary critic who wrote a brochure on your work. Prior to that, in *Critique* in 1963, he wrote, "Singer's knowledge of the Jewish psyche and tradition is deep, certain, indeed ancestral."

SINGER: I am very much rooted in the Jewish tradition, but not in the Yiddish tradition, which is sentimental, Socialistic, and not really my way of thinking.

RIBALOW: Baruch Hochman, writing on you in *Midstream,* observed that "Singer works, for all his unconventionality, as a Jewish writer."

SINGER: That is what I am. I call myself a Yiddish writer also, but I am not in the Yiddish tradition.

RIBALOW: You once said to Brian Glanville, an English Jew, who writes on sports as well as novels and literary criticism, "It's true that in being a Jewish writer you limit yourself. . . . In a way I feel that to be a Yiddish writer is to be isolated in a very terrible way from the world of literature."

SINGER: It is true that in the beginning I felt isolated, but just the same I made peace with it and when I got a little recognition, as I told you before, I considered it a pure miracle, or a bonus. Naturally, if you write in Yiddish and no one translates you, you speak to a small audience, which is getting older.

RIBALOW: Now *In My Father's Court* there are forty-nine sketches; there must have been hundreds you didn't include.

SINGER: No, no. There were about sixty. Not all of them were used. But four of them were included in *The Isaac Bashevis Singer Reader.* These four didn't appear in the earlier book.

RIBALOW: There are many stories in your other collections that would easily have fitted into *In My Father's Court.*

SINGER: Sure. Since they are autobiographical, of course.

RIBALOW: So it's hard to tell where the fiction begins or ends.

SINGER: No. *In My Father's Court* is *completely* autobiographical.

RIBALOW: Completely? You didn't make up any of it?

SINGER: I don't guarantee that the dialogue is completely so, but every story is a true story.

RIBALOW: In a chapter on *The Magician of Lublin,* Buchen, in his book on your work, speculated that "Yasha's conversion is like his own situation as a Jewish writer,"—meaning you—"the temptation to turn away from Jewish materials for the wider. . . ." But you have concluded that the Jewish writer would be crippled or impotent if he pulled himself away from his own roots. How true is all this?

SINGER: Of course a real writer must be rooted in his environment. If he is not, he is finished. There isn't such a thing as a cosmopolitan writer. There may be perhaps a cosmopolitan painter. But the writer must belong somewhere. He may quarrel with his environment, but he cannot really tear himself out of it.

RIBALOW: Do you prefer the short stories or the novels?

SINGER: In a way, I like the short story because you can plan it better. In a novel, no matter how many plans you make, after a while the novel is stronger than all your plans. It has its own life. In a short story, the writer can still control the story. He can still make it the way he wants it to be.

RIBALOW: In the novels, the people take over.

SINGER: The people take over? The *action* takes over.

RIBALOW: Without getting into your vegetarianism, I have a note here in relation to a story you wrote. You are a vegetarian, for among other reasons that you are against the killing of animals. In this story, "The Parrot," a creature says, "If your human ears could hear our weeping, you would throw away all your slaughtering knives."

SINGER: Yes, yes. For fourteen years I have been a vegetarian and I have never regretted it for a second. I think this is, in a way, the greatest accomplishment of my life.

RIBALOW: What about your wife?

SINGER: No, she is not a vegetarian. But she loves animals.

RIBALOW: There is a sentence that caught my attention in "Sabbath in Portugal" in *Passions.* Let me read it, "Their wives with dyed hair and heavily made up faces, smoked cigarettes, dealt cards, laughed and chattered all at once. . . . The men were studying the financial pages of the *International Herald Tribune.*" Then you say, "Yes, these are my people, I said to myself. If the Messiah is to come, he will have to come to them because there are no others." This is in line with my earlier observation that your stories are shot through with humor. But there is more than humor in this passage.

SINGER: Not everybody understands it or feels it.

RIBALOW: In your introductory comment to *Passions,* you remark that "clarity remains the ambition of this writer."

SINGER: I don't believe in all this talking which no one understands, whether they call it symbolism or avant-garde. First of all, if you want to communicate, you have to communicate.

RIBALOW: In your recent books you have introduced a short page of explanation. For example, in *Passions,* before you present your stories, you declare, "These people are living right now. In literature, as in our own dreams, death does not exist." Why do you feel the necessity for having any kind of an explanation before you get into the eighteen or twenty stories in the book?

SINGER: I would say that somehow the publisher demands it from me. I don't know myself why I do it.

RIBALOW: I see. Then you write, "I deal with unique characters in unique circumstances, a group of people who are still a riddle to the world and often to themselves." It is clear enough from the tales themselves.

SINGER: One could do without it but it doesn't matter. A few lines will not do any damage.

RIBALOW: Have you written many stories about Miami Beach and its Jews?

SINGER: Two or three. One of them, "Old Love," was published in *Passions*.

RIBALOW: That's a very touching story. It doesn't start out that way, but. . . .

SINGER: It becomes tragic later on.

RIBALOW: In "Old Love" you have this eighty-two-year-old man, Harry Bendiner, who is rich and lonely and has buried three wives. He is completely out of touch with his family and has retired to Miami Beach, where he lives off collected dividends. His neighbor to his left had died, and life is so impersonal that he doesn't even know it. His new neighbor, Ethel, comes along. She is rich, only fifty-seven and just over a nervous breakdown. So you find in Miami Beach the same Jews that you do everywhere else.

SINGER: Why not? What is Miami Beach? It's a part of the world.

RIBALOW: What about "Sabbath in Portugal," where you find that semi-Marrano in Lisbon. Did that happen?

SINGER: Yes, it's a true story, with some variations.

RIBALOW: And "The Admirer." That one is hilarious.

SINGER: Did you read it in the *New Yorker* or in *Passions*?

RIBALOW: In the magazine first. You publish more often in the *New Yorker* than anyone else, don't you?

SINGER: That's not true. Many publish there more frequently. Donald Barthelme is one.

RIBALOW: I assume your agent submits your stories.

SINGER: No, I submit them myself. It's as simple as that.

RIBALOW: Getting back to "The Admirer," this was another instance where I talked to people about your sense of humor and how few notice it.

SINGER: Some do. Some don't.

RIBALOW: Well, when I read criticism of you, it is "heavy."

SINGER: Those are critics. One reader wrote that he was bursting with laughter when he read it.

RIBALOW: I also laughed out loud when I read it in the *New Yorker*. It's about this writer who is visited by a woman, an "admirer," who invades the writer's privacy, gets phone calls from her husband, mother, and lawyer and then falls into an epileptic fit. It is especially funny at the end. When you think the nightmare is over, some other admirer knocks at the door, a professor of English. And unaware of what has been happening, he starts the cycle all over again. It's like a wild Marx Brothers routine, which leads me to ask: Do you know the Marx Brothers, or do you go to the movies?

SINGER: I used to go, but I haven't gone to the movies in a long time.

RIBALOW: But this is strictly Marx Brothers!

SINGER: Really?

RIBALOW: I'm aware that I can't talk with you about a hundred stories. Some intrigue me more than others and it is these on which I have made my notes. For example, I was taken with "The Witch," published in *Passions*. Mark Meitels has a frigid wife. . . .

SINGER: This is a sexy story.

RIBALOW: This spoiled Polish woman is quite familiar to me because I have known the type. The reason we get involved in these stories is we recognize so many of these people, especially those of us who are Jewish. They are clearly drawn from life.

SINGER: Sure. They *are* taken from life.

RIBALOW: Yet Bella, whom your hero gets involved with. . . .

SINGER: The ugly one.

RIBALOW: Yes. It is interesting that you deliberately make her physically unappealing.

SINGER: At the same time, she attracts him.

RIBALOW: At the end, when they bed down for the second time, in the light of the sun she suddenly becomes beautiful which, I suppose, means that she has enraptured him and enveloped him.

SINGER: Exactly. Also in the light of the shining sun everything becomes beautiful. It has two meanings.

RIBALOW: In this particular story, why do you have the leisurely asides. When your hero is walking through the streets, he is reflecting on life in Poland, its anti-Semitism and Pilsudski.

SINGER: You have to in order to make it authentic.

RIBALOW: But so many of your other stories are compressed.

SINGER: In this case I decided to make it real. It also shows that he is a man who keeps away from everybody. Through these reflections, he shows it. He's not really a Jew, he's not really a goy.

RIBALOW: In the beginning, I got a hint when you called him "highly disciplined." And I said to myself, "Something is going to happen to this man."

SINGER: Which is the opposite of discipline.

RIBALOW: I found "The Fatalist" particularly good because of its closing line. Benjamin Schwartz believes all is preordained and performs a brave and daring act in order to get Heyele to marry him. Would he do it again?

SINGER: "Not for Heyele."

RIBALOW: That gives it a twist.

SINGER: You know already that his life wasn't so sweet, in spite of his great love.

RIBALOW: "The Yearning Heifer" first came to my attention when it was published in the *Southern Review*. The whole Catskill *milieu*, the Yiddish writer who is at first not welcomed by the two women at the farm, but then fawn on him because he is a writer—all this is equally familiar to many of us. Then there is the symbolism. . . .

SINGER: Of the heifer itself.

RIBALOW: Right. Desiring a bull in the country summer. And then there is the fine gentile, Palmer, who behaves so graciously to him.

SINGER: I think his name is Porter.

RIBALOW: My note says "Palmer" and I reread the story only recently.

SINGER: Maybe "Palmer." I will tell you why I now say "Palmer." The real man was called "Porter."

RIBALOW: I see.

SINGER: In this story I make some small changes in the book. Not in the story but in the words.

RIBALOW: This is by the way. The person who is the narrator through so many of these stories, if you read them in the compressed period in which I read them, is a very likable human being.

SINGER: I make him likable. Why shouldn't I?

RIBALOW: Now the story "Sam Palka and David Vishkover" is, on the face of it, not credible.

SINGER: You would be surprised how many incredible things happen.

RIBALOW: Yet the reader believes, when he is reading it. What is more interesting, he doesn't disbelieve when he is finished.

SINGER: You would be surprised how many incredible things are happening right here, near us. There are millions of things which happen which, if you tell them, you think can't happen. The impossible is very possible. Somewhere in *Enemies, A Love Story,* it is stated that the impossible is very possible.

RIBALOW: The hero leads this double life and the second woman, in her twenties, is naive and likable and one understands why the man is attracted to her.

SINGER: He loves her.

RIBALOW: And also, he will never tell her who he really is—rich, unhappily married and unable to marry her.

SINGER: If he would tell her, she would be destroyed.

RIBALOW: Throughout your work, you deal with writers as though they are not the nicest people in the world. You know, my father was the editor of the *Hadoar* and writers were always coming to our home. Bialik visited us and so did Tchernichovsky. Schneour and Aaron Zeitlin and S. Shalom were others we knew. My mother has always said, *"M'zoll zei nit kennen, nor durch den schreiben."* (You should know them only through their work.)

SINGER: She was right.

RIBALOW: In your story, "The New Year Party," you express your unwillingness to meet with other writers. Leftists scold a writer for not promoting world revolution, the Zionists for not dramatizing the struggle for the Jewish State. You're better off not meeting them. Do you really hold to this?

SINGER: I hold with it very much.

RIBALOW: Do you socialize with writers?

SINGER: Very, very little.

RIBALOW: At one point you said, "To write, what you need most is an eye." You need more than an eye.

SINGER: Ah, it's just a saying. You need a heart.

RIBALOW: In "Three Encounters" you encourage Rivkele to lead a new life but then you detach yourself from her miseries. Part of it seems autobiographical. In "The Briefcase," the lecturer—you—loses a briefcase, notes, and money. Do you draw heavily from your personal experiences?

SINGER: These incidents are based on my life. I would, on reflection, call these stories semi-autobiographical.

RIBALOW: In "The Captive," a story about a painter and a woman, you have a passage in which you ask one character why he doesn't leave Israel. Here, you write movingly and passionately about Israel.

SINGER: Yes, he says you get enchanted with it; you get enslaved.

RIBALOW: From time to time, you do allow a certain feeling for Israel to enter your work.

SINGER: Why not? I'm not an anti-Zionist. I love Israel, but I couldn't be there always. It would be difficult.

RIBALOW: To live there?

SINGER: Yes. Settle there, because it's a country where Hebrew is spoken, not Yiddish.

RIBALOW: I assume most of your work has appeared in Hebrew.

SINGER: A lot of it. My son is translating two of my stories into Hebrew.

RIBALOW: New stories?

SINGER: No, but they never appeared in Hebrew before.

RIBALOW: I would like to end with "A Crown of Feathers," which I think is a beautiful story. Your heroine is Akhsa. . . .

SINGER: It's a name from the Bible. In *Shoftim,* Judges, there is a woman called Akhsa.

RIBALOW: I see you are doing what the Israelis do. They go through the Bible to look for uncommon names.

SINGER: In the first chapter of *Shoftim* there is Akhsa.

RIBALOW: She is the rich granddaughter of Naftali and she refuses to marry anybody. She walks away from Zemach, but she is accosted by the devil, who has woven a crown of feathers with a cross. She converts to Christianity, marries, repents and finally marries Zemach. There is much self-torture and in the end there is another cross of feathers with the Hebrew letters for God: Yud, Hay, Vov, Hay. It's a marvellous image and now I am going to ask a naive question. How do these images come to you?

SINGER: I don't know. About "A Crown of Feathers" I read somewhere that a woman wrote in a letter that she found in a pillow a crown of feathers. That's all I read. That's all I needed.

RIBALOW: When she goes through all this torture, pain, retribution, and salvation, then you end with this, "If there is such a thing as truth, it is as intricate and hidden as a crown of feathers."

SINGER: And how! And how it is! We'll never know the truth. Not in this world.

RIBALOW: These are the wonderful lines that remain with me.

SINGER: What is there to say? Thank God I am doing my work. I thank God there are readers like you, who read and understand and appreciate. These are the real people.

A Conversation with

Jack Ansell

Grimly struggling to regain his health, Jack Ansell has lived in hospitals for the past five years. From a hospital bed, he has produced at least three novels, a play, and a cluster of short stories.

A small-boned man, he is painfully thin and frequently wracked with pain. He was very weak. We were unable to complete our conversation in one sitting. Instead, I visited him three days in July 1976 at Lenox Hill Hospital in New York City.

Ansell is a man of great charm and patience. A Southerner, he speaks in an unhurried drawl still unaffected by his years in the East. His hospital room (and life) reflects something of the man. He loves flowers and plants, handles them lovingly and watches leaves and buds develop with the intensity of a man in isolation, cut off from the teeming outside world. The hospital routine is terribly familiar to him and he keeps meticulous records of when he requires pills, medicines, and other medical treatment. Often in pain, he maintains a gracious manner. He is on very good personal terms with nurses, gray ladies, interns, and specialists. He is surrounded by books, including his own, and scores of magazines. He is constantly being called on the telephone by friends checking on his condition. Presently, he sees few people and has not allowed me to photograph him, for obvious reasons.

In the course of the conversation that follows, much of Ansell's background, education, and business experience emerge. Still, it is worth noting here that he has written many novels, a collection of short stories, and an unproduced and unpublished play. His work breaks down to novels and stories about life in the South and novels dealing with the entertainment and business worlds of radio and television. Jews are both major and minor characters in all he writes.

201

His early novels, *His Brother, The Bear* and *The Shermans of Mannerville*, are set in a small Louisiana town. The books are inhabited by Southerners on all levels of society. We meet judges and sheriffs, businessmen, Christians and Jews, and blacks, both of an older generation and of the revolutionary 1960s. His short stories are diverse and wide ranging and some reiterate or anticipate the themes of his larger works.

Gospel is an ambitious in-depth study of American business which captures the evangelistic fervor, the almost religious power, of American business. *Jelly* is a short, intense novel about a "defrocked" rabbi who throws away his rabbinical post, his place in society, and his loyal wife for a wild, sexually uninhibited young woman. It is a study of a man trapped in the embrace of lust.

Dynasty of Air and *Giants* are large, ambitious novels about radio and television and are peopled by scores of characters. Here Ansell is in his element for he was himself a TV executive with a major network for many years.

Commercially successful, Ansell's books have been issued in paperback editions in this country and in hardback editions in the United States and abroad. Although widely reviewed in the daily press, in business and trade journals, his books have not gained the attention of academics or the literary arbiters of our time. Yet his Southern and Jewish material make his work relevant and interesting. His business and radio and TV novels utilize meaningful material with authenticity.

Ansell is thoughtful, speaks easily and with the awareness that he is working under extraordinary handicaps. He is a stubborn, determined, and very brave man—and a very fine writer.

*   *   *

I have decided to retain this introduction as originally written, although a week after I wrote it, on Monday, September 20, 1976, Jack Ansell died of cancer at Lenox Hill Hospital. He was fifty years of age.

RIBALOW: I am curious about your background, especially your Southern background. You write about a "Mannerville." Where are you actually from?

ANSELL: I'm from Monroe, Louisiana. Of course, Mannerville is Monroe. I've never hesitated to say that it is. I fictionalized it mainly because I work better within a fictional framework. I'm from the South and in many ways it was the varied backgrounds I had that began my thinking in terms of fiction rather than nonfiction. As far as a writing career goes, I was writing from the time I was born, practically, so it never entered my mind I would not write.

RIBALOW: I keep hearing that from all writers.

ANSELL: Of course, settling into a form or finding the place where you belong is the difficulty, especially in a world where every housewife who leaves a note for the milkman is a writer. You have extreme competitive situations here. It was with the recognition that, by golly, I was unique, had a very unique background. . . .

RIBALOW: You realized this when you were young?

ANSELL: Yes, I realized that when I was young. The Southern and Jewish ethos, as they merged together, were always in conflict with each other. Out of this stemmed the conflict in what today we call the liberal-conservative element, so that all of the political elements, the social elements, the creative elements—all of these were merging together and yet were in conflict with each other. I realized what an interesting, fascinating background I had to write about. When I wrote *His Brother, The Bear,* that was the first piece of fiction—I think the *New Yorker* said so anyway—of Southern Jewish life as an entity. By that I mean, in *His Brother, The Bear* I rather deliberately set Jewish life aside from the mainstream, so to speak.

RIBALOW: In terms of time, that was quite long ago. The novel was published in 1960.

ANSELL: That is correct. Long ago. I wrote it in '58/'59.

RIBALOW: That is almost a generation ago.

ANSELL: A different generation. Oddly enough, some people who had reread it—people I admire, my peers—say it holds up even today, which is interesting to me.

RIBALOW: So you are from Monroe. Where did you go to high school? Did you attend local schools?

ANSELL: I went to high school in Monroe. I was born in Monroe. Then, when I was six months old, we moved to Tennessee and I lived in Tennessee until I was ten years old, and back to Monroe, Louisiana.

RIBALOW: What did your parents do?

ANSELL: My father was in hardware and my mother was a housewife. It was my mother who did most of the encouraging as far as my work as a writer was concerned.

RIBALOW: Where did you live in Tennessee?

ANSELL: In Winchester, a little town not too far from Nashville.

RIBALOW: So you really were born and lived and raised in very small communities.

ANSELL: Yes. I went to high school in Monroe and still have most of my relatives there. My father is eighty-seven years old and he is still living there.

RIBALOW: And where did you go to college?

ANSELL: I went to college at a very young age. I was only fifteen when I went to the University of Missouri, which was a long ways from home. I was there a year and then Louisiana State University for a year, and then went into the Army, into Counter Intelligence. When I got back out, I returned to Missouri and got both my bachelor's and my master's degrees at Missouri.

RIBALOW: How Jewish was your upbringing?

ANSELL: It was not. There was the *feeling* of being Jewish. I went to Temple. I went to Sabbath school, what we call Sabbath school, anyway, although it really was more or less a Sunday school. Very little Hebrew in the services. . . .

RIBALOW: Reform?

ANSELL: Yes. Most of the things in *His Brother, The Bear* and *The Shermans of Mannerville* you will find are quite authentic, even though there are notes of satire and irony throughout. It was not a great Jewish background, except the aura of being Jewish, the feeling of being Jewish—and my own research. I did more research into being Jewish, I read more about being Jewish than most Jewish children in the South. It fascinated me that I *was* Jewish. It did not fascinate me that I was *Southern* because I never really thought of the difference between the Southerner and any other until I went to the University of Missouri. The moment I opened my mouth, everyone was laughing and I did not realize that I had one of those accents they say you can't cut with three knives.

RIBALOW: How long have you lived in the East?

ANSELL: I've been in New York now for around eighteen years. This is home.

RIBALOW: Do you think of yourself as a Southern writer?

ANSELL: At one time I thought of myself as a Southern Jewish writer.

RIBALOW: That was my next question: Do you consider yourself a Jewish writer?

ANSELL: It gave me a uniqueness: a Southern Jewish writer. Now, I don't. Basically, I am too eclectic a writer. I take from so many moods and modes. A work that I am on right now, for example, which is going to take place partly in the South and partly in the North, I feel equally qualified for both. I feel I have had so much of America. . . . You see, having been with a television network for so many years, I have traveled all over the world and much of America I have traveled a hundred times.

RIBALOW: Let me return to your background for a moment. How did you get involved with television. You say that after you got your two degrees from the University of Missouri, it's about then that you came North?

ANSELL: I came to New York for just a few months at that time, in 1950. There was a death in the family. I went back to Louisiana and remained there.

RIBALOW: What did you do when you were there?

ANSELL: Well, first I wrote a column for the newspaper, a weekly column.

RIBALOW: This was in Monroe?

ANSELL: In Monroe. Then I went into broadcasting—a radio station in Monroe, just as we were about to go into television in 1953. I stayed on and became a vice president of the station and remained there up until 1960, when I came to New York. I was brought to New York by *Sponsor* magazine and went to work for the magazine. Meanwhile, the first novel, *His Brother, The Bear,* sold. Doubleday bought it right away.

RIBALOW: You wrote that in the South?

ANSELL: I wrote it while I was in Monroe, yes. I stayed with *Sponsor* for about a year and I took off and free-lanced. Wrote another novel . . . it has not been published but it's going to be.

RIBALOW: That was the gap between 1960 and *The Shermans of Mannerville,* which came out in 1971.

ANSELL: That is a very *large* gap, because by that time I had gone to work for the ABC Television network and worked my way up to where I was assistant to the president of the network for the last four years—five years. I just left there, you know, last year. No, that eleven years seems a very large gap except for one thing. I did an extraordinary amount of work which is coming to fruition. I did much of the research on *Dynasty of Air* and *Giants* at that time, because I knew I was going to do a work of fiction on broadcasting. My master's thesis had been a history of broadcasting. So I had already begun an enormous research project on that. I also wrote two full-length books during that period.

RIBALOW: Novels?

ANSELL: One was a novel and one was a group of tales. Both are going to be published within the next two or three years.

RIBALOW: You say "tales." You must mean short stories.

ANSELL: They are short stories that are interrelated. They belong together as an entity and I kept them out of *Summer*, a collection of my stories. Then I began *Gospel* during that period and also wrote a number of the short stories which later formed the basis for *Summer*.

RIBALOW: How would you define a Jewish writer?

ANSELL: That is a very difficult question. I'm not sure that you could call Saul Bellow, for example, any more a Jewish writer than you can call Michael Arlen Armenian. How can you? These are American writers with Armenian or Jewish backgrounds. A Jewish writer, it seems to me, is still someone like Moshe Leib Halpern or Isaac Bashevis Singer, for example, who write within a traditional Yiddish mold. But a Jewish writer as such— they make so much over people like Philip Roth and Bernard Malamud and Bellow being Jewish writers—Saul Bellow, I know, resents it to a great extent and I do not blame him.

RIBALOW: Yes, he complains. He calls himself, Malamud, and Roth the Hart, Schaffner, and Marx of American literature.

ANSELL: That's very good. I don't blame him in the least because he is really much more representative of America in the midseventies, right now, at this moment, than he is of Jewish life, even though his characters for the most part are Jewish in background. Well, so are mine, even in the broadcasting books all of the major characters are Jewish, mainly because I am more familiar with them and also I chose that particular *milieu* because they were Jewish, most of the founders in entertainment were Jewish, the founding fathers, so to speak.

RIBALOW: I found a quotation the other week which I would like you to reflect on. A literary critic named Barbara Hardy, in a book, *Tellers and Listeners,* published in London in 1976, expanded on an article she had written in 1968 in an academic journal, *Novel*. She says that man is a storytelling animal, that human life is made up of narrative and that "we constantly tell stories about ourselves and each other . . . and the identities of individuals and societies depend on a degree of coherence and continuity in the personal and collective story." Bernard Bergonzi reviewed her book in the *Times Literary Supplement* in London, in the issue of April 23, 1976, and he added that B.S. Johnson believed that telling stories is telling lies. In which camp do you belong?

ANSELL: I do not think there is any contradiction in substance or tone here in any way whatsoever. I think we are storytelling animals who essentially tell lies. We exaggerate our lies in order to give them drama, in order to give them dignity, to give them all the trappings of lies.

RIBALOW: Your first novel, *His Brother, The Bear,* was published in 1960. So you really are a veteran writer. Why do you think you are not as well known as some other Jewish writers? You know, when I tell people the writers I am interviewing, your name is least familiar to them. And yet some of your books have been in paperback: *Dynasty, Jelly, Gospel, Giants.*

ANSELL: All of them. And I am now being published in England.

RIBALOW: The reviews of your books are generally very good.

ANSELL: It is very interesting what has happened. I think one of the reasons is that my work is very diverse. I have never stayed with any one particular subject or group of subjects. I started out with Southern Jewish background novels and then I did a novel which was in a completely different vein, *Gospel,* which is one of my major novels. It was really not of a Jewish nature.

RIBALOW: Do your books sell?

ANSELL: The books sell extremely well in paperback. I am beginning now to be known by mass audiences. It is odd because my reputation is taking the reverse of most, which start out with critical appreciation. Mine now has reached a crossroads where I am becoming well known by the masses because of the paperbacks. The critical attention is being paid in the later stages.

RIBALOW: I was going to ask this question earlier, but we didn't have a chance to get to it yet: What is it like to be a Jew in the South? Were there many Jews in Monroe?

ANSELL: Yes, there were. Monroe happened to have a large Jewish community which Mannerville, of course, does in all of the novels that I have the Mannerville figures into. Mannerville is probably in every one of my books. It is mentioned in some way or other or someone is from there. It is like Hitchcock in his movies; it is a symbol of luck to me. As to how it feels to be a Jew in the South, I *never* felt I was a Jew in the South.

RIBALOW: That's interesting.

ANSELL: It is only in latter years, when someone like you looks at me and says, "How did it feel to be a Jew in the South?" that I start thinking about how it felt to be a Jew in the South. I knew what it was to be a member of a minority within a large constituency, a majority, that was of a fundamentalist religion, Baptist for the most part. I certainly knew what that meant, growing up. I knew what it meant to be Jewish, let's say, within a framework of a large community, but not necessarily a Southern community. I was *so* Southern myself and still am to an extent. My background is just as Southern, if not more so, than it is Jewish. My tastes in food, the entertainment, the influence of writers. The writers who influenced me most, when I was very young, were Faulkner; I went through the Thomas Wolfe period probably much more headily and dreamily than most American writers because it was closer to where I lived. Even the earlier plays of Tennessee Williams were much more affecting and played a great part in the evolvement of my own styles.

RIBALOW: I don't see anything of Faulkner or Wolfe in your work.

ANSELL: I know, but I feel their influence while I still have maintained my own style. Actually, I do not think you can compare me to anybody. Let me ask you, do you feel that I am on a comparison with anybody else as far as style goes? I don't think my material is derivative.

RIBALOW: No, I don't. You are hard to pinpoint.

ANSELL: Well, good. I like that.

RIBALOW: When were you last in the South?

ANSELL: About a year and a half ago. All my family is there and I still have interests there. They are interested in me there, too. *The Shermans of Mannerville* was burned publicly by the then mayor of Monroe. Afterwards he admitted that he had not even read it. He tore it out of his wife's hands while she was in the middle of the novel.

RIBALOW: The title of *His Brother, The Bear*, as I understand it, is based on a fable or parable you wove into the novel. The fable is based on the premise that when Man emerged from the animal state, only the cave bear and Man survived. Man then devoured the bear in order for Man to survive. That's the explanation of the title, I gather.

ANSELL: That was really the basis, the symbolism, the metaphor of the book itself, because it was the bear that first stood up beside Man, that was Man's closest ally, closest friend, when Man stood on his two feet. But the first one Man turned against was the bear. Of course, that is the metaphor of the book itself, the turning against one's own.

RIBALOW: Your major character in the book, Julian Black, is a businessman married to Evelyn Barrow. I mention this as I do because in later books you have a lot of similar relationships, where men are married to women who come from the lower levels of Southern society and who feel they are marrying upward.

ANSELL: I have seen so much of it.

RIBALOW: So these Southern women, who do not become "Jewish" princesses, become princesses anyway. This recurs on so many different levels, even in *Giants*, when you have some of the Robert Abrams' marriages, which remind me of the marriages in *His Brother, The Bear.*

ANSELL: That is interesting. You are telling me some things I hadn't really realized. I can't answer your question because your question is almost the answer.

RIBALOW: And the young girl in this novel, Charlotte, who is in love with Irving Kaufman, reappears in *The Shermans of Mannerville,* by this time long married. It is almost like the same book, except that the main characters are different ones.

ANSELL: The same book? Oh, no. I don't think I was writing the same book at all. One dealt with Jew against Jew, what the Jew does to his own brethren. *The Shermans of Mannerville* did not at all. *The Shermans* did have a to-do with the denial of one's background and faith, but it really was a much more explosive novel in the contemporary scene, especially where the black was concerned.

RIBALOW: Yet in both books, the voice of reason and rationality and tolerance comes from a Judge Sam Aiken, a character who appears in both novels. He also preaches to the central Jewish characters in each book.

ANSELL: To an extent. Yes, he is in both books but then also there are a number of these characters who are also in a number of stories in *Summer*. Also, you will see some crop up in *Jelly* because, you see, I have a continuity. That is one thing I have always admired in writers like Faulkner—the continuity of character. Even in some of the work I am doing now, I am going back to books with major or central Jewish background.

RIBALOW: On *His Brother, The Bear*. . . .

ANSELL: One of your questions bothers me . . . on being well known. I think one of the reasons is that I have not been known exclusively as a Jewish writer. Everybody else you are interviewing, the minute you mention their names, I think, "Jewish writer." I resist the term just as Bellow does, and yet I think of it.

RIBALOW: The reason is that, by and large, almost everything they have written has been Jewish. In *His Brother, The Bear* you have a sort of villainous character, David Black, the son of Julian. He impregnates a girl back North, who later kills herself. Again you have the pattern where a few young women are involved with men who are not very worthy, and the women commit suicide.

ANSELL: You are telling me things about myself that I am finding very interesting. Do go on.

RIBALOW: The patterns have not hit you the way they seem to have hit me?

ANSELL: No, they haven't. But if patterns of one's writing stay too much within the consciousness of any writer, then I think that writer is suffering.

RIBALOW: That is probably true. Then you have David Black returning to Mannerville and he is no better a person than he was when he left. In the North, he was trying to pass as a non-Jew.

ANSELL: I have the counterpart to that in a short story in *Summer,* called "I Passed for Yankee." That is the comic side of it.

RIBALOW: Yes, I made a note on that story. That is the one where the hero goes back to his thick Southern drawl and returns to his roots, so to speak. At one point you give a reason for David's going North. He heard "one horrendous deafening roar, 'Jew, Jew, Jew.'" And then he leaves for New York. The burden of being a Jew is overwhelming to him. Did you know many Jews in the South who felt that way?

ANSELL: Yes, I did. I never did, but I knew those who did and who resented being Jewish to such an extent that when they went away to college they generally denied it to get into non-Jewish fraternities.

RIBALOW: I would like to make a point of one of the special gifts you possess. Your confrontations with people are very good even though they are not lengthy. The one I am thinking of at the moment concerns David, who goes to meet his Jewish girlfriend, Joyce, in New York. Instead, he meets Clara Rosen, who sees through him just by looking at him. She enters into a series of touching observations in which she points out that Joyce is a nice Jewish girl who has no special talents, has a good body, is pretty and really has nothing else. But it really is such women who simply want to marry honorably who are the foundation of our world.

ANSELL: Right.

RIBALOW: It has struck me that in many of the novels you have brief confrontations which are successfully done.

ANSELL: Well, thank you very much. One of the reasons, I suppose, if there is a question there, the answer would be that I see life as a continuum of confrontation. Not necessarily as something that one uses as a central dramatic piece. The reason, probably, that the confrontations are so short is because they are a natural flow.

RIBALOW: So many books lead up to one major climax or explosion.

ANSELL: I know. I never was that kind of writer.

RIBALOW: I may add that although some of your books are long in terms of words, in many respects they are tight.

ANSELL: Thank you. That is a compliment, too. Again that is because I see life as—I call it a continuum of confrontation. Do you? Aren't we always confronting, if not some one, some thing?

RIBALOW: Sure. In *His Brother, The Bear,* Julian, at one point, gets into an argument with his mother, Estelle, and he asks her, "Is being Jewish so almighty important?" We should remember that the story commences on Rosh Hashanah. She replies, "Perhaps not. But being *something* is."

ANSELL: I think you will find in all my books, from *His Brother, The Bear* all the way through *Giants* so far, there has been that identification thing.

RIBALOW: Not only with Jews.

ANSELL: No, in *Gospel* it was just a story. The whole idea of belonging is so important to it. We are so vulnerable, all of us, we are so defenseless, we are such air that the seeking of earth, that little soil, that little patch of ground, is so vital and so important, that is what I meant by, "if not Jewish, *something.*" It is being an amalgam of nothings that is so dangerous, I think, to the human character.

RIBALOW: I must bring up a problem that develops in talks such as this one. When I am talking with you, the writer, you, of course, know what your books are about and so do I. But the third person, the reader, may not be familiar with the writer's work. So it is a problem as to how to indicate to the third party what the stories are about.

ANSELL: That is right. But let me get to something else. One of the disadvantages in waiting so long between publications, as I did, between *His Brother, The Bear* and *The Shermans of Mannerville* is that I got enormous critical attention with *His Brother, The Bear.* The *New York Times* and the *New Yorker* did a full two or three pages on it. But so many years elapsed that people who are familiar with me are less familiar with *His Brother, The Bear* than with the other books, which is a shame because I think it is one of my better books.

RIBALOW: In this novel, the central Jewish character is Julian Black, a highly regarded businessman, in the midst of a crisis. He tries to keep another Jew, Aaron Kaufman, out of a local club. What is his reason? He feels that Kaufman, a glove manufacturer, is not good enough or that he, Black, wants to be the only Jewish member of the club. Is that accurate?

ANSELL: Yes, he did not want the neighborhood to "disintegrate."

RIBALOW: Also, we do not learn until late in the novel that Kaufman was, in effect, the last invitee. Other Jews had been invited and they had turned down the invitation.

ANSELL: That is the irony of it.

RIBALOW: So Kaufman allowed himself to be used and he was the Jew against whom Julian Black was fighting!

ANSELL: Right!

RIBALOW: Why is it that Sam Aiken turns out to be the one who is more perceptive about these matters than the Jews are?

ANSELL: I don't know. Maybe it is because I knew two or three people like Sam Aiken. He is modeled on Sam Ervin, to tell you the truth.

RIBALOW: Sam Aiken's father was a red-neck bigot. He saw this prejudice in his own father and consciously tried to take it out of himself. It is Aiken who says that "we live in a pretty shallow society" and makes the point that belonging to or joining this club is not worth all that much, so why fight it? It seems to me he is the voice of the new South.

ANSELL: He is the voice of reason, the voice of understanding. He is the mellowing point. I deliberately did not make him Jewish mainly because I knew within the Southern framework non-Jewish Southerners who really were more reasonable. . . . I had experiences when I was a child in which I was the only Jewish child—so far as upper society was concerned —in the town that was accepted, although we had a large Jewish population.

RIBALOW: Why was that?

ANSELL: My family background. My mother's sister had married into a family that had been in that area for over two hundred years.

RIBALOW: Non-Jewish?

ANSELL: No, Jewish. Because of the family situation and reputation, I was thrown more or less with the non-Jewish society as much if not more than the Jewish society. There was a man who was the father of one of the girls

I dated when I was fourteen-fifteen years old who was very much like Sam Aiken. The only time I could ever remember it being said that I was Jewish, was said at a party at their home one night when one of the boys blurted out—I had said something—and one of the other boys said something about, "Well, what would a Jew know about that?" Nobody had *ever* said that to me before up to this. I was so upset over the whole situation that the girl's father made me get into his car with him and he just rode me around a few blocks and he started talking to me. I thought, as I grew older, "What a lovely thing of him to have done!" To have taken that time and have given so much—he gave that whole evening to me! It concerned him so much. He was Sam Aiken in many ways.

RIBALOW: I see. I have a quote here from Sam Aiken, "I am a man. I am an American Christian. Southern. But primarily I'm a *whole man*." That is what you have him say. At some point, you have Julian saying. . . .

ANSELL: Julian is torn apart through most of that book.

RIBALOW: He says, "I am *not* a Zionist, I am an *American* Jew, an *American*, do you hear, I am a *Southern* Jew, *Southern, Southern*, not one of *them*." So he was trying to isolate himself from the Jews who identified with their fellow Jew.

ANSELL: Hence the title, *His Brother, The Bear*. He was slaying his brother.

RIBALOW: Julian has a Christian mistress. You have Christian mistresses through your broadcast novels as well.

ANSELL: Try to find a Jewish mistress in the South! You are really looking for a needle!

RIBALOW: On this subject: has there been much intermarriage?

ANSELL: Yes. Now particularly. But even in the time of *His Brother, The Bear* this was so. The book itself began because of my interest in intermarriages. It was all around me, even in my own family. That is when I began to be so interested in the whole situation and out of that came *His Brother, The Bear*.

RIBALOW: In this novel, I admire your Rabbi Meyer Silverman. Especially in a confrontation, when he talks with Julian. He calls Julian a Gentile Jew. What do you mean by that?

ANSELL: Well, if you have known most of these people in the South, that is what they are. They are Gentile Jews. They are Jews who have spaghetti suppers at the Temple, if you know what I mean.

RIBALOW: Silverman has been a rabbi in town for twenty-three years and later, in another of your novels, someone succeeds him and the reader learns that he has retired.

ANSELL: One of the reasons I have kept this continuity of characters from book to book is that even though I wander into different channels, such as the broadcasting books, which were a tremendous job, and in the books I am working on now, I find I am picking up the same characters years later from *His Brother, The Bear* and *The Shermans of Mannerville*. . . . You might be interested in knowing that the final drafts—and this you could not have known—of *Gospel*, of *Dynasty of Air*, and of *Giants* were all written in a hospital bed. The entire works.

RIBALOW: I guess one can learn to write everywhere and anywhere.

ANSELL: That is where I have been living mostly for the last three to four years.

RIBALOW: When you say you "write," do you write longhand or at the typewriter?

ANSELL: In hospitals, *this* is the way I work.

RIBALOW: Pencil, in a spiral notebook.

ANSELL: I am on two novels and a play simultaneously.

RIBALOW: So you write in longhand, in pencil. Who does the typing? You?

ANSELL: When I was at ABC my secretary did the transcribing. Now I do my own if I am well enough. If I'm not, I have to bring in a typist.

RIBALOW: You have a reference in the novel where the rabbi says to Aaron Kaufman something that is interesting but not too many people think along this line; that "tolerance is at best a tepid thing." And that Kaufman wants only to be tolerated. The fact that Kaufman wants to get into the club simply to be tolerated bothers the rabbi, who feels that tolerance is not what one should seek.

ANSELL: You are almost more familiar with this than I, because you have read the book more recently, whereas I have not read *His Brother, The Bear* in a decade.

RIBALOW: The rabbi also stresses that there are two things certain in life: death and taxes. For the Jew, it is death, taxes, and being a Jew. Also, the rabbi fights *for* the conception of Jews as a chosen people, which surprised me in a way. But he means "chosen to have no choice." This reminds me of a story I heard from my wife, who teaches in a yeshiva, which has a black janitor. The executive director asked him to do something say remarking, "Joe, you've got to do this." The black man replied, "I don't have to do nuthin' 'cept die and be black."

ANSELL: Yes, that is true. It is a very interesting thing about being Jewish. You asked earlier in our dialogue about its meaning, or how it feels to be a Jewish writer. You never really get away from it even though you do not define it or find it explicable at all times. Being Jewish is something that the black understood when he said, "All I've got to do is be black and die." He understood it; it is the same thing.

RIBALOW: Both have no choice.

ANSELL: You have no choice. You can become a Catholic and you are still a Jew. However, a Baptist who becomes a Catholic is no longer a Baptist. It is a great difference.

RIBALOW: You also say, or Julian says, that he does not want to wear neon lights advertising he is a Jew. He emphasizes that "this is a Christian society." Does he really think he can become part of it?

ANSELL: You see, he is the second generation. His is that peculiar problem facing the second generation where he has a loyalty to his father and he also feels his loyalty to his wife. It is a false loyalty, but he feels it. He is torn between these two philosophies.

RIBALOW: Then you have Charlotte, Julian's daughter. She *wants* to become Jewish when she discovers that her brother David was responsible for the suicide of his Jewish girlfriend back East. It is a kind of affirmation or sense of belonging. May I then ask, does the book end on a downbeat or upbeat note? It is hard to say.

ANSELL: It ends on neither a downbeat nor upbeat note. I think that it ended with certain rays of hope for the family, but I am not so sure that there was any hope for a marriage that was doomed in the first place. I think there is hope only in one of his children and that is Charlotte. That hope is fulfilled and carried out in later books.

RIBALOW: *The Shermans of Mannerville* was published eleven years after *His Brother, The Bear*. It has the same scene, the same town, some of the same people. Why, then, the long silence?

ANSELL: It was not a silence at all and much is coming to fruition.

RIBALOW: Arthur Sherman is your fifty-year-old businessman who kills a black boy in a hit-and-run accident while driving with his mistress, Binnie Lamb. Sherman's wife is called by you "the smartest richest Jewish girl in town." She is the most sympathetic Jew in the book; the others, by and large, are unsympathetic.

ANSELL: Really? You did not think that the son, Arthur Jr., was sympathetic? I think he was. He was torn between and among a number of moral fibers. He was very sympathetic; I disagree there. If he did not come across that way then it was a failure on my part. I certainly intended his mother to be the strength and backbone of the Jewish family itself. I hope I succeeded there.

RIBALOW: Yes.

ANSELL: She certainly affected me as a person. I became deeply involved with her.

RIBALOW: Arthur has a sort of honest relationship with his mistress, Binnie. Arthur, Jr., has a relationship with a black girl, Callie Smith. You seem to describe quite consistently relationships between the Jew and the non-Jew in sexual entanglements.

ANSELL: You see, that is because the assimilation process has gone so much further in the South than it has in other areas. Being thrown with non-Jews is a normal course of events.

RIBALOW: You also introduce deep-dyed villains, a mean sheriff, a greedy judge, and blackmailers of Arthur.

ANSELL: This book gave me a lot of difficulties because it depended upon a very delicate turning of the plot, which so many of my novels do not. Many of my novels have been of an epic nature or saga nature, where the turnings and twistings of plot were not as vital to the basic solutions of the novel, whereas in this one, *plot* was almost as vital as character. It made the novel a very difficult and delicate balance to hold.

RIBALOW: What initially prompted me to think of talking with you was that you were writing about a sociological element of Jewish life that so few are concerned with. For example, in this novel, you describe the United Jewish Appeal spokesman and how he is treated in the South. You talk of the delicacy and straddling the Southern Jew engages in when Northern B'nai B'rith people and libertarians come down without being aware of the impact of what they do to the Southern Jew. What really does happen in the South when the B'nai B'rith in New York decides to take a national policy stand which is opposed by most Southern Jews? What happens to the Jewish in Southern communities, who frequently accuse the Jews of the North by saying, "You go home but we have to live here."

ANSELL: That's right. I have attended countless meetings called because of B'nai B'rith decisions in the North. There is a line of demarcation between the Southern and Eastern or Northern establishment Jew and it is only in very recent years that much of this barrier has been broken down because what existed between the Yankee and the Southerner existed between the Yankee Jew and the Southern Jew.

RIBALOW: The crux of this story lies in the fact that Arthur Sherman does not know whether or not to admit he killed the black boy. Finally, Sam Aiken presses him on ethical grounds. Arthur confesses, first to his wife and then, more or less publicly, to Aiken.

ANSELL: I have been charged in many quarters of having followed more closely someone like Arthur Miller, say, in my dramatic emphases, than, say, someone like Tennessee Williams or Thomas Wolfe or others of that nature, who merely create the sordid Southern scene, so to speak. Miller, however, creates a moral atmosphere for all of his works and is given to moral solutions, or at least, if not solutions, moral groundings. I have often been accused, you might say, of being of that school, the moralistic school, in my writing. I had not noticed it so much myself. It would be someone like you who would be able to answer that for me, but some of my situations and plots have been compared to those of Miller, for example, *All My Sons* or *The Death of a Salesman,* to an extent, where the moral dilemmas that are posed have had a similarity to my work. I have never, frankly, seen myself in that particular genre, but others have.

RIBALOW: Young Arthur ultimately falls in love with Peggy, but love comes too late because he is killed by his black childhood friend, Lukie.

ANSELL: Yes, Lukie Birding. I think he is one of the best characters I have created. He gave me a hell of a lot of trouble at first. In fact I rewrote the entire book because of that son of a bitch, if you'll pardon the expression.

RIBALOW: Well, he and Arthur started off as childhood friends. Lukie's mother works for Arthur's family.

ANSELL: That's right. The families were interconnected, of course, through the old, almost plantation, system.

RIBALOW: Yet Lukie becomes extremely bitter—and the two boys share the same girl!

ANSELL: Right.

RIBALOW: In the end, Lukie kills Arthur. Is that symbolic?

ANSELL: Yes, it is symbolic. There was quite a bit of symbolism in that fire at the end. I know it was a use of melodrama of which I usually disapprove because trying to wind everything up, create a denouement, do the great big fire which comes to symbolize everything you try to say in a book is an old and, I think, pretty trite device. In this particular case, because of the large industry that was involved, because of the particularizations of character, it was the only thing to do. I do not regret it even now, looking back on it these many years later having created that fire as the symbol, or even better, the metaphor for the entire book.

RIBALOW: Again, in this book as in so many others, your people wrestle with their Jewish identity. One of them says, "Being a Jew means being persecuted because your house is cleaner than other people's."

ANSELL: Yes, this came about through something my mother had said at one point, about being Jewish and going into Jewish homes and non-Jewish homes. All of these things that you are bringing up and bringing out now have some basis in the things I heard and saw throughout my entire childhood in the South. Identity—I was thinking from some of the questions you asked yesterday and some of my answers—the Jewish identity and the Southern identity being in conflict as they are by their very natures *do* create an enormous conflict in the Southern Jew that he is often not aware of. It is an unconscious conflict, but it is there. It is always seething beneath the surface, and I really had not realized it to the extent, but then I should have realized it because at least one half of my work has been based upon that premise, hasn't it?

RIBALOW: Yes.

ANSELL: And I notice that in some of the work I am doing now, in the groundwork for the future, it is appearing again. So obviously, this question of identity is always with me and it goes back to something that you brought out yesterday about the sense of belonging. If you are not a Jew, be *something*.

RIBALOW: As a matter of fact, in line with this, in your next novel, in *Jelly,* you also raise the question of identity—in a way. It is the story of a youngish rabbi, Jacob Weiss, who ends up with an uncontrollable passion for a young girl.

ANSELL: A very young girl, very wild and, again, a *shiksa.*

RIBALOW: Weiss is married to a girl named Miriam who, again, is a rather unattractive daughter of a rabbi. Weiss met her at a Hebrew Union College dance. He is a Reform rabbi yet her father was Orthodox. She maintains an Orthodox home and life. The young girl, Jelly, is the daughter of a Baptist evangelist. She is tall, sexy, and totally uninhibited. Weiss changes his name and becomes Jack White.

ANSELL: Who plays piano in a saloon in New Orleans.

RIBALOW: In a whorehouse.

ANSELL: You know, I thought it was a damned good piece of work, if I say so myself.

RIBALOW: I found it, knowing your first two novels, so different, so different.

... Again, as I said yesterday about your patterns: When Miriam becomes pregnant and loses her child, in the end, she, too, commits suicide. So now two or three girls in your books have killed themselves when they have had a problem.

ANSELL: I guess what you are trying to say is that even with the differences in my books, there is a certain kind of continuity in my thinking, in my approach. You are making me much more aware of it. By the way, the original title of *Jelly* was *Goodbye, God*. If it is ever reissued, as it may be, I want it reissued as *Goodbye, God*.

RIBALOW: Well, the word "Jelly" has various connotations.

ANSELL: Yes. That was a very tight story. It brought out something that has not been done before, so far as I am aware of. There have been many novels or pieces of fiction about priests and their love for girls, even work on Protestant ministers. But it has not been done on a rabbi. Frankly, almost every major Jewish publication in the country took up *Jelly* viciously. It was not well received. Later, I did a series of lectures and was received with a great deal of hostility and animosity.

RIBALOW: You understand there are those who feel that anybody who writes about Jews should make sure that the Jews emerge in a favorable light, or "What will the Christian say?" *Mah yomru hagoyim*?

ANSELL: Keep your dirty linen to yourself!

RIBALOW: Yet in this book you make references to many Jewish scholars like Kaufman Kohler, Mordecai Kaplan, and the old French writer, Edmond Fleg. Does this all come from your research?

ANSELL: It comes from research and it also comes from the fact that two young rabbis helped me very extensively with this book. They read it in progress and in first, second, and third drafts, so that I had authentic help with it. When I say "help" I mean on whom to read for philosophical background. I had to spend a lot of research on this novel, more than I did on, say, *The Shermans of Mannerville*. That novel flowed naturally and it came from an experience, whereas *Jelly* demanded scholarly attention.

RIBALOW: One of the ironies to me is that Jelly, the uninhibited, "free" girl, is the one who resists getting married. And Jacob, who is doing all the revolutionary things, wants the propriety of marriage.

ANSELL: He is still basically a conservative.

RIBALOW: Then she says that the marriage will be no "fun." In the end, she is right.

ANSELL: She is very right. She was right all along. She is a delightful creation if you can get past some of her sexual aberrations. She is a perfectly marvelous person.

RIBALOW: Then, when she goes off, Jacob returns to Judaism, at least partially.

ANSELL: As the marriage begins to fail, he again seeks comfort or at least some hiding place back in the womb of his fathers. I like that, don't you? Because the womb of his fathers is not the womb of the mothers. But that is where he seeks his solace and comfort.

RIBALOW: Where did you come up with the concept of a rabbi getting involved with a sexually wild creature? It is an odd combination.

ANSELL: It is. It actually happened one day while I was having lunch in an Italian restaurant with a friend. I can't tell you why; it just suddenly hit me. I said, "I'm going to start a book tonight called *Goodbye, God* and it is going to be about a rabbi who falls in love with a very young, wild, mad, hippie type of girl who is the daughter of a Baptist evangelist minister. He looked at me and said, "And the title?" I said, *"Goodbye, God."* He said, "When did you decide this?" I said, "Just as I was having a bite of lasagna!" His answer was, "You are a madman, you really are, all writers are."

RIBALOW: When I say that on the face of it, *Jelly* has an incredible plot, I am reminded of my conversation with Isaac Bashevis Singer. One of his stories is quite incredible in a number of ways. It is "Blood," about a shochet who gets involved with a married woman whose husband is passive while she is still very passionate. She takes a lover and, whatever they do with one another, they ultimately must go beyond that to gain sexual satisfaction. When I remarked that the story stretches credulity, Singer said something extremely interesting and profound, "Anything that is conceivable to the mind of man is possible."

ANSELL: I agree. Wasn't it Flaubert who said, "Nothing human or nonhuman is foreign to me?" I am the same way. I think any writer worth his pepper has to enter into the arena of his own creative consciousness with this in mind: he is totally open to all. That is why you rarely find very many "conservative" writers.

RIBALOW: Is *Jelly* a "Jewish" book to you?

ANSELL: It certainly is concerned more with a Jewish moralism than a lot of the other books, although *The Shermans of Mannerville* and *His Brother, The Bear* are concerned with it too, although in different *milieus* and in a different light.

RIBALOW: *Gospel* is a totally different novel from the first three. I see echoes in this book of characters in the earlier novels. The two brothers, Carey Wade and Emory Wade, come from the South, Mississippi, not Louisiana.

ANSELL: Right. They come from Mississippi, but from the Gulf Coast of Mississippi, which is another area altogether. I hope I evoked that pretty well in the earlier part of the book. That is a particularly interesting part of the country. The Gulf Coast area is really an adjunct of New Orleans.

RIBALOW: Carey started out as a hosiery salesman and Emory as a preacher. In the end, they come together in business. Where, may I ask, did you get the idea for this novel which focuses so closely on the business world?

ANSELL: This novel actually came about because I was at one time president of an organization I abhorred. It was Sales Executives of Louisiana. We used to bring down speakers from all over the country. It suddenly occurred to me during this period that I was serving as president, as. . . .

RIBALOW: What was the precise name of the organization?

ANSELL: The parent organization is Sales Executives of America, Inc., SEA. And this was Sales Executives of Louisiana. It occurred to me that many of these speakers were of an evangelical nature and that they were actually trying to create a new religion in selling.

RIBALOW: You make that point throughout the novel.

ANSELL: That is how the book came into being. I listened carefully and suddenly realized what was happening and saw the religious fervor going through the audience.

RIBALOW: I have a quote here on that subject. When Carey is selling Kraftee Hosiery, he is told by the company's boss, Millard Lampkin, who hired him, "When you sell Kraftee, you're not just selling an accessory. You're selling America. You're right out there selling America." Then Carey says, "I'm a selling man." Later, Emory sees the philosophy of selling very much like being a preacher. When Emory fills in for Carey and makes his famous speech, he says "The dream, the hope, the vision, however vague, of a better life, a softer passage through the harsh halls of his life—these, my friends, are the salesman's product."

ANSELL: You are hitting one of my favorite scenes.

RIBALOW: ". . . these are the precious goods he bears in his sample case. These are the treasures of the American dream. . . ." Then, the Jewish character, Stein, who is later outmaneuvered by Carey, says, "For you, Carey, the American dream isn't an illusion, a myth. It's the whole bloody reality. In fact, I'd say that you, actually, *are* the American dream." So the evangelical theme is there throughout. And you seem to know the business world very well. This is not the common material of the American novelist.

ANSELL: I have been in business. That was the reason. I was part and parcel of organizations that were in business.

RIBALOW: There is another fine section, where Emory spends those few years with his wife when he is a preacher and falls under the influence of the man with that wonderful name—Bob Apricot.

ANSELL: Oh, yes. Preacher Bob. The homosexual.

RIBALOW: Emory spends some difficult years. At the outset it does not really seem relevant to the story, but then it connects.

ANSELL: It becomes very important later on.

RIBALOW: Let me get back to your talent for names. You have Bob Apricot for one and there are others.

ANSELL: Thank you. I have a lot of fun with names; I make up lists of them all the time. Sometimes, when I can't write or have a mental bloc, I sit with my long yellow pad and make lists of names. Names are important to me. I cannot tolerate to start a paragraph and suddenly come to a name and have a blank and I will sometimes hold myself for an hour or two days until I have the right name. Names are our memorables.

RIBALOW: In referring to your thought that selling can be evangelical, like a religion, you have a fine paragraph in *Gospel* which struck me as good writing, but is also thematically valid. It is about the two brothers: "Just starting their journeys, one towards the East, the other West, one to sell stockings, the other salvation."

ANSELL: Well, that is the book. I had that line, by the way, before I ever started the book.

RIBALOW: I am glad I picked it up.

ANSELL: Because that really is the metaphor of the book.

RIBALOW: When you indicated that *The Shermans of Mannerville* has a lot of plot, well, so has *Gospel*.

ANSELL: Yes. This was a *difficult* book to do. It took a number of years to do ... writing, rewriting, starting, false starts, finally reaching plateaus, having to go back to others. It was a *difficult* book to write and some day I think I would even like to rewrite it. But I would like to do that with a number of my works, but that one in particular because I am not sure but I think it just missed being a great American novel. I think it was so ambitious, trying to strike so much within the American framework that had not really been touched upon by the serious fictional writers of this country. I think here and there I missed and it is those misses or near misses that I would like to go back and try my hand at redoing. I know one thing: I wanted to do a play which would actually have been a play covering a whole week of plays, out of this book. That is how deeply involved I was at one time with it.

RIBALOW: Emory's son, Jonathan, takes up a great deal of space in the novel. He is angry with his father, turns homosexual and gives the reader the impression he is doing all this to spite his father.

ANSELL: He is the result of the decisions made by his father and his uncle.

RIBALOW: Emory marries Maud Honeycutt, whose father is a faith healer and she eventually becomes a drunk. There are many such women in your work who come to a dead end.

ANSELL: My women have some pretty rough trials, don't they?

RIBALOW: They surely do.

ANSELL: But then my men do not fare that well, either. They go through some traumatic experiences themselves.

RIBALOW: I know now that you picked up a lot of the business background from your own jobs. Any other research?

ANSELL: I also spent a good deal of time going to a number of tent evangelical happenings, especially among the Baptists. I had friends take me to them during this period that I became interested in writing the book.

RIBALOW: You write about American business with more knowledge than almost any contemporary writer. There are very few who have your background. Not many American novelists are aware of the drama inherent in the business world.

ANSELL: But there is. One of the problems is that writers in America mostly turn to the academic for their livelihood or their extracurricular livelihood. However, when you think about it, business is so fundamental to the American character that for its great writers to have ignored it is to have ignored much of America itself. Even though there is a great deal to be said for something like *Mr. Sammler's Planet* or *Humboldt's Gift*, the core is missing and that is American corporate life, the American corporate world which these people know nothing about. But I *do*. I have been in it. When you serve as I have as assistant to the president of one of three major national television networks, you learn about corporate life.

I was in offices everywhere from General Motors and General Electric all the way to MCA. I had it all, the entire range of American business and industry. I was familiar with them all, I was at luncheons with them, I was honored by them at dinners and at lunches, even though much of me, to be very honest, was repelled by what I saw and what I heard and a great many of the people I was with. I stood it under circumstances that would have driven other writers to drink. I stood it because I realized that until I had the whole damn thing in my pocket, I could not be a major American writer in all honesty and with integrity and with the responsibility that I think many of our American writers today do not have for either themselves, their work, or their country.

RIBALOW: Your collection, *Summer,* has fifteen stories. I have made notes only on some of them. One is "I Passed for Yankee," in which a Mannerville boy goes into the advertising field, works hard to lose his Southern drawl, and "passes" for a Yankee. Ultimately, he becomes homesick and reverts to type.

ANSELL: That is a farce, a comic piece.

RIBALOW: One of the stories surprised me a good deal because it is quite unlike anything else you had done. It reminds me a little of the early Erskine Caldwell.

ANSELL: I have read most of Caldwell.

RIBALOW: He has written some remarkable short stories. Your story, "One Day Is Pretty Much Like Another," reminds me of Caldwell in that you deal with an inarticulate heroine. She submits always to men, first to her father and then to her husband who is so much older than herself.

ANSELL: I have known people like that.

RIBALOW: When she bears a son, she likes to think of the boy as her own special possession. Yet she sees her husband slowly take possession of the young child. She then kills the boy and herself. It is written in a totally different mood from your other work.

ANSELL: Yes. At the same time, it was part of my experience. I had known people like this, I am sure, or there was some mood I was in that created the story. There are a number of stories in *Summer* which are diverse from each other. They all take place in the summer, which brought the book its title. The story they say is my masterwork, even above all the novels and everything else, is the story called "Blackberry Winter," which is the major story in the volume. I am not sure. I would not comment on that to save my life. Were you impressed by that particular story? What do you think?

RIBALOW: When I picked up your books to reread, in preparation for this conversation, I read the short stories first, although I remembered your work quite well. I saw a lot of traces of your themes in "Blackberry Winter." It takes place in one given day, where the blacks prepare to demonstrate in Mannerville, which has two hundred Jews. There is an old Jew in the background who is dying and you have some phrases which I say carry forward some of your themes: "In the end, they were Jews, in the end they were vulnerable." Then you observe, "*Jew* came as easy to their tongues as nigger. . . ." And Willie Mae, who works for the Jewish family for twenty-one years now, is the mother of Walter, who leads the sitdown. Walter himself has worked for the central Jewish family for eighteen years, and Willie Mae worries about her son.

ANSELL: Yes, in a few pages it did bring together much of my philosophy.

RIBALOW: It appears that the Jews have to look out for Jews, who are on trial twenty-four hours a day. The kicker at the end, after some of the Jews place their personal societal role on the line, is that the Jews do not get any thanks from anyone.

ANSELL: That is right, and you will see this thing carried even further in a play I have been writing, called "To Die in Dust."

RIBALOW: As I said earlier, this story line is expanded in one of your novels, and that aspect is expanded somewhere else. I do think "One Day Is Pretty Much Like Another" is more artful.

ANSELL: Do you? It is interesting that the story that has been most anthologized, in the United States and Western Europe, is the first story in the book, "The Only One in Town."

RIBALOW: That is the story about Marcus and Lillian Greenbaum, who run a dry goods store near Mannerville, of course.

ANSELL: This is suggested by an actual incident.

RIBALOW: They are the only Jews in the town of Twosboro, with 1,074 whites and 663 blacks. The Jews refuse to join the White Citizens Council. They are not particularly smart Jews, or brave Jews, yet Marcus refuses to join. The Jew in him rebels. His store is wrecked and he and his wife are forced to leave town. Again, as in your other story, they do not get any sympathy from the blacks for whom they put themselves out.

ANSELL: That is the irony and this is what happened, to a great extent in this particular case, although I did it as artfully as possibly, I hope, as fiction. My job there was almost a reporter's job.

RIBALOW: Let's talk a bit about "Can't We Come Back Yesterday?" a story in which Charles Gardner, a non-Jew, is married to Ruth Greenberg, a Jewish woman. He has not worked in a year and their relationship is crumbling.

ANSELL: This story, too, is based on an actual incident. I was not exactly a reporter here because I changed the story considerably and spent a great deal of time working on the approach the story should have, because it had to be a very *short* story in order to have the emotion I wanted to come across with the story.

RIBALOW: And you do have a wide range. For example, "A Kind of Light," about the reflections of a senile old Jew, has to be read very closely for the reader to realize the effort that went into it.

ANSELL: Many of my stories are very different from my novels, and are different from one another. That is one of the reasons—to get back to an earlier question of yours. Yesterday you asked me why I was not as well known in certain circles as some of your other Jewish writers. That is one of the reasons. A number of these stories in *Summer* do have Jewish backgrounds; some do not. I think I am much more diverse in my subject matter than some of the others you mention. As you say, I can go from a tiny farm situation, a tragic red-neck situation into the chambers of big business and almost do it in a single leap. I have been so diverse—*Variety* will headline me because I am writing books about entertainment or show business, and *Business Week* and the *Wall Street Journal* headlined me when *Gospel* came out.

RIBALOW: Your novel, *Dynasty of Air* is, to me, simply the first part of a longer work which concludes with *Giants*.

ANSELL: The two originally were going to be one big volume, which would cover all of broadcasting. It just did not work out that way. They were published as two books, although they are companion pieces and one does follow the other.

RIBALOW: These novels are different in style from your other fiction. The prose is dense, there is much journalism and you employ many writing techniques. Speech material, journals, newspaper reports of actual events and you even include factual happenings.

ANSELL: In these works I finally got into the epic or saga fiction.

RIBALOW: David Abrams and Bernie Strauss are the partners who are in on the birth of commercial and network radio. David and his son, Robert, are, to me, David and Robert Sarnoff.

ANSELL: There were hundreds of reviews that suggested that, I am sure. I paid relatively little attention to that.

RIBALOW: There is a tremendous amount of the history of radio contained in the novels. You include a detailed account of the development of the various radio companies as well. How did you go about the research?

ANSELL: The research? It was *astronomical*! I do not know how I ever got through it.

RIBALOW: How does one research a growing industry?

ANSELL: Don't forget I did my master's degree on it, so I had the basis. At that time, while I was still in college, I had gotten a number of the private papers from NBC, which I never would have had access to, but as a student, I did. Consequently, I had made copies of many of those papers. I was able to use that material. However, the research in later life for these two volumes was just enormous. I must have read over one hundred volumes in addition to the research through encyclopedic material and papers and biographies.

RIBALOW: You also have an *enormous* number of people in these books. Do you plot and outline your novels? I might have asked this question sooner, but it fits now.

ANSELL: In this particular case I knew where I was going. I had a general feeling for *Dynasty* and *Giants*.

RIBALOW: You manipulate literally dozens of characters.

ANSELL: I know, and it was not always easy. I have great big boards at home that I keep records on as I go along, so they are always before me and I am constantly changing them. Some of them are represented by different colored pens, because these are broad canvasses and both books together form the enormous canvas of being *the*—I will say it myself—*definitive* fictional story of broadcasting. I went everywhere, from the performances to the studios, into the managerial offices. There was not much I omitted, except the news operations, on which I am planning another book.

RIBALOW: I don't know how I can talk to you about all of the people in these books. . . .

ANSELL: It is impossible.

RIBALOW: Still, I want to start with Ellen Curry, David's mistress.

ANSELL: And the heroine of both books.

RIBALOW: She marries Bernie Strauss, David's partner, when Bernie is close to death. Prior to that, she was married to a homosexual program director because she and David were unable to marry. She convinced David not to leave his wife for her. Ellen thought such an act would destroy David's career. Ellen Curry is the most interesting, most likable and most vivid person in these two books.

ANSELL: She certainly is the vitality, I hope, of both books, because they were built very solidly around her. She is central to everything that happens.

RIBALOW: Her relationship with David is particularly affectionate and that is important because to the outside world David was a forbidding, unliked man.

ANSELL: But not to you, the reader.

RIBALOW: Not to me primarily because of his relationship with Ellen. You have so many Jews in this novel about a major industry. Is that because they are really there?

ANSELL: They really are. And another thing. I had the background to bring in what was very interesting. They had Southern backgrounds, the Jews at all three networks, as well as the non-Jews.

RIBALOW: One is Steve Lilly who reminds me of characters in many of your other novels and stories.

ANSELL: Also David's wife, from Atlanta. Arabella is a major character. I was able, because of my unique background, to bring in these divergent characters, Jewish from the South, and from the East. I had to do a lot more research on Jewish life in the East, particularly in cities like Newark, New Jersey, at the time when David and Bernie grew up. Anna, Bernie's sister, was also a difficult character to draw.

RIBALOW: She finally goes mad and kills her own mother, which ultimately influences her daughter, Jocelyn, to turn into a nymphomaniac.

ANSELL: There is always a continuity in my work in regard to the people in the novels.

RIBALOW: One of the minor characters, Tom McCarthy, is clearly an anti-Semite. Are there many anti-Semites in the radio-TV business?

ANSELL: You can bet your buttons there are!

RIBALOW: There is something else that struck me, without going into the scores of relationships in these works. There are many sexual liaisons and relationships. It is all that prevalent in the industry?

ANSELL: The answer is, yes, it is. The truth is I guess I have been involved in the networks for so long and have seen so much that it was just second nature to me to write it as I saw it. It has been happening in corporate life for many years and there is nothing new about it. I could not write the book honestly and vividly unless I did bring that out.

RIBALOW: Although there are many Jews in these novels, they do not really play an active role as Jews in their private lives. Is there any special reason for that?

ANSELL: It would have been impossible to deal with that. At one point, David and Bernie were going to have large involvements with their temples. I had written about their commitments but after much discussion with my publishers, we deleted a lot of that material. One reason was that I was really trying to bite off more than I could chew. I had described Jewish life elsewhere. To attempt it in books about broadcasting, even with numerous Jewish characters, would have been detrimental to the basic theme I was concerned with, and that was broadcasting itself.

RIBALOW: *Giants* is a continuation of *Dynasty of Air*. It concerns the same people but is set in the world of television rather than radio. I am particularly impressed with your knowledge of and control of what goes on in the executive suites.

ANSELL: It comes from firsthand knowledge.

RIBALOW: I recall *Variety* giving *Giants* a very big play. But I am sure that the TV executives did not read the novel as fiction.

ANSELL: No, they did not. I had a very mixed reaction. There were those who found it honest and well done. There were those who said some critics underrated the book, and I do think some did. I hope no one overrated it. At the same time, some feel it is going to be much longer lasting than some of the scholarly tomes that are coming out on the history of broadcasting. The Broadcasting Center in Washington has a special shelf of a number of copies of both *Dynasty of Air* and *Giants*. The Library of Congress also has put in copies of the two novels, which is unusual, I was told, because they do not usually take fiction of that nature. They called it documentary fiction.

RIBALOW: This confirms a theory of mine that if you want to get a good picture of the Jews of America, you get a better one from the novels than you will from the sociological and statistical studies. Apart from the stories coming alive in *Dynasty* and *Giants*, you list the radio and television programming, you deal with those who conceive the ninety-minute TV movie and the various talk shows.

ANSELL: You see, much of that was actual history and I build the fiction around it.

RIBALOW: My overall impression is one of shock and sadness over the cruelty in these books, the unappetizing people, the over-sexuality, the throat-cutting. Is this characteristic of all business?

ANSELL: Yes, it is, but don't forget, but remember the goldfish bowl nature of the television business. It is not all that different from Hollywood. Do not forget that the two are allied. One is an offshoot of the other. Yes, I am afraid that I have given a vividly true picture.

RIBALOW: David and Ellen marry each other late in life, she after having had two husbands and he stuck with Arabella.

ANSELL: David and Ellen were best friends even though they were lovers.

RIBALOW: David and his son Robert have a tortuous relationship. Robert, by the way, always marries women somehow beneath him. You also have an interesting observation on the relationship between David, who was without a formal education, and Robert, who is a bit of an intellectual. David remarks that Robert really detached himself emotionally from his father when the boy was only five years old, "because his Daddy had never heard of Marcel Proust." This shows an awareness on the part of the successful man in the popular field who realizes that the intellectuals will never appreciate what it is that the crowd pleasers do.

ANSELL: True.

RIBALOW: Another important person in your story, Mark Banner, who is obviously slated to move up the executive ladder, tells an underling, "This is a desperate industry."

ANSELL: I had trouble in making Banner as real as possible.

RIBALOW: He is a decent and sympathetic person. Yet the fact that his wife becomes a drunk and their marriage becomes a hopeless one is as much his fault as hers.

ANSELL: Basically, he is a man of integrity.

RIBALOW: But Mark does say, "This is a desperate industry." David likes Mark Banner, which is the reason Mark finally obtains a top post in the company. Ellen Curry knows David's feelings and when David dies, she arranges for Mark to move upward.

ANSELL: You know, I have created more sympathetic characters than you think I did.

RIBALOW: In *Giants*, yes, because it is such a big book. So David tells Mark somewhere, "We both got philosophies. Most people in this business, they don't have philosophies. You want to entertain, maybe *enlighten*. It's a philosophy." There are not too many times when these people sit reflectively and talk to one another. They live at such a hectic tempo.

ANSELL: I hope I brought that tempo into the novel. That is the way we live.

RIBALOW: Your Steve Lilly reminds me of many of the people in your previous books. He is a Southerner, is charming, has a simple wife.

ANSELL: He makes love to anybody.

RIBALOW: And he drives his infatuated office mistress to suicide. Joel Greer, born Griebsberg, is a decent fellow who dreams of being a novelist himself.

ANSELL: The networks are full of such people. I am one of the very few who succeeded.

RIBALOW: When Mark Banner offers Joel an important job, you know that Joel will accept it and forget about writing his novel, a project which his wife urges him to continue. You have the impression that Banner has chosen a decent man to work with him.

ANSELL: There is always a chance he will get out. At the time, he is caught up in it just like everybody else. Once you are caught up in that kind of maelstrom, it is hard to break away. I think I brought that out in the book.

RIBALOW: It must be the power and prestige.

ANSELL: It is habit forming. It is a narcotic, an opium.

RIBALOW: You appear to have detailed knowledge of FCC regulations.

ANSELL: One of my jobs in being assistant to the president was writing not only all of his speeches throughout the country but also all of his reports, both oral and written, to the FCC. I became very involved with the government at that time. This is why you will find my knowledge is pretty extensive in *Dynasty of Air* and in *Giants,* of government as well as business. You see, they are inseparable in the case of broadcasting.

RIBALOW: You deal with a lot more than that: the TV blacklists; the dropping of Paul Robeson from a show; the Red-baiting in the McCarthy era; the quiz-show scandals.

ANSELL: There was not much in the history of television I did not cover. There is one area I would have done more about and that was the news area. It is touched upon but it has not been given the depth it requires. I saved some of the material that I deleted from the final drafts and I tucked them away for another novel which I plan to do on television news. This is something to look forward to, I think, because the material is just as exciting, if not more exciting, than some of the material I had on the entertainment functions of the network.

RIBALOW: I have made some notes on your writing techniques. There is a lot of crisscrossing in the dialogue that moves the story and develops character . . . letters that people write to various members of their family . . . Mark Banner, for example, writes long letters to his father.

ANSELL: You have to use a certain amount of mechanical devices in a novel as epic as this. It not only has a story of a contemporary nature and of a continuing nature. It also brings in the entire history of the medium. Between the two, if you do not use a number of these bridges, then you are going to leave the reader pretty lost because he has to be carried along.

RIBALOW: There is so much stage dialogue in your work. Which leads me to my next question, one I passed over when you first mentioned it, but now that I have had an opportunity to read your play, I would like to discuss it. It is *To Die in Dust.* Is it your first play?

ANSELL: Yes, my first full-length play. It actually was done as a therapy for myself since I was hospitalized and have been for most of the last four-five years. It has been in the back of my mind for many years, as all of my works are. None of my works spring forth full-grown overnight. As I say, it is my first and it has allusions to many people, living and dead, so that if any of my works were comprised of composites of people, I would say that this, more than any other, is.

RIBALOW: I am particularly interested in having read it since I saw you a few days ago, because it reiterates many of your themes. Again, when we talked about the women in your books who commit suicide, here in this drama there is another woman who has killed herself.

ANSELL: You know, you are making me terribly conscious of this. I have already made notes for the next six or seven novels and five or six plays in which I am going to have at least one major male character commit suicide to balance the women and just to throw you off the track.

RIBALOW: You repeat some of your scenes, in the play and in the novels and stories. One more time, you have an elderly Jew dying upstairs.

ANSELL: Yes, I did that in a long short story in *Summer,* "Blackberry Winter." I deliberately took that same situation because I felt it played so well. I have almost always created a character as a composite of someone I knew. In taking the character of the Old Testament prophet father—Yahweh Himself almost—lifting it from "Blackberry Winter," I felt fully justified in taking that particular idea and incorporating it here. It fit too beautifully and too well and, as long as I was stealing from myself, I had no compunctions.

RIBALOW: Just as your earlier novels deal with Jews, white Southerners, and blacks, this is a play that deals with Jews as members of the Jewish family and its relationship to the outside world—a subject I do not remember being treated on the stage.

ANSELL: That is what others have said. The Southern *milieu* is, of course, by now standard and in many ways substandard on the stage.

RIBALOW: And stereotyped.

ANSELL: That is what I meant. Certainly there have been plays with Jewish themes that have had certain degrees of success. However, to my knowledge and to the knowledge of those of my peers who have read this play, this is the first time that the Southern Jewish *milieu* has ever been depicted on a stage in a theatrical or dramatic fashion.

RIBALOW: We ought to say that it is based on a Margaret Mitchell type, in a way, a woman who has written one major best seller, has gone North, committed suicide there and now she is being buried in the South by her relatives.

ANSELL: She happens to be Jewish, which is important to the play.

RIBALOW: The whole family is Jewish.

ANSELL: Well, both the Southern and the Jewish background are vital to this play. The other thing I can say about this play is that through the years—as you started chronologically with my works from *His Brother, The Bear* on to *The Shermans of Mannerville* and *Jelly* and *Summer* and *Gospel, Dynasty of Air* and *Giants*—I have incorporated strong Jewish and Southern backgrounds. What I have tried to do in this play is not necessarily to bring all these diverse facets together, but I believe I am through a maturity and the much suffering I have had on my part through these last years when I have been so painfully ill, is that there is a growing sophistication in me. I think this play reflects a maturity that I am not sure I got into some of my earlier novelistic works. I say that without knowing and I am trying to be objective about my own work, which it is very difficult to be, as you know. I have noticed that even in a new play that I have just begun, I carry the sophistication even further. When I say "sophistication," I certainly do not mean that in the chi-chi sense. I mean there is, I think, a greater depth in my understanding of the whole Southern Jewish *milieu* and how, in so many ways, here, more than in any other of the works, it is comparable almost to the end of the era that Chekhov was writing about. At least I felt that while I was writing it.

RIBALOW: Your references to "Three Sisters" in your own play is quite Chekhovian.

ANSELL: Yes, I made the reference which I am not sure was so necessary because the play itself, if it can be said with modesty, is Chekhovian in a sense.

RIBALOW: I have found it surprising that you have written novels and short stories and here is your first play—and it is as good as anything you have done.

ANSELL: Well, I appreciate that.

RIBALOW: Although I read it only the other day, it stays in the mind. Yet it can be butchered by a producer or director who does not have the sensitivity to stage it the right way or it can be terrific. It has so much byplay and so many subtleties.

ANSELL: Especially when it comes to the Jewish part, because these people *are* Jewish even though they are living within and are an integral part of the Southern *milieu*. It is not easy to depict people of conflicting cultures on a stage and that was one of my difficulties in writing it—to stay very subtly and delicately within the balances of these two genres.

RIBALOW: Everything you write brings Jews into it. This play did not *have* to be Jewish.

ANSELL: No, I could have treated this as Lillian Hellman treated *The Little Foxes*, if I had wanted. My play does not have to be compared with it, but it is a family play which has a crisis about which all is built. In this case, it happens to be the death of a beloved. No, it did not have to be Jewish, but because these people *are* Jewish, I think it gives it several dimensions that it would not have had otherwise. The whole conflict of life and death itself is built into the conflict of the Southern and Jewish backgrounds.

RIBALOW: I don't know how familiar you are with the plays of Arnold Wesker.

ANSELL: I have read one or two. I have never seen Wesker performed.

RIBALOW: I wrote a book on him years ago. But what I wanted to get at is that in one of his plays, *Roots*, there is a girl named Beattie Bryant, who leaves

London and returns to her family in Norfolk. She has been turned inside out psychologically by her relationship with a young man, Ronnie Kahn, who is one of the ongoing characters in a Wesker trilogy. Ronnie, who is the most vivid person in the play, is never on stage. You have a similar situation in which the dead writer around whose funeral the whole story revolves, is never on stage. She, too, is almost the most potent character in the play itself.

ANSELL: That was deliberate.

RIBALOW: But it is carried off, through a letter, or comments about her, or the interrelationships others have had with her, and other techniques as well. It very much reminds me of *Roots*, where Beattie says, Ronnie taught me this and Ronnie said that. And while Ronnie is never there, what he has done to influence her makes him very much alive to the audience which never really meets him.

ANSELL: Here, too, while it is a play, I hope, of great vitality and life, the very center of it is death in the person of the young and brilliant writer.

RIBALOW: Meanwhile, the old man is dying upstairs and is holding fiercely onto life.

ANSELL: That is right. There is the interplay among and between all of them.

RIBALOW: I might say that the blacks in the play are interesting people. The black woman and the old man, who is on the surface a shuffler and subservient, really isn't.

ANSELL: He is not. Of all the characters I had to rewrite so many times in the play, he, I think, was more difficult to create than any of the others. It would be so easy to have him shuffle across that stage. He does not. Not really. At first you think that he does. . . .

RIBALOW: He is a salty old man and has a sexual relationship with the black woman that, in the beginning, you never suspect. Yet she is an intelligent woman who sees everything as it truly is.

ANSELL: Most of the characters are intelligent people who are brought to great destruction by emotion. That is another theme of the play, which has many themes. So many that it is quite difficult to talk about them all. They can be read or seen on many levels.

RIBALOW: That makes a good play.

ANSELL: I suppose so.

RIBALOW: Having read you in a single sitting, so to speak, you seem like two writers to me: Southern and Northern industrial.

ANSELL: That is very funny.

RIBALOW: I was going to ask how it happened.

ANSELL: I have had two lives, haven't I? I have had more than two lives. My worldly experience has been wide and diverse and it has helped me as a writer. It has not harmed my reputation as a writer but it has held me back to an extent because I am not of a singular nature.

RIBALOW: Now that you have "done" radio and television, what are you planning next?

ANSELL: A book of tales of interrelated stories which I am rewriting and to which I am also adding. Another novel, of which I have completed a first draft and I am rewriting that book. Still another novel that I am two-thirds of the way through. It is in an entirely different vein from anything I have written before. I have also started another novel which is going to take a number of years to complete because it is a rich saga of American-Jewish life in the South and the North.

RIBALOW: How does that differ from what you have already written?

ANSELL: I do not want to get into it, but it brings together a life's work, you might say.

RIBALOW: When you say a "saga," do you visualize it as a trilogy or a single novel?

ANSELL: I am not sure it is going to be a single book or a trilogy. Right now there are certain elements of it that make me think it could be six or more volumes.

RIBALOW: Does any of this work have Jewish material?

ANSELL: Most of them do. All have Jewish characters.

RIBALOW: Let us hope you get to do all of them.

ANSELL: For someone who is pretty ill. . . .

RIBALOW: If you were perfectly healthy, it still would be an enormous task to complete so much work as you outline it.

ANSELL: I am just damned if I am going to give up. I have got to make plans for these things, whether they see fruition or not. And if I die "in the middle of the last tycoon," God bless me.